W9-CRM-681

BURNING DOWN THE HOUSE

BURNING DOWN THE HOUSE

HOW LIBERTARIAN PHILOSOPHY WAS CORRUPTED BY DELUSION AND GREED

ANDREW KOPPELMAN

ST. MARTIN'S PRESS
NEW YORK

First published in the United States by St. Martin's Press, an imprint of St. Martin's Publishing Group

 Printed in the United States of America. For information, address St. Martin's Publishing Group, 120 Broadway, New York, NY 10271.

www.stmartins.com

The Library of Congress Cataloging-in-Publication Data is available upon request.

ISBN 978-1-250-28013-8 (hardcover)
ISBN 978-1-250-28014-5 (ebook)

Our books may be purchased in bulk for promotional, educational, or business use. Please contact your local bookseller or the Macmillan Corporate and Premium Sales Department at 1-800-221-7945, extension 5442, or by email at MacmillanSpecialMarkets@macmillan.com.

First Edition: 2022

10 9 8 7 6 5 4 3 2 1

For Ruby and George, again.
I think they would have been pleased.

CONTENTS

INTRODUCTION 1

1. PROSPERITY 25

2. RIGHTS 74

3. TYRANNY 107

4. NANNY 151

5. LIBERTY 173

6. MOOCHERS 187

CONCLUSION 230

Acknowledgments 239
Analytical Table of Contents 242
Notes 246
Index 301

BURNING DOWN THE HOUSE

INTRODUCTION

> So far as direct influence on current affairs is concerned, the influence of the political philosopher may be negligible. But when his ideas have become common property, through the work of historians and publicists, teachers and writers, and intellectuals generally, they effectively guide developments.
>
> —Friedrich Hayek[1]

The fire department was run by idealists. That is why it ignored the homeowner's pleas and watched his house burn down.

He had neglected to pay his bill. What happened then tells us a lot about libertarianism, the increasingly influential philosophy of minimal government. Many libertarians took it to show the stern seriousness of their ideal. Their enemies on the left thought it revealed how repugnant it is to leave such important matters to the market. Both sides thought that it revealed the essence of the libertarian tradition. Both were wrong.

Obion County, Tennessee, uses the fire protection services of the nearby City of South Fulton. But the county doesn't contract with the city on behalf of all its residents. It leaves them each to pay a seventy-five-dollar fee to the city. Fire protection in the county is essentially privatized: it is up to individual homeowners to contract with the city fire department.

Gene Cranick, who lives in Obion County, had paid the fee for years. In 2010 he forgot. His grandson burned some trash in his backyard, and the fire got out of control and began to spread. Cranick called 911, but the operator told him the fire department would not come. His wife told the operator that she would pay "whatever the cost," but that was not an option. The department arrived several hours later, when the fire threatened the house of a neighbor who had paid. It sprayed the neighbor's land up to, but not across, Cranick's property line. Three dogs and a cat died. Cranick's son punched the fire chief and was arrested.

Glenn Beck, the conservative radio and television host, explained why the department had done the right thing. In America, "we are going to start to have to have these kinds of things." It would have been wrong to put out the fire. "If you don't pay your seventy-five dollars, then that hurts the fire department. They can't use those resources and you would be sponging off of your neighbor's seventy-five dollars." Soon there would be no fire protection: "As soon as they put out the fire of somebody who didn't pay the seventy-five bucks, no one will pay the seventy-five bucks."[2] Jonah Goldberg, writing in *National Review Online*, said that letting the home burn was "sad," but he thought that it would "probably save more houses over the long haul," since people will now have a strong incentive to pay their fees. Other conservative writers soon converged on the same view.[3]

The fire chief was not, so far as is known, an ideologue or a philosopher. But the decision to let the house burn reflected two key tenets of libertarianism: that people are appropriately understood to be on their own in the world, responsible for their own fate, and that need does not make a claim on others' resources.[4] Beck thought that the fire illustrated the importance of those principles, and that those principles had implications for the then-pressing debate about Obamacare: its protection of people with preexisting medical conditions created the same perverse incentives that saving Cranick's house would. The same principle demanding that houses be allowed to burn also entailed that millions of people should be allowed to go without health care.

The broader philosophy that Beck embraces would radically transform our society. In modern America, government protects people from not only fire and disease but also dangerous workplace conditions and toxins in the environment. It provides education, maintains roads and bridges, funds medical research and disaster relief. It protects against destitution through Social Security, unemployment insurance, and food stamps. Obamacare built upon Medicare and Medicaid.

The most influential forms of libertarianism aim to radically curtail all of these in order to lower taxes, particularly taxes on the most prosperous Americans. "I don't want to abolish government," Grover Norquist, the president of Americans for Tax Reform, told National Public Radio in a 2001 interview. "I simply want to reduce it to the size where I could drag it into the bathroom and drown it in the bathtub."[5] The organization's pledge to oppose all tax increases was signed in 2012 by 95 percent of Republican members of Congress and all but one of the Republican presidential candidates.[6] Were its ideal realized, there would be a lot of Gene Cranicks: people who discover that they can no longer rely on the government to protect them. The party did not always endorse that ideal. This development is the result of an intellectual movement.

Within Obion County, there is disagreement about how the tax burden should be apportioned: farmers don't want their taxes raised to protect homes from fire.[7] It is a problem that obviously could be addressed by imposing an annual seventy-five-dollar tax on residences but not farms. Everyone I spoke with in Obion County agreed, however, that raising taxes is politically impossible. Two years after Cranick's fire, South Fulton enacted a new law allowing the fire department to respond to all calls within a five-mile radius of the city. But homeowners who had not paid the fee would be charged $3,500 per call.[8] There is a persistent squeamishness about the tough discipline that was administered to Cranick.

The individual firefighters were troubled. "Most everybody has been compassionate and neighborly," Cranick told a reporter. "I understood some of the firefighters went home and were sick. Some of them even cried over it." His wife, Paulette, said, "You can't blame them if they have to do what the boss says to do. I've had firemen call and apologize."[9]

But perhaps those firefighters just didn't understand that doing what's right can be hard. Beck and Goldberg argued that letting the house burn would make America into a better, more self-reliant society.

Beck described Cranick as though he were deliberately "sponging." Kevin Williamson, in *National Review Online*, wrote: "The world is full of jerks, freeloaders, and ingrates—and the problems they create for themselves are their own."[10] Cranick, who was sixty-seven years old, had paid for fire protection for years, however. "I'm no freeloader, I've worked all my life for everything I've got."[11] He remembered paying up every other year except one. "But humans forget. It seems like I do more than I used to. I just don't think they done right."[12] The implications of Beck's views are harsher than he realizes. Suppose there were children in the house. If the firefighters rescued them, wouldn't that also create perverse incentives, encouraging other parents to sponge?

Leftists sneer at Glenn Beck. But he is a smart man who is good at his job. Journalism is an intensely competitive business, and he has been a remarkable success. His ideas matter. They have a huge constituency. He knows how to mirror and shape the moral convictions of much of contemporary America.

Libertarianism takes multiple forms. The kind that let the house burn is a corrupted variety. Libertarians once defended free markets, and the inequalities that markets inevitably generate, without claiming that those inequalities are deserved or that people's needs count for nothing. Free markets were valuable precisely because they offered the most promising path toward satisfying the needs of the worst off. Its commitments did not include letting houses burn.

This valid core of libertarianism has prevailed across the political spectrum, so completely that the label "libertarian" is no longer meaningful as a way to describe it. What was valid in libertarianism has been assimilated into mainstream liberalism. Except for a politically impotent fringe, the American left aims for a generous welfare state—more generous than the present one—in the context of capitalism. Although Senator Bernie Sanders calls himself a socialist, he envisions "an economy in which you have wealth being created by the private sector, but you have a fair distribution of that wealth, and you make sure the most vulnerable people in this country are doing well."[13] The American right, too, has embraced the welfare state in some form. Few Republicans propose to abolish Medicare or Social Security.

Libertarianism is a mutated form of *liberalism*, the political philosophy that holds the purpose of government to be guaranteeing to individuals the freedom to live as they like. The distinctive claim of libertarians is that the best way to guarantee this freedom is to impose severe limits on government, barring much of the regulation and redistribution that today is routine. It is radical because it proposes to dismantle political institutions that are in fact now delivering freedom to millions. It is an infantile fantasy of godlike self-sufficiency. People in fact cannot be free in isolation. There can be no freedom without institutions. Structures of responsible regulation, and nonmarket transfers of income and wealth, are necessary preconditions of liberty.

The story of the corruption of libertarianism is a sad tale with a hopeful ending. It has pitted decent Americans against one another, the left suspecting the right of blind rapaciousness, the right suspecting the left of malicious envy. The encouraging news is that they are less far apart than they think. Libertarianism is most persuasive when it shares the commitments of the political left. The disagreement is not about ends. It concerns strategy. Too many on the left fail to grasp that the original libertarian strategy has been massively vindicated. The capacity of markets to alleviate poverty has been so overwhelmingly demonstrated in recent decades that it is silly to keep denying it. Too many on the right fail to grasp that unregulated markets cannot deliver a livable world. Moderate libertarianism can bridge some of the bitterest divisions of contemporary American politics.

When Glenn Beck defended the burning of Cranick's home, he thought he was promoting the ideas of the most important libertarian thinkers. One of his most prominent interventions in American political discourse was his advocacy for the late economist Friedrich Hayek. Four months before the Cranick fire, Beck devoted a section of his show to Hayek's 1944 book, *The Road to Serfdom*. The book denounced socialism and argued that people should be made to rely on themselves rather than on the state, that central government planning was wasteful and tyrannical. Beck's endorsement catapulted it to the top of Amazon's bestseller list. In the following month, it sold a hundred thousand copies.[14]

Beck is also an admirer of the novelist Ayn Rand, and made a cameo appearance in a 2014 film based on her didactic novel *Atlas Shrugged*. Rand, too, worries about mooching by unproductive parasites.

What Beck takes from both is a deep suspicion of government as the enemy of individual freedom. He aims to free us from those who would impose coercive taxation in order to provide guaranteed fire protection. (Or other guarantees. Obamacare similarly used tax dollars to protect people from nasty surprises.)

Contemporary libertarianism promises freedom from overbearing government and unproductive leeches. It categorically condemns regulation and redistribution. It has become the kind of idealism that, carried to its logical conclusion, leads firefighters to watch houses burn. The quest for a free society mustn't be compromised by sentimental weakness.

The American left hates Beck and everything he stands for. But many leftists agreed with him about this much: what happened to Gene Cranick reveals the true face of libertarianism.[15] More: they think that libertarianism is the true face of capitalism. It shows where we are headed if we tolerate huge inequalities of wealth, abandon tariffs or rent control, or entertain claims that regulators of business are sometimes incompetent or corrupt. This is the future capitalists want: a pitiless world in which only the strong prosper, a world casually cruel to the old, the weak, the sick, and the poor. Cranick's story was pounced upon as a paradigmatic illustration of capitalism's moral bankruptcy. Even the most basic needs, such as help when one's home is on fire, count for nothing unless the claimant pays. The lesson, for some, is that the ideology of the free market must be rejected wholesale. The state must aggressively redistribute and regulate to make sure that society's resources are devoted to people and not profits.

Libertarian political philosophy thus looms large in the imaginations of both right and left. But both focus on a corrupted variant.

I use the term *corruption* in two related senses. It sometimes means an accidental transformation in which the original message is garbled, as with corrupted computer code. It also means, more invidiously, the abuse of authority for personal gain. Both meanings are relevant here. Malign interests have benefited by garbling the original meaning of libertarianism. The ideology of small government attracts two very different groups: principled ideologues like Beck, driven by philosophical commitment, and predators who want to hurt people without interference from the police. As libertarian rhetoric becomes more common, the second group increasingly likes to masquerade as the first.

Beck embraces both Hayek and Rand. The left demonizes both. But there are crucial differences between them. Libertarianism has deep fault lines.

Rand worships strength and despises vulnerability. Human weakness terrifies and repels her. Old people who forget to pay their bills deserve what happens to them. In this, Beck is her faithful acolyte.

But modern American libertarianism began with Hayek, who starts with entirely different premises. He shares the left's concern for the poorest members of society. It is unfair to lump him together with Beck and Rand. Hayek's disagreement with the left is that he thinks that the way to attack poverty is not redistribution—there isn't yet enough wealth in existence to give everyone a decent life—but the opportunities created by free markets. The state mustn't block those opportunities. Any attempt to direct the economy will end in tyranny. But that doesn't rule out protection from random accidents, such as fires.

More is at stake here than clarity. The right's embrace of Rand—and there is a whole lot of embracing going on—reinforces the left's suspicion that any libertarian argument based on concern for the poor is a lie, a mask for amoral greed and selfishness. These ideas have produced some awful behavior. The firefighters who let the house burn are not creations of socialists' fevered imaginations. It really happened. Political philosophy matters.

The fundamental error of the anticapitalist left is focusing on inequality when its most pressing concern should be poverty. Effectively addressing poverty will require acceptance of substantial, undeserved inequality. Attacks on capitalism foolishly hurt the very people they are intended to help.

The fundamental error of the libertarian right is its proclivity for justifying inequality on the grounds that the winners in market competition are better, worthier people than the losers. Those on the bottom recognize the cruel stupidity of that claim and they will not endure it. With friends like the Randians, who praise capitalism in a way that makes it seem morally repellent, markets need no enemies. Neither of these factions recognizes that capitalism takes multiple shapes, and that the choice of capitalisms is necessarily a political choice.[16]

There is a middle path, one that captures the best commitments of both. Unlike Beck, Hayek does not presume that those who cannot pay their way in a market are sponging off their betters. He acknowledges the arbitrariness and unfairness of markets. It is precisely their amoral tendency to maximize productivity, in unpredictable ways, that makes them the hope of the world. He brings to economics a tragic perspective that is entirely absent from Beck. Precisely because he sees the arbitrariness of markets, he does not rule out government action to protect citizens from disasters. The welfare state he defends is too stingy: he fears that income stabilization measures, such as Social Security, are a slippery slope to socialism. He is nonetheless far from Rand and Beck.

Hayek is a hero for Beck and other libertarians. On the left, he is the bad guy who invented the ideology that let Cranick's house burn. Both sides have only the dimmest idea of what he actually wrote. He is better than either of them.

Hayek's forgotten middle way shows that libertarianism need not, and originally did not, take the reprehensible form that looms so large in the imagination of the left, and that has captured the souls of so many on the right.

I'm writing this book for two audiences—audiences that, as it happens, fear and despise each other. I'm going to try to persuade leftists and libertarians that your ideals are not so far from each other as you believe, and that you need not be enemies.

Both positions, in their strongest forms, rely on contestable judgments that are sometimes false. Each should be open to the possibility that the other is sometimes right. At the deepest philosophical level, they agree. They hate poverty and they want to make people free and prosperous. A moderate libertarianism—libertarianism, as it happens, in its original Hayekian form—can accommodate both.

Let's pause for a moment to clarify what we're talking about. What is libertarianism?

Libertarians themselves like to say that their philosophy is centrally concerned with human freedom: "Libertarianism is the view that each person has the right to live his life in any way he chooses so long as he respects the equal rights of others."[17] "Libertarians believe that so long as we do not violate others' rights, we should each be free to live as we choose."[18] "The idea of libertarianism is to maximize individual freedom."[19] "Libertarians agree that liberty should be prized above all other political values."[20] The trouble with these definitions is that these specific beliefs are shared by many who find libertarianism repugnant. They leave out what's distinctive about libertarianism. It's like saying that what defines Protestantism is a belief in God.

Here's a better description: "Government, if it has any purpose at all (and many libertarians doubt that it does), should be restricted to the protection of its citizens' persons and property against direct violence and theft."[21] That claim has big policy implications: "Limited government means a very small one, shorn of almost all of the apparatus we have come to take for granted during the last sixty years."[22] The freedom at which it aims is precisely *freedom from government*.

Libertarianism is committed to free markets and private property.

It aims to radically limit the scope and size of government. More and more people are drawn to it—by some accounts, as many as a third of voters.[23] It is a powerful force in the Republican Party.

If you're tempted by it, you need to know what you're buying. If you're not tempted, you still need to understand what your fellow citizens believe, whether those beliefs make sense, and how they are shaping American politics.

Libertarianism comes in different forms, with very different visions of human freedom. This book examines the most influential ones.[24] One version imposes strict conditions on economic regulation and redistribution. The other, increasingly influential, rules them out categorically, and so threatens to turn America into an oppressive plutocracy in the name of liberty.

Political philosophy sounds abstract, but it is inescapable. If you have any political opinions, then you have a philosophy and are acting in accordance with it. Politics is not merely the pursuit of interests. Ideology matters. For example, Charles Koch, who has been funding libertarian causes for half a century, is often depicted as a greedy man hoping only to line his own pockets. This is a massive misunderstanding. Koch is an idealist. (Whether his actions have been consistent with his ideals is another matter.) To understand and critique him, it is necessary to understand the creed to which he is committed. Similarly with former House speaker Paul Ryan's efforts to privatize Social Security, or the antiregulatory efforts of Donald Trump.

I became interested in libertarianism by accident. In 2010 I was invited to give a presentation about recent constitutional challenges to Obamacare. I teach constitutional law, but I hadn't followed that litigation. So I prepared by reading the two district court cases that had recently declared part of the law unconstitutional.

I got upset. The reasoning was so flagrantly bad, so manifestly driven by the judges' political views, that I was shocked to see such stuff coming out of the federal district courts.[25] More decisions like that followed. With only a few exceptions, judges appointed by Republicans accepted arguments that were inconsistent with nearly two hundred years of settled law.

I eventually became persuaded that the judges were in the grip of a philosophy that was no part of the Constitution, but which they found so compelling that they felt sure it had to be in there somewhere. It rested on a weird understanding of liberty, which conjured up a right previously unheard of: the right not to be compelled to pay for an unwanted service. If people wanted to go without insurance, it was tyrannical for the state to force it upon them. Government, however, provides myriad services, paid for by taxes without asking whether the recipients want them. The proposed "right" repudiated sources of economic security that most Americans depend on. More broadly, the implication was anarchy. Why should anyone believe there was such a right?

As I learned more about the origins of this litigation—a story I eventually told in my book *The Tough Luck Constitution and the Assault on Health Care Reform*—it became clear to me that its deepest source was libertarian political philosophy. There were two fundamental objections to Obamacare: One was that it expanded the size of government. The other was that, while it concededly provided health care to millions who were doing without, it did so by raising taxes on prosperous people who had not themselves done anything wrong.

I thought both objections repellent. How could people believe them? And they attracted unlikely fans. In a revealing moment during the March 2012 Supreme Court argument over the constitutionality of the law, Solicitor General Donald Verrilli argued that the state legitimately could compel Americans to purchase health insurance, because the country is obligated to pay for the uninsured when they get sick.

Justice Antonin Scalia responded: "Well, don't obligate yourself to that."[26]

He was saying, in effect, that there is no real *obligation* to care for sick people who cannot afford to pay for their own medical care; that any assumed "obligation" is really a discretionary choice. You can choose to obligate yourself or not.

Verrilli replied that the Constitution did not "forbid Congress from taking into account this deeply embedded social norm." Scalia didn't challenge that, but he still was not satisfied. A bit later, he suggested that under the Constitution, "the people were left to decide whether they want to buy insurance or not."[27] This would mean that any federally required insurance scheme was unconstitutional. Scalia clearly did not mean that. But then, why was he saying these things?

The arguments against Obamacare frequently took a Manichaean form: interference with market processes, in order to provide health care to those who could not afford it, was taken to be tantamount to Stalinism. Laissez-faire capitalism or totalitarianism were the only choices that existed. Many of those who made these arguments, I discovered, were entirely sincere. They massively misunderstood Obama and what he was trying to do. How could educated people be captured by such delusions?

I wanted to understand. Investigating philosophical debates in the law is what I do. I soon found that libertarianism comes in flavors, some more bitter than others.

I was not reading libertarian writers in a generous spirit. I was predisposed for a fight. So I was surprised to discover that, while some of them were as callous as I had expected, others were animated by a deep humanitarian impulse, tied to powerful and persuasive arguments about how economies work. The thinker who most clearly reflected that impulse was Friedrich Hayek, the founder of the movement. He changed my mind about some major issues: he made the case for tolerating substantial inequalities of wealth better than anyone I'd read before (and my embrace of that position here will make many of my friends on the left feel betrayed). So now I faced a puzzle: How did libertarianism come to take such different forms?

That question led me to the story I'm about to tell you.

I write from a peculiar political position. On the American political right, libertarianism competes with Christian fundamentalism and Trumpian racist, xenophobic nationalism. (Traditional Burkeanism is barely breathing.[28]) On the left, there is growing enthusiasm for socialism, although there is considerable ambiguity about what that means.[29] I am a pro-capitalism leftist. There exists no sustained critique of libertarianism from this perspective. Hence this book.

I've been uncomfortable with abstract libertarian slogans for a long time. In the field of legal studies, people are often motivated to develop new ideas when they perceive injustice in the world. When I was a law student in 1986, the Supreme Court casually dismissed the idea that gay people had a right to privacy in their sexual relations as "at best, facetious."[30] That made me angry. But I had a problem: I didn't like the story that everyone on my side was telling. The standard defense of gay rights was simple: people should have a right to do whatever they want as long as they don't violate anyone else's rights. I thought it was *too* simple. The principle had two embarrassing implications. First, it meant that the law could impose no restrictions on self-destructive conduct: corner stores would have to be allowed to sell heroin and methamphetamine. Second, it undercut all of antidiscrimination law, which forces people into transactions that they would prefer to avoid. The world was just more complicated than that. So I was led to defend gay rights on an entirely different basis. (I argued, and still think, that discrimination against gay people is a form of sex discrimination.[31])

Here is what I have learned in my investigation of modern libertarianism.

Two libertarian factions matter in modern American politics. The ideas of Hayek, valuing markets because they promise a better life for everyone, are today commonplace in the Democratic Party—a major ideological shift that almost no libertarians have noticed. Capitalism is embraced—it was not always thus on the left, and even today the Marxists are full of passionate intensity—but it must be tempered by regulation and redistribution. Democrats do not all accept that. Every Democratic president has. The Republicans once had a similar view, and some still do. But the Hayekians have lost ground to a different, more extreme libertarianism, which opposes nearly everything that government does. Its most important proponents have been the economist Murray Rothbard, the philosopher Robert Nozick, and Rand.

Hayek defends capitalism because price mechanisms transmit more information than any central planner can possibly know. Markets, he thought, can generate astonishing levels of prosperity, and thus offer more of that prosperity to the least advantaged members of society than socialism could.

Hayek's views were scandalous when he first developed them in the 1930s. The Great Depression had produced a broad consensus in America and England that capitalism had failed and that central economic planning was necessary. Hayek's courageous protest led him to be labeled a crank, and for many years he faced ridicule and indifference. In 1974, to the surprise of many (not least himself), he won the Nobel Prize in Economics. In the 1980s, his ideas triumphed when his admirers, Ronald Reagan and Margaret Thatcher, came to power.

It has turned out that Hayek was right. A huge range of policies that were once unquestioned—tariffs, subsidies for failing industries, wage and price controls, rent control, price supports for farm commodities—are now widely agreed to be counterproductive and wasteful (or at least, they were before Trump's enthusiasm for protectionism).

His defense of inequality is particularly pertinent today. When businesses succeed, this signals unmet demand, and the surge in profits gives them the means to respond quickly to that demand. It's very expensive to enter some markets, so monopolies will form unless some investors are wealthy and intrepid enough to take the risk. Even luxury consumption often benefits everyone: today's new toys of the rich often will end up improving the lives of the masses.

In order for the worst-off members of society to prosper, some must be extraordinarily and undeservedly rich. Redistribution is fine, so long as it does not tax so severely as to destroy the accumulations of capital that a well-functioning market requires.[32] What the poor need most, however, is not redistribution but economic opportunity that can produce enough wealth for everyone.

This argument is distinctive because it is coldly instrumental. Of course the rich do not deserve their good fortune. Markets do not consistently reward virtue. Businesses often prosper or fail for reasons that could not have been anticipated by anyone. But if you want more for the poor, you shouldn't try to equalize. You should make the economy grow, and that means letting the rich keep quite a lot of what they have. ("Quite a lot" is not necessarily every penny the market gives them.)

Hayek's strategy of removing restraints from free markets has succeeded. After the collapse of Communism and the abandonment of socialism by such major powers as India, the proportion of the world population living in desperate poverty plunged. Economic growth consistently helps the poor in countries that protect rights and have the rule of law. There the correspondence between real GDP growth and the income of the lowest quintile is approximately one to one.[33] In 2013, 10.7 percent of the world's population lived on less than US$1.90 a day, compared to 35 percent as recently as 1990.[34] For the first time in history, more than half the world is middle class or wealthier.[35] Most of the remaining poor live in failed states. It's not the promised land, but it is better than the human race has ever seen. It is one of the most spectacular developments in history. It has been even more impressive than Hayek anticipated. The rise of the global economy has of course had losers, most prominently the semiskilled workers whose wages became unsustainable in the face of competition from poorer countries. Globalization produced so much new wealth that it could have made them better off as well. The fact that it did not was the product of political choices that could and should have been different.

Hayek's view did not entail minimal government. It rather imposed strict conditions on intervention in the economy. He thought that regulation is appropriate to deal with what economists call "externalities," side effects on third parties that aren't reflected in prices, such as pollution. It should prohibit fraud and manipulation. It should fund public goods that the private sector will not adequately provide, such as roads, education, social services, and basic scientific research. But the state should act only on a clear showing of market failure.

Hayek's libertarianism soberly assesses the advantages of a free market, including the inequalities that markets engender, and demands justification for any interference with the knowing choices of consenting adults. It views with suspicion proposals to regulate and subsidize. It is likewise suspicious of paternalism absent a clear showing of incompetence or deceit. It redistributes in ways that minimally impact markets. These presumptions can be overcome with evidence. (In 1960, Hayek proposed the outlines of Obamacare, requiring citizens to buy health insurance in the private market, with subsidies if they need them.)

Here again Hayek has triumphed, particularly on the moderate left: defenders of regulation typically presume that markets should be allowed to operate freely, and then try to show how markets fail in this or that sector of the economy and how intervention can help. This Hayekian view is evident in the policies of the Obama and Biden administrations, which demanded (here expressly following Hayek's acolyte Reagan) that proposals for regulations prove that the benefits exceed the costs.

Rothbard and Rand (and, in a complicated way, Nozick) were romantic individualists. No cold Hayekian calculations for them. Their vision of the individual breaking free from society's stultifying constraints broadened libertarianism's concerns from economics to ideas of personal liberation. Policy calculations were secondary. Their libertarianism was based on rights. Instead of Hayek's presumption against interference with markets, they posited an absolute bar: property is sacrosanct, and anything that enfeebles the state is good for freedom. Any government action, beyond (perhaps!) the protection of property and enforcement of contracts, violates human rights. The consequences of minimal government don't matter.

Rothbard's philosophy is the most influential of the three. Many who would not recognize his name embrace his ideas in some detail. He was an anarchist. He thought that whatever government does, including police protection, can be provided better by private businesses. Markets reward those who look after themselves. Taxation is theft. He surrounded himself with young libertarian intellectuals, notably Nozick, who came under Rothbard's influence while he was still a student, and Randy Barnett, the mastermind of the legal challenge to Obamacare. He wrote for Representative Ron Paul's newsletter, and Senator Rand Paul writes that Rothbard "was a great influence on my thinking and when I was a young man I was lucky to meet him."[36] In 1976 Rothbard persuaded Charles Koch to create new libertarian institutions, such as the Cato Institute. The state is not likely to disappear. But the platform of today's Libertarian Party mirrors Rothbard's views in many ways, and the Republican Party, increasingly under Koch's sway, has been moving in his direction.

Nozick is the most prominent modern libertarian philosopher. He thought Rothbard's anarchism could be rebutted. But the most that could be justified was a minimal, laissez-faire state, which would protect property, enforce contracts, and do nothing else.

Ayn Rand, a less sophisticated thinker, reached the same minimal-state conclusions, which she defended in apocalyptic terms. Any interference with markets operates to elevate "the weakling, the fool, the rotter, the liar, the failure, the coward, the fraud, and to exile from the human race the hero, the thinker, the producer, the inventor, the strong, the purposeful, the pure."[37] She is certainly the most widely read libertarian, and her influence is cited by Donald Trump, Paul Ryan, Gary Johnson, and many others. Her arguments matter less than her portrayals of good and evil in her novels: the magnificently self-sufficient heroes, Howard Roark in *The Fountainhead* and John Galt in *Atlas Shrugged*, and the despicable moochers and looters who try to suppress their genius.

Rothbard, Nozick, and Rand all thought that the poverty of those who cannot prosper in an unregulated economy is simply justice. All three aimed to redistribute *upward*—to cut social services in order to ease the burden of taxation on the richest citizens. None of them understood markets as well as Hayek did, and all rely on philosophical premises that crumble under even brief scrutiny.

Externalities such as pollution create difficulties for them all: Rand never seriously addressed the problem. Rothbard thought about it a lot, but his response is radically unstable, oscillating between opposite conclusions: either externalities must be tolerated wholesale because the state can't price them, or most of modern industry must be prohibited because its effects trespass on property. Nozick, the most sensible of the three, thought that a society should "permit those polluting activities whose benefits are greater than their costs."[38] He thus approached agreement with Hayek, but he did not pause to consider that cost-benefit analysis, if it is to be done competently, requires a huge scientific bureaucracy, not a minimal state. He also did not explain how this moderate stance could be consistent with his property absolutism.

All these philosophers, even Hayek, make the same mistake. They have an excessively crude understanding of their core concept: private property. All of them imagine it to be absolute dominion over some part of the world, unencumbered by affirmative duties or liability to taxation. Property rights have never been like this. They think they are defending existing property rights, but what they envision is an otherworldly fantasy. Moreover, if the value of property is that it gives individuals independence and autonomy, then this function is nicely performed by streams of government-generated income, such as Social Security and Medicare. Abolishing those, as many libertarians propose, would be a disaster not only for liberty but for property as well, depriving millions of what they had worked for. Libertarian philosophy perversely threatens to destroy what it most cares about.

Libertarianism is also susceptible to abuse by predators.

Wealth in the United States is increasingly concentrated at the very top. In 2019, the mean income of the top 1 percent of adults was $1.4 million, and that group had 39.6 percent of the nation's wealth.[39] Between 1983 and 2019, the top 20 percent of households received 94.9 percent of the growth in wealth, with the top 1 percent getting 41.6 percent of the total, and 14.9 percent going to the top one-tenth of 1 percent.[40] Between 2007 and 2019, income grew at a rate of 7 percent for the bottom quintile of workers, 22.6 percent for the top quintile. With income as with wealth, the growth is concentrated at the top of the top: "Among the 600,000 or so that constitute the lower half of the top 1 percent, average pretax income roughly doubled between 1979 and 2014, from $275,000 to $500,000. Among the 12,000 households that make up the top 0.01 percent, average income quadrupled during those years, from $7 million to $29 million."[41] Between 1979 and 2007, after-tax income grew by 275 percent for the top 1 percent of households; 65 percent for the next 19 percent; just under 40 percent for the next 60 percent; and 18 percent for the bottom 20 percent. During the same period, the share of total market income received by the top 1 percent of the population grew from about 10 percent to more than 20 percent. The share of the bottom 20 percent of the population fell from about 7 percent to about 5 percent.[42] From 2002 to 2007, the top 1 percent received more than 65 percent of the gain in total national income.[43]

Income is also more unstable. Economic risk has been shifted from broad social insurance to workers and their families. Jobs are less secure, and a college degree no longer reliably guarantees middle-class status.[44] In any year, 10 to 20 percent of Americans will experience a 25 percent drop in income, and about a third of these do not recover their prior level even a decade later.[45]

Some of the growth at the top is the legitimate effect of the new opportunities created by accelerating technological change and the expansion of the world economy into formerly socialist countries. The astounding wealth of Steve Jobs and Bill Gates is a small fraction of the value they created (though this fact should not immunize them from some redistributive taxation). Billionaires capture about 2 percent of the value that their innovation produces.[46]

The inequality is also in part the result of free trade with low-wage countries, which helped break American labor unions. Had public policy kept those unions strong, the downward pressure on wages could have been resisted in various ways.[47]

Much of the new inequality, however, is not the effect of competitive markets but of a crony capitalism in which large corporations and banks have used their power to skew the rules in order to redistribute wealth upward, toward themselves. Liberals and libertarians ought to be able to join forces against this.[48] That, however, demands that we not treat the present distribution of wealth as neutral and natural. Libertarian rhetoric has been deployed to justify artificial monopolies, and even to expand them. The most flagrant case is the law of copyright and patent, where the notion of "intellectual property" has produced an enormous expansion of monopoly and censorship under the guise of protecting property rights.[49]

Large, sophisticated actors can exploit and hurt people in plenty of ways if the state doesn't intervene. They can destroy the environment and heat up the planet, as the coal and petroleum industries do. They can parasitize sick people and drive up the cost of medical care, as the health care industry does. They can risk another bust on the scale of 2008, as the financial industry does. They can manipulate and deceive employees and consumers with exorbitant and deceptive home loan and credit card schemes, and contracts that nullify legal remedies. Such pests are likely to be hostile to regulation, and so they piously recite ideas of small government.

The most important of these bandits is the fossil fuel industry, which has deployed libertarian language to make the Republican Party the only major political party in the world that denies climate change science. This license to profit by hurting people and destroying their property betrays the most basic commitments of even Randian libertarianism.

If the minimal prohibitions of force and fraud were made effective, inequality, to the extent that it is the product of this kind of robbery, would at least be ameliorated. That is, however, a reason for these leeches to try to make sure that these rules are not enforced, at least not against themselves.

Hostility to government also has crippled public services that capitalism needs. In the name of freedom, roads and bridges deteriorate, funding for medical research disappears, science is starved. America's pandemic response capability, disastrously gutted in the early Trump years, is another example. The enfeeblement of the state is self-defeating even from the selfish standpoint of business, which depends on functioning infrastructure.

It is curious that this philosophy has captured the imagination of so many billionaires, whom Koch has gathered into a powerful fundraising network. Once more, greed can't explain its appeal for so many of America's superrich. In most times and places, wealthy elites are conservative in the old-fashioned sense: they fear change and want to keep society operating along traditional lines. Social welfare programs are a conservative strategy: they were invented by Otto von Bismarck in nineteenth-century Germany to pacify the working classes. But in America, Bismarck would be on the marginalized centrist wing of the Republican Party, which has become the party of upheaval and revolution. Today's recklessness is evident in the crusade against Obamacare. You need to embrace a mighty tough libertarianism in order to cheerfully strive to take health care away from millions of people.[50]

The most consequential effect of libertarianism, under Koch's leadership, has been the spread of climate change denial and the effective blocking of any coordinated effort to address the greatest danger that the human race has faced in many millennia.

If the hollowing out of the state allows economic behemoths to do whatever they like, then what libertarianism licenses, in the garb of liberty, is crass predation and the creation of a new aristocracy. The hamstringing of environmental regulation empowers a small group of industrialists to impose massive costs on the rest of humanity. This is just a different kind of mooching and looting. It is a new road to serfdom. It reinforces the prejudices of those on the left who repudiate capitalism. The libertarians who embrace it, thinking that they are thereby promoting freedom, are useful idiots, like the idealistic leftists of the 1930s whose hatred of poverty and racism led them to embrace Stalin. John Galt is a sap.

Even in its most attractive form, libertarianism is an inadequate political philosophy. Rights depend on a culture, institutions, even individual personalities, that sustain them. In order to be free to live the lives they want, people need more than a minimal state. Libertarianism points beyond itself.

Freedom is not the absence of government. It is the capacity of people to shape their own lives. Libertarianism is at its core a protest against the massive apparatus of regulation and redistribution that arose in the twentieth century. That apparatus has done a lot of stupid things, but without it we would be less free.

The philosopher to whom modern libertarians are most deeply indebted is John Locke, who developed the classic defense of liberty and property in the seventeenth century, and whose views influenced the nation's founders. Locke aims to bring about a world in which human effort is likely to be rewarded: "God gave the World . . . to the use of the Industrious and Rational, (and *Labour* was to be *his Title* to it;) not to the Fancy or Covetousness of the Quarrelsom and Contentious."[51] Libertarians misread Locke when they claim that America's foundational commitments entail absolute property rights, which in turn limit or even bar taxation.

The twentieth-century philosopher John Rawls, whom many libertarians regard as their bitterest adversary, argued persuasively that in a fair social contract, such as Locke contemplated, inequalities must somehow benefit the least advantaged members of society. If state authority is not to be mere brute force, those on the bottom need a reason to support the rules that put them there. Rawls did not fully appreciate the virtues of capitalism, but he was right that its systemic effects matter. Hayek had something important to add to this conversation: he showed that free markets with their attendant inequalities can go a long way toward satisfying Rawls's principle. Economic growth will do more for the poor than redistribution can.[52]

Of course, there will always be people who cannot possibly provide for themselves in a market: the old, the sick, the orphaned. Hayek saw no principled objection to a state-funded minimal income. That is one difference between him and the other libertarians. Rothbard regarded property rights as so absolute that one may have an obligation to die of starvation rather than violate them. Rawls's powerful response is that no one could reasonably agree to such brutal terms of social cooperation.

The inadequacy of the libertarian account of freedom is revealed, in a different way, by two fields of regulation that it cannot account for, the ones that bothered me when I was a law student: addictive drugs and discrimination. An autonomous life requires a certain degree of self-control. Unrestricted availability of heroin, cocaine, fentanyl, and methamphetamine would destroy many people's lives. Those people are freer today because the law has kept them from learning how much they would like those drugs. (This is not to endorse contemporary America's vicious and counterproductive antidrug policies.)

Discrimination, when it is pervasive, frustrates the Lockean aspiration in a different way: effort is not rewarded when ambition is obstructed on the basis of race or sex or other arbitrary categories. People do not have a fair range of opportunities when the dominant culture consigns them to subordinate status the day they are born. This happens all over the world, wherever one tribe has conquered another: Dalits in India, Catholics in Northern Ireland, on and on. Antidiscrimination law appears to be an unavoidable aspect of a decently functioning modern capitalist system. These two cases show that genuine freedom requires both internal and external preconditions. Neither is delivered by a minimal state.

The Lockean aspiration is also thwarted if the world is so open to upheaval by market forces that it is impossible to plan a life. Even Hayekian libertarianism, the most reasonable of the variants, calls into existence a world too unstable and destructive for most people to endure without protest. Its operation will unleash, indeed is unleashing, forces that endanger both democracy and free markets. Libertarianism has no language to cope with those forces.

Libertarianism is at best a useful corrective to a political left that does not grasp the virtues of capitalism. Liberalism will be more attractive if it incorporates Hayek's insights. A few academic political philosophers understand this, and have been developing an attractive synthesis of Rawls and Hayek.[53] This book draws freely on their arguments. But their work is mostly unknown outside the universities. The result is that the moderate wing of the Democratic Party, instantiated by the presidencies of Bill Clinton, Barack Obama, and Joe Biden, does not know the best justification for what it has been doing.

I said at the outset that you probably have a political philosophy.

Everyone with political opinions does. A philosophy is implicit in Donald Trump's crude nationalism. You ought to be a libertarian—of a certain kind, and only up to a point. This book is not only a critical description of libertarianism. It aims to marry what is best about libertarianism with the agenda of the left. It proposes to harness the enormous productive energies of capitalism for the benefit of everyone, not just those who succeed in the market.

Chapter 1 explains Hayek's libertarianism. Chapter 2 turns to the question of rights, which Hayek neglected; it considers Locke's philosophy and Rawls's critique. Chapter 3 critically examines Rothbard, Nozick, and Rand. Chapter 4 addresses paternalism, focusing on drug policy and consumer protection. Chapter 5 takes up antidiscrimination law. Chapter 6 assesses libertarianism's impact on American politics, showing how Hayek's thoughtful defense of free markets has been corrupted into a tool of looters and moochers.

1

PROSPERITY

> I think what is needed is a clear set of principles which enables us to distinguish between the legitimate fields of government activities and the illegitimate fields of government activity. You must cease to argue for and against government activity as such.
>
> —Friedrich Hayek[1]

In the late 1930s, the world's most admired economic managers were Joseph Stalin and Adolf Hitler. The Great Depression had devastated most of the world's economy. In the United States, for example, between 1929 and 1933, real output fell by 29 percent. Unemployment rose from 3.2 percent to 21 percent (not counting 4 percent in government make-work programs). The Standard & Poor's index of stock values dropped from an average of 26.02 in 1929 to 6.93 in 1932.[2] Unemployment remained stubbornly high in the world's other leading democracies, Great Britain and France. Meanwhile the Soviet Union, which had always been a rural backwater, was industrializing rapidly. Germany, which only a few years earlier had devastating inflation and unemployment, was booming, stimulated by huge military and public works spending.

Most leading American and British politicians and intellectuals agreed that the only way back to prosperity was a scientifically planned economy. Even those who were unhappy about the dictators' methods agreed that capitalism had failed. They thought that, if there must be planning, it should be democratically controlled. It was, historian

Angus Burgin reports, "a period of extraordinary isolation for academic opponents of government intervention."[3]

A dissenting view had developed among a small group of Austrian economists, who argued that central economic planning could not work, because it would not be possible to calculate where capital should be invested. This movement began in the late 1800s as a direct response to the then-recent work of Karl Marx and was elaborated after World War I, when its leading scholars anatomized the baleful effects of the trade barriers that were developing between the nations that had previously been parts of the Austro-Hungarian Empire.[4] In 1931 one of their students, Hayek, was offered a job abroad that he could not refuse. "If you are at thirty-two a professor at the London School of Economics," he recalled, "you don't have any further ambitions."[5]

As the consensus grew for a planned economy, Hayek felt impelled to respond. He thought that the arguments for planning had already been rebutted by his teachers, but "found that certain new insights which were known on the Continent had not reached the English-speaking world."[6] He produced a series of writings in the 1930s, arguing that efficient economic decisions could not be made without private property and competitive markets. But his objections went beyond efficiency. He argued that central planning would inevitably become tyrannical.

The question of planning became more urgent with the outbreak of World War II. In wartime, centralized planning really is unavoidable: the government commandeers factories for war production, diverts resources from capital investment and consumer goods, fixes prices to avoid inflation, and sets up systems of rationing.

Hayek desperately wanted Hitler to be defeated, but he was also worried about what would happen after that. Many thought that state control of the economy ought to be continued in peacetime. The National Executive Committee of the British Labour Party declared in 1942:

> There must be no return to the unplanned competitive world of the inter-War years, in which a privileged few were maintained at the expense of the common good. . . . A planned society must replace the old

> competitive system. . . . The basis for our democracy must be planned production for community use. . . . As a necessary prerequisite to the reorganization of society, the main Wartime controls in industry and agriculture should be maintained to avoid the scramble for profits which followed the last war.[7]

So Hayek, who until that time had written only academic studies in economics, decided to write a popular book making the case against socialism. *The Road to Serfdom* was published in England in 1944. It was rejected by several American publishers before the University of Chicago Press produced a small run of two thousand copies. It was an unexpected bestseller.

A coalition of businessmen had been vainly opposing President Franklin Roosevelt's New Deal, sometimes in apocalyptic terms. The industrialist du Pont brothers founded the American Liberty League to "combat radicalism, preserve property rights, uphold and preserve the Constitution." It deemed the New Deal bureaucracy "a vast organism spreading its tentacles over the business and private life of the citizens of the country." The chairman of the Illinois division said, "You can't recover prosperity by seizing the accumulation of the thrifty and distributing it to the thriftless and unlucky." The league provided a handy foil for Roosevelt, who denounced "economic royalists" in his 1936 reelection campaign—which he won with a crushing 60 percent of the vote, giving the Democrats huge majorities in both houses of Congress. The Democratic Party chairman said that it "ought to be called the American Cellophane League" because "first, it's a Du Pont product, and second, you can see right through it."[8]

Hayek gave the movement a coherent basis for its views. The publication of *The Road to Serfdom* marks the beginning of libertarianism as a distinctive force in American intellectual life.[9]

Libertarianism is the philosophy that aims at freedom from government. In the context of the 1930s, the reason for focusing on that aspect of freedom was clear. The big threat to liberty was socialism—the

Marxist socialism of the Soviet Union, and the National Socialism of Germany. In the nineteenth century, there were plenty of defenders of laissez-faire, the policy of leaving markets unregulated and with no welfare provision. Their adversaries were different from Hayek's. The idea that men had a right to work where and how they wanted emerged in response to slavery in the American South.[10] The labor and populist movements aimed to raise wages and inflate the currency, but they did not propose central economic planning. The ideologists of free markets, such as Herbert Spencer and William Graham Sumner, were opposed to those movements, but they had no interest in restraining the state as such. The few promarket anarchists, such as the abolitionist Lysander Spooner, were politically marginal.

The earlier defenses of property rights were also philosophically underdeveloped, leaving them vulnerable to the criticism that they assumed rather than defending the legitimacy of existing distributions of wealth and power. Intellectuals who supported Roosevelt hammered that criticism repeatedly. His opponents had no good answer until Hayek came along.

Libertarianism is a variety of liberalism, the political philosophy that holds the purpose of government to be, not the dominance of one king, race, or nation, nor the promotion of religious, moral, or martial virtue, but rather peace, prosperity, intellectual progress, and above all personal liberty. Each individual is to be autonomous within a certain sphere which government must not violate. The dimensions of that sphere have been understood differently at different times and by different people. Most modern American political ideologies are variations on liberalism.

Libertarianism is distinctive in insisting on very strong property rights and minimal government. It is suspicious of, and in some forms categorically prohibits, economic regulation and redistribution. It associates these with socialism. Other liberals think that government must take a larger role if people are actually going to be free to live as they choose.

This disagreement can get pretty bitter. But that should not keep us from seeing that this is a family quarrel. Practical philosophy, of which political philosophy is a subset, needs a starting point. If we are going to think together about better and worse ways to act and govern ourselves, then we need some initial consensus from which to begin. We are lucky. We have a consensus on fundamentals. Few Americans are attracted to theocracy or open racism. Few repudiate liberty or equality.

The value of freedom is common ground between libertarians and their adversaries in contemporary American discourse, and to a large extent elsewhere in the world. Libertarians disagree with other liberals about strategy. We fight with each other about what a free society should look like.

It's sometimes said that libertarians differ from left liberals in their conception of freedom. Libertarians understand freedom in negative terms: as Hayek puts it, freedom is "the state in which a man is not subject to coercion by the arbitrary will of another or others."[11] Left liberals have a broader conception, one that includes the capacity to do things in the world. Thus, for example, Roosevelt's emphasis on "freedom from want"—an ideal that became a central war aim in World War II, and was the subject of Norman Rockwell's most famous painting.[12] A person in desperate poverty is unable to have the life he wants.

Hayek doesn't deny that "the range of physical possibilities from which a person can choose at a given moment" is tremendously important.[13] But, he argues, the way to deliver on that is to aim at freedom as he defines it. Central economic planning will deliver neither freedom from domination nor freedom from want. Almost all libertarians follow him in this: they think free markets and a small state together are a powerful engine for generating wealth and thereby positive liberty. They also seek freedom from want—as Roosevelt defined it, "economic understandings which will secure to every nation a healthy peacetime life for its inhabitants—everywhere in the world"[14]—but offer a different and, they think, more reliable path to get there.[15] A free market in food has driven its price down and its quality up. That means a lot less starvation.

Some libertarians misunderstand and mischaracterize their liberal adversaries, making their disagreement appear to be more fundamental than it is. Randy Barnett, for example, claims that the rise of the modern administrative state represents the defeat of the idea that people have rights against government. American political philosophy, he writes, is divided between republicanism, the idea that government exists to protect the natural rights of individuals, and progressivism, the idea that "the only individual rights that are legally enforceable are a product of majoritarian will."[16] It is true that some early-twentieth-century progressives had no use for rights talk, which they associated with the then-ubiquitous judicial invalidation of laws that protected workers. That ended over a hundred years ago. The liberal hostility to rights evaporated during the repressive war hysteria of 1919. The basis of the New Deal transformation was the claim that minimal government would not deliver liberty: in Roosevelt's words, "Necessitous men are not free men."[17] A Hayekian critique of Roosevelt's strategies should understand that this is a disagreement about means, not about ends.

Hayek was born in 1899. By leaving his native Austria for the professorship at the London School of Economics, he inadvertently escaped Nazi rule. In 1950 he was appointed Professor of Social and Moral Sciences at the University of Chicago. He returned to Europe in 1962. For much of his life, his biographer observes, "Hayek was a subject of ridicule, contempt, or, even worse for a man of ideas, indifference."[18] Over time his influence grew. In 1974 he won the Nobel Prize in Economics. He had claimed for decades that Keynesian stimulation of the economy would eventually produce inflation without growth. The stagflation of the 1970s seemed a vindication. Margaret Thatcher introduced him to Ronald Reagan. She once famously brandished a copy of his *Constitution of Liberty* and declared, "This is what we believe."[19] He died in 1992.

Modern libertarianism began with Hayek's attempt to resuscitate the idea of free markets. The decline of faith in markets, he thought, created an opportunity for a clearer articulation of their virtues: economic liberty's "underlying philosophy became stationary when it was most influential, as it had often progressed when on the defensive."[20] Nineteenth-century defenders of capitalism did not have to worry about either socialism or the modern regulatory state. One historian observes that Hayek's great innovation, along with his teacher, Ludwig von Mises, was "to create a defense of the free market using the language of freedom and revolutionary change."[21]

Hayek thought that central planning would inevitably lead to tyranny and poverty, but he also rejected the nineteenth-century ideal of a laissez-faire, minimal state. He sought to delineate a middle path.

The Road to Serfdom got much of its audience through publication of a *Reader's Digest* "condensed" version, which had more than eight million readers. More than a million reprints of the abridgment were distributed (compared with forty thousand copies of the original). The abridgment, however, was substantially different from the original, excluding many qualifications and with some wholly new sentences added. It was widely taken to be an endorsement of a minimal state. In 1945, *Look* magazine published a comic strip titled "The Road to Serfdom in Cartoons," which explained in eighteen pictures how what began as an idealistic effort to plan for everyone's needs would inevitably end in fascism. The final panel shows a firing squad executing an underperforming worker.[22] Hayek's own views were more nuanced, as I will shortly explain. So from the very beginning, American libertarianism was bifurcated into crude and sophisticated versions, with Hayek ironically the spokesman for both.

The book's reception reveals the origins of a fundamental mistake that plagues much of modern American libertarianism. Matt Zwolinski and John Tomasi have noted that, with its core concern about the ills of socialism, twentieth-century US libertarianism resembles nineteenth-century British and French libertarianism more than nineteenth-century American libertarianism, which tended to focus on slavery.[23] After 1848 the Europeans had real socialists to worry about. So did Hayek in Austria and England. The closest America came to that was the early, corporatist National Industrial Recovery Act phase of the New Deal (1933), which Roosevelt soon abandoned in favor of welfare state capitalism. Libertarians nonetheless persistently confused Roosevelt with Lenin. Misapplication of the socialism label is today one of the defining features of American libertarianism.

Hayek continued for the rest of his life to argue against government meddling in markets. In 1947, with funding from some of those same American businessmen, he founded the Mont Pelerin Society, an annual conference of scholars who opposed socialist planning. The society became an important school for libertarians, notably the young Milton Friedman.

Hayek argued that socialist central planning must fail. The basic problem is the immense amount of information that undergirds the complex division of labor: "As decentralisation has become necessary because nobody can consciously balance all the considerations bearing on the decisions of so many individuals, the co-ordination can clearly not be effected by 'conscious control,' but only by arrangements which convey to each agent the information he must possess in order effectively to adjust his decisions to those of others."[24]

Should a farmer grow beans or zucchini? It depends on what consumers want. How can he know what they want? And how can he know if consumer preferences change—if, for example, there is a surge of interest in fried zucchini flowers? Only prices in a market can convey the necessary information quickly and accurately. If the price of zucchini rises, farmers will plant more of it without needing to know anything about culinary fashions, or any of the incalculably many other factors that affect the demand for vegetables.

The irreplaceable virtue of free markets, Hayek thought, is their capacity to manage that flood of information. Mises had argued, against socialism, that without a market, one can't rationally calculate how to allocate capital. Hayek argued, more radically, that the necessary knowledge could not even be collected.[25] Innovation often emerges from individuals' tacit knowledge, inexplicit even to themselves. Its value is not reflected in existing prices, because the innovation does not yet exist. The problem is not the complexity of calculation, but the lack of information. No central authority can know all the competing demands for resources. Individuals often can't articulate their own reasons for wanting what they want. Even if (as "market socialist" economists claimed) central planners somehow could gather all pertinent objective data about consumer demand, they could not detect changes in individuals' knowledge and values.[26] The general welfare "cannot consist of the sum of particular satisfactions of the several individuals for the simple reason that neither those nor the circumstances determining them can be known to government or anybody else."[27]

We are fundamentally mysterious and opaque, to ourselves and to one another. I don't know what I want until I see what I do. What government should provide is not the direct satisfaction of needs, but the securing of conditions in which people have opportunities to provide for their own needs.

Markets respond to information with admirable precision. My zucchini example shows how. If the demand for a commodity increases, consumers bid up its price. That raises the profits of producers, and induces them to increase production and others to start producing the same commodity. Once the new supply matches or exceeds demand, the price falls, and the stimulus to production disappears. No one is managing the process, but the market nonetheless coordinates the productive activities of millions who need not even be aware of one another's existence.

Free markets played a crucial role in what Deirdre McCloskey has called "the Great Enrichment": after scraping by in desperate poverty for about one hundred thousand years, the human race became spectacularly rich beginning around 1800.[28] There is no single explanation for the Great Enrichment. The Industrial Revolution, the growth of trade, the consolidation of strong states, and the advance of science all played a role. The ingredient that Hayek emphasizes is the development and political entrenchment of ideas of liberty, equality, and property rights. People are a lot more likely to invest and cooperate if they get to keep what they produce.

Economic value is what people are willing to pay. People cannot be expected to agree on the purposes worth pursuing, not least because "new ends constantly arise with the satisfaction of old needs and with the appearance of new opportunities."[29] We can't argue about ends, because we often can't articulate our reasons for pursuing the ends we do. Each of us has a "unique combination of information, skills and capacities which nobody else can fully appreciate."[30] Yet somehow we must live together and cooperate. "What makes agreement and peace in such a society possible is that the individuals are not required to agree on ends but only on means which are capable of serving a great variety of purposes and which each hopes will assist him in the pursuit of his own purposes."[31]

Today's political left is often less concerned with putting money in the pockets of the working classes than with cultural imperialism and the oppression of minority identity. The concern with poverty persists but is part of a larger agenda. That agenda inevitably has Hayekian resonances. A right to be different pushes toward localization of power and away from central planning. Engagement with Hayek's ideas thus played a direct role in (temporarily!) transforming the ideology of the British Labour Party into Tony Blair's more capitalism-friendly version.[32] Many on the left repudiate capitalism because they don't grasp the anti-socialist logic of their present views.

There is, of course, a limit to this opacity. If the way to promote society's welfare is to provide what people are willing to pay for, then we will count only the preferences of those who have money to make purchases. If a rich family has a healthy baby, and a poor family has a sickly one, then an efficient market will give the healthy baby more visits to the pediatrician.[33] Rawls summarizes the problem nicely: "A competitive price system gives no consideration to needs and therefore it cannot be the sole device of distribution."[34] That is why Hayek thought redistribution to provide basic needs was an appropriate supplement to a free market. Such a supplement was not central planning, because it left the recipients free to make their own decisions.

Central planners must depend on a set of definite, specified goals. Since they cannot know all the purposes that individuals are pursuing, Hayek observed, they must impose their own. Tyrannical power is thus inherent in socialism.

In short, Hayek argued that a centrally planned economy must be both wasteful and dictatorial. It would deliver neither prosperity nor freedom.

In retrospect, it is remarkable how right he was. There's a tendency on the left to sneer at *The Road to Serfdom* for its exaggerated denunciation of government intervention in the economy. Hayek would eventually make such excessive claims. But they are not to be found in *The Road to Serfdom*. Its target was not the likes of Obamacare—as I mentioned in the introduction, Hayek himself proposed the basic scheme of Obamacare in 1960—but centralized control of the economy.

Increasing numbers of Americans, particularly the young, have favorable views of "socialism." But the term's usage has drifted. At Merriam-Webster they still define *socialism* as "collective or governmental ownership and administration of the means of production and distribution of goods."[35] But this is anachronistic. Today the word is generally taken to mean a welfare state, in which government assures a basic level of health, education, housing, and employment.[36] In 2018, only 17 percent of Americans understood *socialism* to mean "government ownership or control, government ownership of utilities, everything controlled by the government, state control of business," compared with 34 percent in 1949. Only 13 percent of Democrats in the same survey understood the term that way.[37] Thus Senator Bernie Sanders, the most prominent contemporary socialist, declares, "I don't believe government should own the means of production, but I do believe that the middle class and the working families who produce the wealth of America deserve a fair deal."[38] Central economic planning has largely been abandoned by the left. Hayek deserves much of the credit.[39]

One of the most troublesome aspects of the operation of a free market is the inequality that it engenders. During the 2008 presidential campaign, then-Senator Barack Obama was asked about his proposal to raise taxes on high-income households. His response: "It's not that I want to punish your success. I just want to make sure that everybody who is behind you, that they've got a chance at success too. I think when you spread the wealth around, it's good for everybody." This produced accusations of incipient socialism. Was Obama proposing the kind of dictatorial manipulation of the market that Hayek denounced?

Obamacare, as already noted, was divisive in large part because it did exactly what Obama the candidate proposed: it raised taxes on the rich to subsidize healthcare for people with low incomes. Most of the reductions in the 2017 Republican tax law, on the other hand, benefited the richest taxpayers. The disagreement about that law was precisely about the justice of the distribution of wealth. House minority leader Nancy Pelosi declared that the law would "rob from their future and ransack the middle class to reward the rich." Senator Sanders called the law "the looting of the federal Treasury." Defenders of the bill responded that the law merely permitted Americans to keep more of their own money.[40] Since the rich paid so much more in taxes, it was only fair for them to get a bigger share of any cuts.

Hayek's views of inequality are complex. He refuses to endorse the familiar claim that markets reward the industrious—an argument that was ubiquitous among American defenders of free markets before the 1930s.

The distributions of income that markets produce are efficient, Hayek thought, but they do not reliably reflect merit. Prices, including compensation for labor, signal what is demanded now, not whether producers made virtuous choices in the past. Claims about what's deserved are backward looking. Prices are forward looking. They tell people which of their efforts will be most valued by other people. John may have toiled selflessly for years to produce a product that he knew would greatly improve the lives of consumers, but if some lazy lout happens to stumble upon a better or cheaper substitute, John's business will be ruined. And it should be ruined. No one wants his product, and it would be wasteful to keep producing it. In a free market, Hayek concluded, rewards "will of necessity be determined partly by skill and partly by luck."[41]

He was ambivalent about the sense of entitlement that is typical of those who have become rich in a commercial society: "It certainly is important . . . that the individuals believe that their well-being depends primarily on their own efforts and decisions. Indeed, few circumstances will do more to make a person energetic and efficient than the belief that it depends chiefly on him whether he will reach the goals he has set for himself." But there is an element of delusion. It is unfortunate that free enterprise has been defended "on the ground that it regularly rewards the deserving, and it bodes ill for the future of the market order that this seems to have become the only defense of it which is understood by the general public. That it has largely become the basis of the self-esteem of the businessman often gives him an air of self-righteousness which does not make him more popular." So there is a "real dilemma" whether to encourage those "with whom the over-confidence in the appropriate reward of the able and industrious is strong and who in consequence will do much that benefits the rest, and whether without such partly erroneous beliefs the large numbers will tolerate actual differences in rewards which will be based only partly on achievement and partly on mere chance."[42]

Some readers will object that Hayek underestimates the degree to which markets reward merit. In a free market, those who think ahead and work hard tend to be lucky.

One of the deepest attractions of capitalism is that it realizes, imperfectly but as well as any economic system can, the idea that people deserve to be rewarded for their efforts. In many countries, people tend to support capitalism if they think that hard work, not luck, determines success. Among Americans, 69 percent agreed that "People are rewarded for intelligence and skill," a much bigger proportion than any other country.[43] Rough justice is not the same as injustice.[44]

The constant upheavals of capitalism sometimes produce a *lot* of roughness: huge populations can abruptly find that the skills they have relied upon for decades are suddenly worthless. Opportunities are inevitably unequal. Native talents vary widely, are compensated on the basis of contingent market conditions, and are not themselves deserved. The opportunity to engage in such cultivation, and even awareness of one's opportunities, depends on early education, the economic and social environment, and the values learned from parents and peers.

Hayek also observes that merit is not identical with the capacity to produce goods or services that others are willing to pay a lot for. There neither is nor should be any universal measure of merit. A free enterprise society should be "a pluralistic society which knows no single order of rank but has many different principles on which esteem is based; where worldly success is neither the only evidence nor regarded as certain proof of individual merit."[45]

He is clearly correct about this. There are virtues, including some that confer enormous benefits on others, that get no reward in a market, and which sometimes are even punished. Most people in infancy and senescence depend on unpaid care, usually from women, in a persistent, gendered pattern of custom and duty. The obligation to provide such care often tightly cabins women's economic opportunities—yet another reason why distribution of goods should not be determined solely by the market. When it is, the subordination of women is baked into the economic structure. (And of course some kinds of merit, such as courage in the face of suffering, are not even other-regarding.)[46]

So the winners in a market don't deserve all their gains. Hayek's defense of private property thus doesn't rule out (though it limits) redistributive taxation. One can take from the rich and give to the poor, and then the poor will be able to send their own price signals.

So why not equalize wealth within a market system? Hayek thought that large inequalities of wealth enhance productivity and so should be undisturbed. What "has contributed most during the last two hundred years to increase not only the absolute but also the relative position of those in the lowest income groups has been the general growth of wealth which has tended to raise the income of the lowest groups more than the relatively higher ones."[47]

This, Hayek thought, meant that government should not try to limit the inequality of wealth. Capital accumulation signals unmet demand, drawing resources into markets. Any limit on capital accumulation impairs the economy's capacity to respond to those signals.

Economic progress is not simply "an accumulation of ever greater quantities of goods and equipment." On the contrary, "the growth of income . . . more probably depends on our learning to use our resources more effectively and for new purposes."[48] That progress depends on economic liberty. "Nowhere is freedom more important than where our ignorance is greatest—at the boundaries of knowledge, in other words, where nobody can predict what lies a step ahead."[49]

Any substantial improvement over what is already on offer will beget extraordinary profits. That prospect drives innovators (or at least attracts investors), but any such gains are inevitably temporary. The competition of imitators will soon reduce returns to normal levels. Hayek was right about this: producers capture only about 2 percent of the social returns from technological advances.[50] Such advances are the primary cause of the Great Enrichment.[51]

The creation of new enterprises "is still and probably always will be done mainly by individuals controlling considerable resources."[52] Established corporations or institutional investors are likely to be cautious and bureaucratic.[53] Progressive taxation can frustrate this source of growth:

> The large gains of the successful innovator meant in the past that, having shown the capacity for profitably employing capital in new ventures, he would soon be able to back his judgment with larger means. Much of the individual formation of new capital, since it is offset by capital losses of others, should be realistically seen as part of a continuous process of redistribution of capital among the entrepreneurs. The taxation of such profits, at more or less confiscatory rates, amounts to a heavy tax on that turnover of capital which is part of the driving force of a progressive society.[54]

Thwarting such new formations of capital is likely to "strengthen the position of the established corporations against newcomers," and thus to "create quasi-monopolistic situations."[55] A class of wealthy investors limits corporate power: "What will control the power of large aggregations of capital are other large aggregations of capital."[56]

Today, innovation is in fact a substantial check on monopoly power. Cell phones and internet service, for example, have both steadily improved because of intense competition among enormous businesses. Corporate entities whose dominance seemed permanent, such as Nokia and America Online, learned the limits of their power.

These arguments justify inequality on the assumption that the rich reinvest their wealth and try to become even richer. Some very rich people live unostentatiously, never touching their capital or even buying more stock with some of the income. When this happens, one can reasonably ask in what sense the property is theirs. They are in effect holding it in trust for future generations, not only their own heirs but all those who will be able to consume more in the future because investments are being made now. The common claim that wealth has diminishing marginal utility—that redistribution is good because a dollar is more valuable to a poor person than to a rich one—is false if the redistribution would lead to underinvestment in long-range production. Some resources should be directed not to those who would benefit most from consuming them but to those who will make the most productive use of them.[57]

But of course the rich consume a lot as well, sometimes profligately and wastefully. Can that be justified?

Frivolous expenditures contribute in their own way to progress: "Even the successful use of leisure needs pioneering and . . . many of the toys and tools of sport that later became the instruments of recreation for the masses were invented by playboys."[58] Many new creations will initially be expensive, and therefore will begin as amusements of the wealthy: "The ambitions of the many will always be determined by what is as yet accessible only to the few."[59] Luxury consumption "serves to defray the cost of the experimentation with the new things that, as a result, can later be made available to the poor."[60] The automobile and the bicycle are both examples of what Hayek was describing. In the mid-1800s, bicycles were fashionable, expensive, dangerous playthings for rich young men. In the early twentieth century, the same was true of cars. Only later were ways devised to make them safe and cheap for the masses.[61] Inequality is the price of progress. "If all had to wait for better things until they could be provided for all, that day would in many instances never come."[62]

If there is to be inequality, it is better that it be random than that society try to tie it to virtue or aptitude—an attempt necessarily doomed: "No man or group of men possesses the capacity to determine conclusively the potentialities of other human beings," and "we should certainly never trust anyone invariably to exercise such a capacity."[63] The good fortune of an independent income, then, is best distributed with no attention at all to what anyone deserves: "We can only hope that this rare advantage is not meted out by human will but will fall by accident on a few lucky ones."[64]

Finally, Hayek thought that bequest by inheritance was the least socially destructive channel for parents' partiality for their children. Absent this, parents will try to use their influence to place them in advantageous jobs, which is even more wasteful and unjust. "Such is the case with all societies in which inheritance of property does not exist, including the Communist."[65] Even the unequal opportunities of children are useful. Everyone benefits from "socially valuable qualities which will be rarely acquired in a single generation but which will generally be formed only by the continuous efforts of two or three"—efforts that will give those families' children "the chance to benefit from the better education and material environment which their parents may be able to provide."[66] (Hayek himself was able to pursue an academic career in Vienna only because he could afford to serve first as an unpaid lecturer.[67])

Hayek thinks it is somewhat arbitrary that the rich are the ones who are rich and the poor are the ones who are poor. He admits, indeed insists, that neither deserves their position. Nonetheless, he argues that those at the bottom will have the best prospects if they accept this rather than using the state to equalize wealth. In short, Hayek endorsed the inequality engendered by markets, not because markets give each of us what we deserve, but because they produce growing wealth, which is good for everyone. No human agency is wise enough to do better.[68]

These arguments largely succeed in justifying *some* inequality. What they don't do, however—what they don't *try* to do—is show that the *existing distribution* of property is sacrosanct, or make a case for a minimal state. It is possible to have an expensive system of social insurance while continuing to concentrate wealth. The Netherlands, Denmark, Sweden, and Norway have low income inequality but high wealth inequality (though not as much as the United States).[69] Norway and Sweden have more billionaires per capita than the United States.[70] Germany has a huge public sector, a prosperous working class, steep progressive taxes, and the third-largest number of billionaires of any country. The poor can become better off—in much of the world, they *have* become better off—while a flurry of new billionaires makes inequality wider than ever. Even if America were to develop a welfare state comparable to that of the Nordic countries, there would still be astonishing levels of wealth at the top.

Redistribution need not inhibit growth. From 1950 to 1964, the top marginal tax rate in the United States exceeded 90 percent. During the 1950s, the US economy grew by 37 percent.[71] It has been difficult to establish any clear relation between the top tax rate, the magnitude of social welfare provision, and economic growth.[72] Reductions in the top tax rate historically have been more clearly associated with concentration of wealth at the top of the distribution.[73]

Given the extraordinary economic opportunities created by the modern world economy, it is, however, unlikely that any progressive taxation short of confiscation would prevent, rather than slow, the growth in the number of billionaires.

Consider Jeff Bezos. He is one of the richest people in history. When he started Amazon as an online bookstore in 1994, he warned his investors that there was a 70 percent chance that the company would fail. It was a spectacular success, and he has kept reinvesting his profits. Luck certainly played a role: he started an internet retailing company just when the market was awakening to that industry's possibilities. So did skill: the company operates with remarkable efficiency, prospering with very low profit margins. His wealth spiked during the COVID pandemic, when demand for online purchases became intense. By that time, Amazon had become the most efficient delivery service of all time, fulfilling many orders within twenty-four hours. It is impossible to calculate the benefit to ordinary people (in technical terms, the amount of consumer surplus) the company has generated. It was also impossible to anticipate the benefits of the company's innovations. By making it unnecessary to visit retail shops during the pandemic, Amazon must have saved thousands of lives. Bezos can look you in the eye and argue that you have good reason to consent to the economic structure that made him rich.

One need not claim that Bezos is morally entitled to his entire estate, or bless everything he has done. (And, the argument here is obviously no objection to a progressive income tax: without a substantial redistributive apparatus, Bezos will not be able to say truthfully that the system that enriches him is to everyone's benefit.) Working conditions at some Amazon warehouses are reportedly oppressive. His resistance to unionization, at a time when America so badly needs a reinvigorated labor movement, is reprehensible. But these grievances sting in part because he could remedy them and still be extraordinarily rich. He and his customers were not wrong to do what they have done, his fortune was the inevitable result of his company's success, and the company made everyone else better off.

Hayek's qualms about redistribution did not prevent him from supporting any welfare provision whatsoever. He saw no "reason why the state should not assist the individual in providing for those common hazards of life against which, because of their uncertainty, few individuals can make adequate provision," such as "sickness and accident."[74] The preservation of competition is consistent with "an extensive system of social services—so long as the organization of these services is not designed in such a way as to make competition ineffective over wide fields."[75] Even if we can't know what people deserve, we can detect misfortunes that they don't deserve, and we can remedy them. Hayek's social minimum, it has been observed, entails "more universal healthcare than the Affordable Health Care Act now provides."[76] And, of course, he would have let the state use compulsory taxation to extinguish Gene Cranick's fire.

The solution he embraced was "a certain minimum standard, dependent upon the average level of wealth of [the] country."[77] In a country as rich as the United States, that minimum could be pretty generous. "It can hardly be denied that, as we grow richer, that minimum of sustenance which the community has always provided for those not able to look after themselves, and which can be provided outside the market, will gradually rise."[78] He left unresolved, and therefore open to political contestation, the question of where to draw the line, as Keynes immediately noticed.[79] He opposed price controls, subsidies, a minimum wage, and other efforts to tinker with the operation of the market. A social minimum would not prevent markets from performing their informational function.[80] It remained unsatisfactory from the standpoint of justice, since "to confine to the citizens of particular countries provisions for a minimum standard higher than that universally applied makes it a privilege and necessitates certain limitations on the free movement of men across frontiers."[81] What could raise wealth across national borders was not redistribution but trade.

He resisted those aspects of the welfare state that go beyond a social minimum, including some that have become familiar parts of the American safety net and which have not produced the dire effects he feared. Insurance against income loss in old age is universal among rich countries; the richer the country, the more generous the insurance tends to be (with the United States a stingy outlier).[82] Consider Social Security. That program's benefits are tied to one's level of earnings: those who have earned more before retirement collect more after retirement. Social Security provides more than subsistence. It protects many retirees' middle-class status.

Hayek rejected all state efforts "to direct private activity towards particular ends and to the benefit of particular groups."[83] He thought that there could be no principled basis for any system of social insurance beyond "a limited security which can be achieved for all and which is, therefore, no privilege."[84] Once one goes beyond that minimum, "there is no limit to the demands that will be pressed for."[85] (Here one sees his fear of democracy, about which more anon.) Pension payments would exceed prior contributions, imposing an unfair burden on the young. The required contribution also paternalizes the present generation of workers, who "would be better off if the money were handed over to them and they were free to buy their insurance from private concerns."[86]

This issue made him hysterical: "Concentration camps for the aged unable to maintain themselves are likely to be the fate of an old generation whose income is entirely dependent on coercing the young."[87] He wrote that in 1960, after Social Security had been in place for decades. In 1976, he declared that "the extensive redistribution of incomes through taxation and the institutions of the welfare state" would lead "slowly, indirectly, and imperfectly" to "central economic planning."[88]

His terror of a slippery slope is perhaps understandable after experiencing the Nazis, but this is silly. Elizabeth Anderson observes that Social Security in fact has the virtues that Hayek emphasizes about property: the benefits are distributed "on an impersonal, nondiscretionary basis, independent of anyone's judgment of what a particular individual needs or deserves."[89] Recipients need not justify their financial choices to anyone. Social Security is tied to income, but that level is set mechanically, with no investigation into individual recipients beyond their level of contribution. Means-tested benefits, on the other hand, such as Supplemental Security Income, Temporary Assistance for Needy Families, Medicaid, and food stamps, require applicants to document that they are poor. Such programs therefore demand that people spend down their assets, and punish them for saving or even receiving gifts. Hayek thought that social insurance "would not make the private citizen in any way the object of administration; he would still be free to use his knowledge for his purposes and not have to serve the purposes of an organization."[90] Means testing in practice betrays this promise.

Hayek doesn't fully understand the concept of property. He knows that it can be specified in various ways: "The recognition of the right of private property does not determine what exactly should be the content of this right in order that the market mechanism will work as effectively and beneficially as possible."[91] But his imagination is limited. In an influential 1964 essay that Hayek evidently never read, Charles Reich observed that one function of property is "maintaining independence, dignity, and pluralism in society by creating zones within which the majority has to yield to the owner."[92] An income from government sources will accomplish this so long as it is effectively guaranteed: "There is no surer way to give men the courage to be free than to insure them a competence upon which they can rely."[93] Social Security accomplishes this.

In so doing, Anderson observes, it also benefits the young:

> First, by keeping up with rising standards and hence costs of living, it enables many parents to live in independent households, so they don't have to move in with their children—the overwhelming preference of both generations in the modern day. Second, it helps liberate women, primarily, from the need to drop out of the wage labor market so they can provide direct care to their parents or in-laws at home. Third, it helps spare the young from the burden of having to deal personally with the financial demands their parents would otherwise make on them, along with accompanying resentment, humiliation, guilt, needling, and supplication. The emotional costs of elder provision are dramatically lower when such provision is mediated by an impersonal entitlement system.[94]

Compare David Boaz's libertarian complaint that Social Security has "weakened family bonds by reducing parents' reliance on their children."[95]

Hayek's critique of Social Security thus inverts his fundamental commitments. Within the terms of his philosophy, it is an error, the result of his excessive fear of government interference with the economy. Yet, as we shall see in chapter 4, it is an influential error, generating endless schemes to privatize the program and cut its benefits.

In short, Hayek defends inequality, but he is vague about just how much inequality is necessary. He does not categorically rule out redistribution, and he may tolerate quite a lot of redistribution. It all depends on the likely consequences.

What did Hayek think about regulatory interference with markets? A lot of modern libertarians are uncomfortable with it, but the standard justification for most of the regulation we have now is Hayekian.

Market transactions generally make both parties better off. Trade makes the world richer. We can understand the value of trade even if we have no idea why or what people are trading. That is Hayek's core insight: the parties have information that we don't. Deliberate, consensual transactions are the building blocks of a free market. They spontaneously combine into a vast web of mutual cooperation. Without them there would have been no Great Enrichment.

As we have seen, in order for there to be a lot of trade, the parties need to be sure that it's safe to become richer, that bandits (including those in police uniforms) won't appear and carry off their gains. Adam Smith observed that those whose property is not secure "in this defenceless state naturally content themselves with their necessary subsistence; because to acquire more might only tempt the injustice of their oppressors."[96]

The consent of all the parties is how we know that the transactions are in fact making the world richer. If third parties are affected, then we don't know that. An indispensable condition of "the usefulness of the system of competition and private property," Hayek wrote, is "that the owner benefits from all the useful services rendered by his property and suffers for all the damages caused to others by its use."[97]

If A produces goods to sell to B, but his factory produces pollution that injures C and D more than the widget benefits B, then the world isn't richer after all. A and B have merely conspired to injure C and D. They are a new sort of bandit. (Chapter 6 will show that bandits of this kind tend to talk a lot about freedom.)

Markets often have effects on people who aren't buying or selling. Economists call these *externalities*. The parties to any transaction have no incentive to take externalities into account. If they ignore them, as A and B do in the example above, market prices won't reflect the real costs or benefits created by the transaction, and prices won't perform their Hayekian information-encapsulating function. Pollution regulations are a burden on businesses, and they may feel that their liberty is being infringed. But if they are making money by shortening the lives of their neighbors, then this infringement is justified.

The point is nicely illustrated by the political struggle over the regulation of fine particulates. These are particles of air pollution that are so microscopic that they can move through membranes from the lungs into the bloodstream. Particulate exposure has been associated with aggravated asthma, difficulty breathing, irregular heartbeat, lung cancer, kidney disease, chronic bronchitis, and premature death in people with preexisting cardiovascular or lung diseases. It is especially dangerous for old people, pregnant women, and children. In children, it passes directly into the brain, where it damages the development of their central nervous systems. There is no known safe level of exposure.[98]

The Obama administration imposed heavy limits on particulates. Those limits were so effective that they were the primary reason why the overall benefits of Obama-era regulations far exceeded their costs. Under Trump, EPA staff scientists continued to study the effect of particulates, and concluded that levels should be lowered still further. They estimated that doing so could save between 9,050 and 34,600 lives a year. The Trump administration declined, consistent with its broader quasi-libertarian program of rolling back environmental regulation.[99] It fired its panel of experts charged with studying the effects of particulate inhalation.[100] More generally, while earlier administrations required that regulations be justified by cost-benefit analysis, showing that the benefits exceeded the costs, the Trump administration focused exclusively on the costs of regulation to businesses, either ignoring the benefits or attempting to conceal them.[101]

The benefits of Clean Air Act regulation in the period 1990–2020 exceed the costs by a ratio of more than 30 to 1.[102] Taken as a whole, this regulatory structure does impose considerable costs on businesses, but those costs are massively outweighed by the harms that the regulation prevents. If one is to assess this regime from the standpoint of liberty, one must take account of the liberty not to breathe poisonous air. From a libertarian standpoint, toxic pollution should be impermissible for the same reasons that murder and robbery are impermissible.

That's the argument for regulation. When the market can't be trusted to get it right, government interference can be a gain for human freedom.[103]

Externalities can be positive as well as negative. Education, for example, benefits not only the student who pays for it but the society as a whole: educated people are more productive, less likely to commit crimes, better democratic citizens. If education is left to the market, there won't be enough investment in it. Similarly with basic science: it can't be patented, so there's not enough incentive to produce it.

Even with respect to technology, which can be patented, government-funded research or contracts have produced "semiconductors, integrated circuits, nuclear power, satellite communications, GPS, radar, the microwave (used in communication as well as cooking), jet engines, the radio (and its sister technology, television), and a dazzling range of high-tech materials and innovative methods for making them, from titanium to powder metallurgy."[104] And that's just the nonmedical technologies. The iPhone is a triumph of modern capitalism, but its major components—GPS, lithium-ion batteries, cellular technology, LCD and touch screen displays, connectivity to the internet—were created by research that was either funded or directly conducted by the government.[105] Infrastructure, transportation, sewers, reliable police, and courts are all undersupplied by markets.

Hayek understood that, where there are externalities, law may need to intervene.[106] This argument will not, however, necessarily justify the regulations that actually exist. Another ubiquitous theme in libertarian thought is the danger that regulators will be incompetent or venal or both. All transactions have *some* externalities. They have not prevented the Great Enrichment.[107] It is an open question whether intervention in any particular case will improve or worsen matters. In any specific area of policy, imperfect markets need to be compared with imperfect government.[108]

In a democracy, small, well-organized groups often are more likely to get their way than diffuse, unorganized groups. Legislators and administrators sometimes dole out political goodies to unworthy special interests. The "public choice" hypothesis, which almost all libertarians embrace, is that such organized interests are likely to advance their policy goals even when their gains involve greater losses for others who are unorganized. The consequence is legislation and regulation that stifle competition, pointlessly burden economic activity, and are likely to benefit wealthy stakeholders who know how to work the system.[109]

For instance, large farming interests spend a lot of money to keep their subsidies, artificially cheap high-fructose corn syrup finds its way into most processed foods, and the mass of citizens endure obesity, diabetes, tooth decay, and inflated food prices. Regulation is susceptible to "capture": established economic actors learn to influence their regulators, and use them to stifle competition. For decades, the Interstate Commerce Commission, which was created to protect farmers and consumers from monopolistic railroad rates, was the servant of the trucking industry, routinely stifling competition and raising shipping prices by denying new firms permission to carry goods across state lines.[110] So, whatever the defects of an unregulated market, the effects of regulation are sometimes worse. Hayek worried about that, and the struggle against this kind of pork is one of the most valuable things that modern libertarians do.[111] This undeniable pathology has led many libertarians to conclude that the regulatory state is irredeemable.

Fortunately, the public choice hypothesis is testable. It is falsified whenever the state delivers broad benefits to unorganized citizens at the expense of organized groups. And it is in fact constantly being falsified.

Consider the fact that the air you're breathing and the water you're drinking are both cleaner than they were when the Environmental Protection Agency was created in 1970. The administrative process insulates regulators from political pressure in numerous ways, and beneficial regulations have been enacted over the protests of both the president and Congress.[112]

Even libertarians—at least, the ones who are not anarchists—concede that *some* state actors, such as police and judges, usually are immune to bribery. They have to believe that, or their minimal state couldn't be trusted to do its job. If *those* officials can develop an internal culture that insulates them from capture, it is hard to see why, in principle, it is impossible for other agencies, agencies with far more expertise at detecting market failures, to do the same thing.[113]

Culture matters. Hayek understood that. He observed that some people pursue ends other than economic gain. Morality can be a powerful motivating force.[114] The abuse of state power, he thought, was prevented in successful democracies by a "background of unwritten traditions and beliefs."[115]

Legislators and government bureaucrats may be cozy with established business interests. On the other hand, they may be coldly distant from them and dedicated to their missions. Cass Sunstein, Obama's first head of the Office of Information and Regulatory Affairs, which oversaw the entire federal regulatory bureaucracy, recalls that whenever the views of interest groups were pointed out to him, he would respond, "Get your mind out of the gutter."[116] Deeply immersed in Hayekian economics during the many years he taught at the University of Chicago, Sunstein was fairly obsessed with refuting the capture hypothesis by insisting (here expressly following a policy laid down in the Reagan administration) that the benefits of any regulation demonstrably outweigh its costs.[117] His insistence on quantification does give him a basis for saying with reasonable confidence that the first three years of regulation under Obama produced net annual benefits of $91.3 billion.[118]

Even idealistic regulators make mistakes, and these are not disciplined by the market. Cost-benefit analysis necessarily involves a certain amount of guesswork.[119] But making mistakes is not the same as being captured by special interests. Externalities must be addressed, and the market won't address them.

Although anti-New Deal businessmen embraced Hayek, he wasn't really their ally. American government's share of gross domestic product (GDP) rose precipitously in the twentieth century. In 1900, government spending was 6.9 percent of GDP. It has risen continuously, with a few spikes in wartime, and is now about 36 percent.[120] The businessmen longed to reduce the size of government. They felt betrayed when Eisenhower, the first Republican president in twenty years, embraced big government and even expanded it, with massive military spending and the Interstate Highway System.

But most of that can be justified in Hayekian terms. The most expensive programs, Social Security and Medicare, function as a variant of the social minimum that Hayek endorsed, since most of their beneficiaries lack significant other income. (Social Security benefits are more than half of pension income for all but the top fifth of retirees, and it is 31 percent even for them.[121]) There are elements of flagrant waste and rent seeking. But even if you cleaned all that up, government spending wouldn't be much less than it is now.

"Regulation" is really too crude a category to rely on for any purpose, because it isn't analytically distinct from law in general. Regulation is just a kind of law, the kind that agencies are authorized to promulgate. It makes no sense to be against regulation as such. Law can be good or oppressive, but one needs to get into the specific case for any measure before one can tell.

Hayekian suspicion of government has its uses. It is the source of the most valuable contributions that libertarians have made. But it also shows their limitations.

When scientists test hypotheses, they use standardized terms to refer to their mistakes. A type I error is the (false) detection of an effect that has not in fact occurred. A type II error is the failure to detect an effect that has in fact occurred. When a doctor mistakenly diagnoses a disease that you haven't actually got, and orders unnecessary surgery, that is a type I error. Of course, it's just as bad if she commits a type II error—declaring that you're not sick when you really are, or that you'll get better without treatment. Good doctors are constantly alert to both kinds of mistake.

Now imagine a doctor—let's call him Dr. Pangloss—who worries obsessively about unnecessary treatment, to the point where he's agonizingly reluctant to interfere with the body's capacity to heal itself. He will become dangerous if he routinely remains passive when medical intervention is necessary. If he's almost never willing to risk type I error, he should not be a doctor.

Libertarianism presents that kind of danger. In the context of regulation and redistribution, unnecessary government intervention is type I error, and the failure to intervene is type II error. Libertarianism focuses on type I error and is oblivious to type II. In practice, then, just like Dr. Pangloss, it produces a *lot* of type II error. It is biased against intervention, either because it is excessively optimistic about the virtues of unregulated markets and excessively pessimistic about honest competent regulation (Milton Friedman, Richard Epstein), or because it regards regulation as a violation of rights (Rothbard, Rand). Hayek is often taken to have the same bias, but as we have seen, he is carefully agnostic on the question of when intervention is warranted.

The focus on type I error can be valuable. If you make it your mission in life to find it, you sometimes will find it. You will then have made an important contribution to our knowledge. Dr. Pangloss shouldn't be treating patients, but he could be a fabulous medical researcher, saving lives by showing that some treatments are useless or harmful. Libertarians who are confident that the state can do nothing right have produced first-rate scholarship about abuses of regulatory power. That doesn't mean they ought to be in charge of government.[122]

Antitrust is ripe for renewed regulation. In a well-functioning market, competition tends to drive down profits. Yet some firms are managing to maintain abnormally high profits for years. Among firms that were making returns on invested capital above 25 percent in 2003, 85 percent still had returns at that level in 2013.[123] Meanwhile there is "higher concentration in industries as diverse as banking, agribusiness, hospitals, wireless providers, and railroads."[124] The rate of new business formation, the size of new firms, and the share of American workers employed at young firms have all fallen since the 1980s.[125] All of this suggests that something is suppressing the competition that Hayek placed his faith in.

Libertarians will claim that monopolies happen only when politically connected businesses manipulate government for their own benefit.[126] But another source of concentration is the abuse of market power, which fits less comfortably into the libertarian narrative.

The United States has some of the highest broadband prices, and the slowest speeds, among advanced nations: its average peak internet connection speed is nearly 40 percent slower than in Hong Kong or South Korea, and many Americans have no access because they can't afford it. Once cable is laid, no one else has an incentive to lay new cables. Some countries have stimulated competition by building fiber lines with public funds and then leasing them to private operators. In America, cable companies have spent millions to block similar efforts.[127]

Monsanto's genetically modified seeds are used in 90 percent of soybeans and 80 percent of corn planted in the United States. The seeds are engineered to resist Monsanto's herbicides, but they don't produce seeds of their own, and so farmers have to buy new seeds each season. Monsanto has bought up most of its competitors, and seed dealers who carry its products are contractually barred from stocking competitors' seeds. Since 2001, it has more than doubled the price of its seeds. It has managed to obtain favorable legislative treatment with expanded patent protection, sued other companies for patent infringement, and even prevented independent scientists from studying its seeds. Its former and future employees hold top posts at the Food and Drug Administration and the Agriculture Department, and staff congressional committees dealing with agricultural policy. It managed to end a two-year Justice Department antitrust investigation.[128]

In many labor markets in the United States, industry has consolidated to the point that employers have enough market power to hold down wages. Aside from the way in which this market distortion enhances income inequality, it leads workers to underinvest in skills, drives some workers out of the labor market altogether, and depresses the overall return on capital.[129]

Hayek was ambivalent about antitrust law. In some moods, he was Panglossian: no one will be able to maintain a monopoly for long, so no intervention is necessary. But he was too keen an economic observer to believe that this was always the case. Deeply suspicious of administrative discretion, he was troubled by the fact that no clear set of rules could delineate how much market power is too much. It is thus easy for later Hayekian students of antitrust to lapse into uncritical Panglossianism.[130]

The deployment of libertarian rhetoric to constrain government regulation has crippled its capacity to respond to indisputable harm. In the 1970s, Congress would certainly have enacted significant legislation in response to the Upper Big Branch Mine disaster, in which flagrant violations of federal safety regulations killed twenty-nine workers, or the *Deepwater Horizon* oil spill, the largest oil spill in the history of the petroleum industry.[131] Both disasters happened in 2010, however, and Congress did not respond. As I will explain in chapter 6, the most important accomplishment of libertarianism is preventing, for decades, any significant response to the danger of global climate change.

The big difference between Dr. Pangloss and libertarian politics is that no one's interests are served by type II medical error. Dr. Pangloss is confused, but he isn't corrupt. But sometimes, when the state fails to intervene when it should, someone gets rich. Libertarian hyperbole is often abused in the service of mooching and looting.[132]

The pathologies interact. Some of the very complexities that libertarians complain about can generate opportunities for capture, leading to type I error. But those complexities arise in response to real failings of the market, so a response that cripples the government generates type II error.

To show how this is so, I'll consider one pathology of big government. And I'll show that the only way to counter it is with another aspect of big government.

A chronic defect of complexity in the modern administrative state is what Steven Teles calls "kludgeocracy." The term, Teles explains, "comes out of the world of computer programming, where a kludge is an inelegant patch put in place to solve an unexpected problem and designed to be backward-compatible with the rest of an existing system." The programmer sees something wrong with the program and throws together a fix that has nothing to do with the program's overall design and can unexpectedly screw up other aspects of the program. "When you add up enough kludges, you get a very complicated program that has no clear organizing principle, is exceedingly difficult to understand, and is subject to crashes. Any user of Microsoft Windows will immediately grasp the concept."[133] Much of policy is like that: an uncoordinated accumulation of legislation enacted to solve particular problems, producing an incoherent patchwork.

An example is poverty programs. Each of them made sense as a way to address a problem, but taken together, they are an incoherent mess. In some cases, they trap people in poverty by imposing marginal tax rates in excess of 100 percent: for every dollar you earn by working, you lose more than a dollar in eligibility for payments from various, unconnected welfare programs.[134]

Kludges make the system more susceptible to capture. The harder it is to understand the system, the more any policy area is necessarily dominated by specialists. Those specialists increasingly are the lobbyists of interested groups. It's often claimed that government's capture by rich special interests is the consequence of unlimited campaign spending. But the more potent source of their power is the state's dependence on them for information. Brink Lindsey and Steven Teles observe that because most policymakers "are consumers, rather than producers, of information . . . those in a position to produce information that is taken as credible by policymakers have a profound advantage in politics."[135] Lobbyists have influence, not only because they can threaten to spend or withhold campaign money but because they also provide specialized information. The information that is provided is biased in favor of organized interests, and so tends to promote upward redistribution.

Policymakers can resist this tendency toward capture, Lindsey and Teles write, only if they become less dependent on lobbyists for expertise and information. But at the same time as the number of lobbyists in Washington has soared, Congress's capacity to process information has been enfeebled: "Starting around 1980, Congress stopped hiring, then began cutting. House committee staff plunged by almost 40 percent between 1979 and 2005. Today, the Government Accountability Office employs 40 percent fewer staffers than it did in 1979, while staffing at the Congressional Research Service, which provides nonpartisan policy and program analysis to lawmakers, is down 20 percent."[136]

The only way to resist the biased information flowing from lobbyists, they conclude, is "staff with a great deal of sector-specific knowledge and a high level of technical capacity."[137] Given the tendency toward kludge, Congress will periodically need to overhaul and streamline this or that area of policy. Either it will have the independent analytic capacity to do that or it will produce a Christmas tree of special favors for the politically connected.

Notice how this conclusion cuts against libertarian orthodoxy. It's commonly claimed that the cure for capture is to reduce the number of government regulations and government employees. It turns out, however, that an informationally weak state is chronically susceptible to capture. Information requires money and personnel. Simultaneously avoiding type I and type II errors is a complicated business, demanding an expensive army of specialists. To realize the Hayekian aspiration, we need a bigger state.[138]

The possibility of a state that is not corrupt brings us to a major theme of Hayek's thought, overlooked by many of his followers: the importance of ideals in explaining behavior. Markets work because of evolved rules of conduct, such as honesty and respect for property.[139] Fear of the law is not why people generally respect other people's property rights. They do that even when the cops aren't watching, because they've been socialized to think that this is the right thing to do. So have most of the cops.

Socialization creates us: "It is not only in his knowledge, but also in his aims and values, that man is the creature of civilization."[140] People act on the basis of learned rules and norms, and these are necessary to a peaceful society. "Coercion can probably only be kept to a minimum in a society where convention and tradition have made the behavior of man to a large extent predictable."[141] And necessary to a complex economy: "Living as members of society and dependent for the satisfaction of most of our needs on various forms of co-operation with others, we depend for the effective pursuit of our aims clearly on the correspondence of the expectations concerning the actions of others on which our plans are based with what they will really do."[142]

Knowledge is not only intellectual. It also includes "habits and skills, our emotional attitudes, our tools, and our institutions." All of these are "adaptations to past experience which have grown up by selective elimination of less suitable conduct."[143]

His defense of markets is not predicated on the notion that everyone is selfish. He does not claim "they are or ought to be exclusively guided by their personal needs or selfish interest," but rather "that *they* ought to be allowed to strive for whatever they think desirable.[144]

"The innermost contradiction in Hayek's system of ideas," John Gray observes, "is between a conservative attachment to inherited social forms and a liberal commitment to unending progress."[145] Hayek thinks that great wisdom is encoded in traditional ways of life. Yet the dynamism of markets tends to disrupt traditions. Entire industries disappear, destroying the communities that depended on those industries. New opportunities free people to resist communal social control.

Hayek never resolved this tension, which remains with us. The economist Joseph Schumpeter famously wrote that capitalism is characterized by "creative destruction," driven by "the new consumers' goods, the new methods of production or transportation, the new markets, the new forms of industrial organization that capitalist enterprise creates." This process "incessantly revolutionizes the economic structure from within, incessantly destroying the old one, incessantly creating a new one."[146] Whole industries disappear: there are no more jobs for watchmakers, carriage and harness makers, blacksmiths, or wheelwrights.

The process of creative destruction continues to revolutionize the American economy, making the lives of most workers increasingly stressful and precarious. To take one dramatic example, driverless trucks will soon eliminate 3.5 million jobs.[147] Manufacturing jobs in the United States are likewise disappearing forever, not because of foreign competition—American manufacturing output is higher than it has ever been—but because automated factories need far fewer workers than they once did.[148]

The competition of foreign laborers has depressed wages, though it's less important than automation. Libertarianism's greatest victory, the collapse of socialism, wasn't good for everyone. "Absent China, India, and the ex-Soviet bloc, there would have been about 1.46 billion workers in the global economy in 2000. The entry of those countries into the global economy raised the number of workers to 2.93 billion."[149] As already noted, this is great news for much of the human race. But it was terrible for American workers, particularly those without advanced education. Increase the supply of anything that much, and its price will inevitably drop. The modern economy offers rich rewards to those with the right knowledge and skills, but the two are unevenly distributed, and workers without them are in trouble.[150]

In America it now takes two working parents to provide the standard of living that one could once manage, and their situation is far less secure. "In 1970, the typical American family had a 7 percent chance of experiencing a 50 percent drop in their income in a given year; since then . . . the risk of such a drop has more than doubled, to 16 percent. The number of households filing for bankruptcy multiplied sevenfold between 1980 and 2005; the mortgage foreclosure rate has multiplied fivefold."[151] Nearly four out of ten American adults would have to borrow money or sell property if they faced a four-hundred-dollar expense, and a quarter of these doubt that they could raise the money at all.[152] Millions have dropped out of the workforce.

From the standpoint of market rationality, this is all a routine adjustment: globalization of the economy increased the supply of labor, robots depressed the demand, and so the price has fallen. The economy may just be able to do without all those workers, just as, after the invention of the automobile, it no longer needed all those horses. But the economic system did not purport to be for the benefit of the horses, and the horses did not vote.

These upheavals have generated a lot of angry people, who signaled their displeasure by voting for Brexit and Trump. There has been impressive growth, but they are not better off. Creative destruction has usually meant that new jobs are created that paid better than the old ones (the wages of a wheelwright weren't so great), but that hasn't been happening. Part of the promise of capitalism is that it will create opportunities. In 1998, 74 percent of Americans agreed that "Most people who want to get ahead can make it if they are willing to work hard." By 2011, that had fallen to 58 percent.[153]

All Hayek can say to those whose lives have been disrupted by the operation of markets is that this is the price of growth. He faces a dilemma: "The necessity of adaptation to unforeseen events will always mean that someone is going to be hurt, that someone's expectations will be disappointed or his efforts frustrated."[154] These effects must, for the sake of opportunity for everyone, be disregarded by the state: "The known and concentrated harm to those who lose part or all of the customary source of income must . . . not be allowed to count against the diffused (and, from the point of view of policy, usually unknown and therefore indiscriminate) benefits to many."[155] But at the same time, too much disappointment and frustration is politically dangerous: "The one thing modern democracy will not bear without cracking is the necessity of a substantial lowering of the standards of living in peace time or even prolonged stationariness of its economic conditions."[156]

Karl Polanyi, the economic historian, observed that capitalism has always been persistently characterized by a "double movement": the expansion of markets elicits political efforts to blunt their disruptive effects.[157] Hayek thought that such political efforts tended to create fields of tyrannical bureaucratic discretion and rent-seeking. Thus he opposed even such mild ameliorative income stabilization measures as Social Security.

The double movement is unavoidable, because there is a limit to how much creative destruction voters will endure. Populations whose ways of life have been smashed may threaten the stability of the entire system. The danger of populist revolt is exacerbated if there is a weak social safety net, as in the United States.[158] Intervention to protect those ways of life can help to preserve the system of free trade, but Hayek feared such intervention, because it empowered the state, unconstrained by rules, to pick economic winners and losers.

The favoritism that Hayek so despised does not always stymie the economic growth he hoped for. South Korea is a spectacular success story of economic development. In 1960, it was poorer than North Korea, which had pursued Soviet-style forced industrialization. Today it is the eleventh-largest economy in the world. Its boom took place under a massively corrupt government promoting crony capitalism. The corruption may even have facilitated South Korean growth by lowering transaction costs and encouraging long-term investments among elites.[159] France nationalized much of its industry for decades, but they were decades of sustained economic growth, and it remains one of the richest countries in the world. It phased out its coal industry (which at its peak employed 350,000 miners) gradually, with a series of planned retirements and retrainings, and managed not to lay off a single worker. Compare the brutal collapse of the same industry in the United States and Britain.[160]

One of Hayek's triumphs was the development of an international trade regime that cabined the discretion of individual nations to interfere with markets.[161] An influential disciple cited his "conclusion that a free system is possible only by renunciation of discretionary policy and by binding all action of the state to general, constitutionally guaranteed legal principles."[162] (Some libertarians carry the point even further, demanding a return to the gold standard.)

The fear of centralized control begot a more general fear of democracy. Hayek eventually laid aside his caution of centralized schemes and became a daffy armchair constitutional designer, proposing a bicameral legislature in which the upper chamber is composed only of people elected at the age of forty-five for a fifteen-year term by an electorate also consisting only of forty-five-year-olds.[163] Liberals since the nineteenth century have regarded democracy warily, and Hayek was no exception. His fear of centralized planning led him to meet and support General Augusto Pinochet, who promoted capitalism in Chile by exterminating its critics.[164]

Democracy offers, at a minimum, the opportunity for those who are ruled to punish abuses of power. That is its deepest affinity with liberalism, an affinity that Hayek did not grasp. He feared that in a democracy, the masses would vote to loot the rich and ruin the operation of markets. In fact, expansion of markets and expansion of the franchise have happened simultaneously, in each case constraining the capacity of extractive elites to loot the masses. With democratic rights came the right to start new businesses without having to depend on political connections. Redistribution has predominantly taken the form of impersonal programs like Social Security that do not manipulate markets.[165]

Even if, as many political scientists think, the people cannot form a common will, and some kind of rule by political specialists is inevitable, elections are a crucial check on those specialists.[166] In most regimes, the rich demand economic controls in order to maintain their privileges. The English Corn Laws, in effect between 1815 and 1846, are a prominent example. The nobility owned most of the profitable agricultural land, so they benefited from laws prohibiting cheap imports of food. Free traders fought these laws, arguing accurately that they tended to starve the poor. In modern conditions, if citizens have no way of controlling government, then the elite-guided rule of law that Hayek aspires to can degenerate into bureaucratic obliviousness or a capitalist version of Brezhnevian kleptocracy. Hayek's trust in unaccountable policymakers here reveals a naïveté about the corruptions of power that mirrors that of Marx and Lenin.

That gap in Hayek's understanding sheds light on one of his most enduring and malign legacies, hostility to labor unions. In recent decades, the proportion of unionized American workers has steadily diminished, partly as a consequence of deliberate Hayekian public policy.

Employers have become increasingly sophisticated in defeating the aims of the National Labor Relations Act, just as taxpayers keep devising clever ways to get around the tax code. The act forbids firing union leaders or threatening employees with dismissal, discipline, or demotion for attempting to unionize. Beginning in the late 1970s, employers figured out that the penalties for lawbreaking were low enough that they could be priced in as one of the costs of fighting unionization. Employers are charged with violating federal law in more than two out of five union election campaigns.[167] Other union-busting tactics that are legally permissible, such as captive-audience meetings, distribution of antiunion literature, and rewarding employees who campaign against unionization, have become employers' automatic playbook. Almost half of nonunion workers polled in 2017 said they would join a union in their workplace tomorrow if they got the chance.[168] Although Congress has constantly amended the law to eliminate tax loopholes, it has done little to stop union busting.[169]

The near-extinction of private sector unions has been one of the principal causes of rising economic inequality. Hayek thought that unions inefficiently raise labor costs, promote inflation, and distort the allocation of investment.[170] On the other hand, organized labor was one of the few mechanisms that mobilized the less advantaged members of society and organized them into coherent voting blocs. Without private sector unions, the political system is under little pressure to respond to those people's interests, including their interests in the basic legal protections that Hayek hoped to guarantee for everyone.

The point here is the one that James Madison made when he defended the Constitution's checks and balances. Abuses will happen whenever there's unaccountable authority. Libertarians tend to focus on the dangers of state power, but are often oblivious of the dangers of unchecked private power. "Whenever modern idealists are confronted with the divisive and corrosive effects of man's self-love," Reinhold Niebuhr wrote in 1944, "they look for some immediate cause of this perennial tendency, usually in some specific form of social organization."[171] A weak state is a recipe for oligarchy.

Market incentives are not always benign. The prospect that investors will take their assets out of a country can dissuade governments from confiscating property or corrupting their legal system. But capital may also be drawn to places with weak environmental and labor rules, where investors can, with state connivance, impose costs on local populations out of all proportion to the benefits. Cheap products will find markets even if they are the result of massive human rights abuses. American antebellum slavery prospered within early-nineteenth-century capitalism. A nation's otherwise well-functioning economy can be devastated by capital flight when interest rates spike on some other part of the planet.

The mechanical application of market rules and elimination of price manipulation can produce catastrophe. In 1997, a wave of financial crises hit Asia, eventually spreading worldwide. In Indonesia, the unemployment rate rose tenfold, and by 1998, GDP fell by 13.1 percent. The International Monetary Fund came to the rescue, but its price was elimination of some of the government-induced market distortions that so troubled Hayek: subsidies for food and kerosene. Riots followed, with revenge killings and attacks on property directed at the capitalist classes, mainly ethnic Chinese. The government pounced on the opportunity to nationalize industrial assets worth billions, and capital fled the country.[172]

The task of the statesman is much like the task of foreign policy. When the liberal order faces chaotic contingencies that threaten its continuing existence, rigid rules that constrain the state, of the kind that Hayek advocated, are counterproductive.

The logic of Hayek's philosophy, in short, yields not a minimal state but the regulatory and welfarist structure of most modern democracies, with more energetic regulation and redistribution than we have now. If one must point to a destination to which Hayek's reasoning leads, it is where Hayekians never look: the Nordic nations.

Denmark, Finland, Norway, and Sweden have big, expensive welfare states. But they also have burgeoning capitalism. Free markets make these nations rich, and the benefits are shared by even the most marginal workers. Their economic systems are not different in kind from that of the United States, which also has a fairly large welfare state. Public provision is simply less stingy, and life at the bottom less stressful and precarious. The expansion of these programs, in the United States and elsewhere, has had no discernible effect on innovation and growth. A welfare state does not necessarily impair the workings of markets, and there is no real trade-off between them.[173]

Categorical opposition to big government is Hayekian only if one assumes either that the market operates perfectly or that the state is too corrupt or incompetent to deal with its flaws. As we have seen, those claims are unsustainable. Yet they are widely believed.

Milton Friedman supplied precisely this optimism. He wrote a column for *Newsweek* magazine from 1966 to 1984, which "pushed reasonably hard-core libertarianism on matters both economic and personal to the largest audience of American readers that would ever see them."[174] His basic framework was Hayekian. But he was far more skeptical than Hayek of the existence of market failure, or of the government's capacity to respond appropriately to such failure. He argued sweepingly that "on the whole, market competition, when it is permitted to work, protects the consumer better than do the alternative government mechanisms that have been increasingly superimposed on the market."[175]

The persistent theme of his popular work is rosy scenarios of what will happen if we privatize everything. In 1962, a couple of years before the passage of the federal Civil Rights Act produced a massive increase in the incomes of Black Americans, he argued that such legislation was neither necessary nor wise.[176] The "appropriate recourse" for those who reject racism "is to persuade our fellows to be of like mind, not to use the coercive power of the state to force them to act in accordance with our principles."[177] That strategy had been attempted for nearly a century without success. "It's extremely hard," Paul Krugman observes, "to find cases in which Friedman acknowledged the possibility that markets could go wrong, or that government intervention could serve a useful purpose."[178]

Hayek acknowledged that markets produced losers as well as winners. Not Friedman. Angus Burgin's history of modern free market economics observes that Friedman's "was not a Spencerian or Sumnerian world in which free markets dealt crushing blows to some in order to contribute to the greater advancement of humanity. Rather, it was one in which incontrovertible benefits redounded, in a display of spectacular beauty, to people of all kinds and in all situations. He represented markets as an unremitting good."[179]

In his valedictory work, *Free to Choose*, Friedman does, in one brief passage, acknowledge that markets can fail, notably because they do not take account of externalities such as pollution. But he immediately shifts his focus to regulatory failure, concluding weakly that regulation should be adopted only if the benefits clearly exceed the costs.[180] He then devotes the rest of the book to cataloging misbegotten economic interventions, many of which concededly were pretty bad. The possibility that any significant regulatory structure could improve human welfare is barely mentioned, and the nonspecialist, at whom the book is aimed, would likely conclude that it never happens.

What Friedman offered, Burgin writes, was far more categorical than his predecessors such as Hayek. "In contrast to their deliberate moderation and rhetorical restraint, he expressed an uncompromising belief that markets would engender better social outcomes than programs administered by the government."[181] The result was ironic. "The rise of Milton Friedman represents both the realization of Hayek's dream of inspiring broad popular support for the benefits free markets have to offer, and the final failure of his ambition to create a new social philosophy that would moderate the excesses of prior modes of market advocacy."[182]

When libertarianism demands a minimal state because that will produce better consequences, it relies on something like Friedman's story, building categorical prescriptions on highly contingent, often false foundations.

The same is true of Richard Epstein, probably the most sophisticated modern Hayekian in the legal academy. He is probably the most influential living libertarian. (His libertarianism is fundamentally Hayekian, which is why he is in this chapter.) A careful assessment concluded that he "has played a key role in challenging the statist Progressive/New Deal consensus that has dominated historical scholarship for decades. His assaults on the welfare state and redistributionist programs have done much to reopen debate about the New Deal legacy."[183] At Clarence Thomas's Supreme Court confirmation hearings, then-Senator Joseph Biden grilled the nominee about a speech in which he had spoken favorably of Epstein's constitutional writings, and dramatically waved a copy of one of Epstein's books. Biden was right to worry. Thomas later embraced a theory of the limits of federal power that looked a lot like Epstein's—one more extreme than any Supreme Court justice had endorsed since the 1930s.[184]

Epstein demonstrates what Hayek does not, that certain understandings of rights—preeminently, the security of persons and property and the enforcement of contracts—are indispensable if the virtues of free markets are to be realized.[185] (Hayek doesn't know how to think about rights.) Epstein elegantly shows that those understandings are *necessarily* reflected in existing legal systems, from ancient Rome to the English common law.[186] As with Hayek, those rights do not preclude regulation, but only lay down strict conditions for them.[187]

Much of Epstein's work exposes dysfunctional state interventions in the economy, with breathtaking mastery of a huge range of policy issues. He shows, for example, that the ban on organ sales has stupidly killed thousands of people.[188] He proposes radical revisions of constitutional doctrine in order to forestall such clumsy interferences with markets.[189]

He is less categorically hostile to regulation than Friedman.[190] The state may "adopt programs that aid in the effective enforcement of private rights when the high costs of private actions make them insufficient to deter or eliminate wrongful behavior," for example when pollution has "multiple sources and/or multiple victims."[191] In such cases, he is willing to let the state regulate aggressively.[192] (His skepticism toward antidiscrimination law will be taken up in chapter 5.) Some libertarians want the state to protect persons and property, but reject administrative regulation. Epstein understands that sometimes administrative regulation is the only way to protect persons and property.[193]

But he would block one crucial aspect of modern regulation. A lot of modern law diminishes the value of property by restricting its uses, for example by prohibiting landowners from draining swamps in order to build upon them. He thinks the state should not be permitted to impose such restrictions, without compensation to the owners, unless the prohibited behavior would be a nuisance at common law.[194] Otherwise, the restriction would be unconstitutional unless the owner were paid for the reduced value of the land. This restriction makes sense, Epstein argues, because "the major political risk is that the government will overclaim private resources that have far less value in public hands than they do in private ones."[195] Judicial toleration of rules that protect wetlands or animal habitat "lets the government operate as if there were no budget or scarcity restraints on their behavior."[196] It is impossible to predict the environmental consequences of his proposed rule, which would require government to somehow raise billions in order to purchase easements from landowners, and allow unrestricted development if the money is not forthcoming. It might be less happy than he predicts. His optimism about an unregulated economy produced embarrassing results when he embraced climate change denial and, disastrously, predicted early in the COVID-19 epidemic that the disease would cause no more than five hundred deaths.[197]

He is even more suspicious of state-mandated redistribution than Hayek or Friedman (who supported a negative income tax): any notion of "a positive right to life and to the wherewithal that everyone needs to survive . . . imposes impossible correlative duties of support on everyone for the benefit of everyone else, which explains why systems of positive rights to life, housing, food, education, and the like degrade and even bankrupt any society in which they are relentlessly applied."[198] The danger is there, but he overstates it. For instance, he condemns Social Security for pitting the old against the young, who will inevitably be betrayed when the system collapses.[199] Hayek made the same confident prediction in 1960. What do you suppose happened to all those people who were young in 1960?

The most promising remedy for poverty, he insists, is not redistribution but economic and technological growth, which misguided state intervention might stifle.[200] Given the ineradicable public support for such programs, he knows he can't get rid of them, but proposes "redistribution last": so long as economic productivity is maximized, "the scope of redistributive policies can be accordingly reduced, given that a large resource base is coupled with a lower level of need."[201]

This is fundamentally right. It is the crucial point that the redistributionist, anti-capitalist left fails to grasp. Growth, not redistribution, has ameliorated both domestic and world poverty, and will continue to do so if markets are allowed to continue functioning.

But at any given time, needs are what they are. And how much redistribution will be necessary to address them depends on unpredictable complexities of labor markets, with the contingencies of automation and globalization that we have already discussed.

Like Hayek, Epstein does not attempt to defend free markets as giving people what they deserve. He acknowledges that there is a lot of moral arbitrariness in the system. He even agrees with Hayek that wealth ought to be redistributed, so that everyone's basic needs are attended to. He believes, however, that the redistribution will be more effective if it is voluntary, and that the voluntary contributions will be forthcoming. Private charity would handle even the fantastically expensive cost of health care.[202] An attractive feature of this proposal is that it out-Hayeks Hayek, by decentralizing decisions about the size and availability of the social minimum. It relies, however, on the speculative prediction that charitable provision will emerge on a scale never before seen in history.

Epstein's reliance on charity does raise a question that should always be asked about state intervention. Even where there is no economic incentive to supply a public good, voluntary cooperation may fill that gap, sometimes better than the government could.[203] But whether this is so in any particular case cannot be resolved without attention to the local evidence. More fundamentally, the networks of mutual trust that facilitate such cooperation don't develop in nations where government is distrusted. Across prosperous democratic nations, and over time, trust in government and interpersonal trust are tightly correlated.[204]

His narrative of the American economy is one of steady decline: before the New Deal, constitutional constraints on government "fueled the rise of the mightiest nation on the globe;"[205] the "intolerable expansion of government power"[206] since then "is disastrous in its relentless efforts to cartelize industry after industry through a set of legal devices that have only served to stymie the economic prosperity and social stability of the United States."[207] Here, too, he is right a lot of the time. There is no excuse for farm subsidies. But he overstates the level of dysfunction. From 1991 to 2012, net of inflation, the US economy grew 63 percent, compared with France, 35 percent; Germany, 28 percent; and Japan, 16 percent.[208] The real gross domestic product of the United

States grew from $299 billion in 1950 to $22 trillion (in 2012 dollars) at the end of 2021, from $14,500 to $59,692 per capita.[209] Some disaster.

Hayek's account of the preconditions of appropriate regulation offers a promising field of battle between the libertarian right and a social democratic left that is reconciled to regulated capitalism. The right will focus on the need for capital to support growth, which may entail reducing taxation especially for those rich enough to invest rather than consume.[210] The left will focus on public investment and a social safety net. The right will be drawn to the hypothesis that any government intervention can be replaced by some market-driven solution. The left will sometimes be blind to the needs of business, the value of multiple sites of concentrated wealth, and the virtues of markets. Focused on the needs of the least well off, it may approach public policy with a stultifying degree of risk aversion. Each side will sometimes be correct, and there will be no way to tell which is correct without burrowing deep into the specifics of the policy at issue. (The temperature of political debate might be lowered if it were recognized that each position often rests on hunches in the face of uncertainty.) Hayek, as we have seen, provides some support for both sides. He is open to all these possibilities, because his philosophy is sensitive to facts in the world. A Hayekian politics is the most appropriate kind of politics for an advanced capitalist society.

If a government restrains economic freedom, it may sacrifice some productivity. (Or, as the case of South Korea shows, it may not.) "That consideration," Gray observes, "will scarcely be conclusive for any ethical theory or political philosophy that is not already committed, as Hayek was, to the strange ideal of maximal productivity."[211]

That strange ideal has become a dominant theme of neoliberalism. The triumph of Hayekian free market ideology has generated a discourse in which all political ends—democracy, equality, liberty, inclusion, constitutionalism, an educated citizenry—are understood as means to economic growth.[212] Historian Daniel Rodgers observes that the image of the market has "moved out of the economic departments to become the new standard currency of the social sciences.... To imagine the market now was to imagine a socially-detached array of economic actors, free to choose and optimize, unconstrained by the power of inequalities, governed not by their common deliberative action but only by the impersonal laws of the market."[213]

That was not Hayek's view. "Strictly speaking, no final ends are economic, and the so-called economic goals which we pursue are at most intermediate goals which tell us how to serve others for ends which are ultimately non-economic."[214] It is clear what he would have thought of a philosophy of education that regards its sole purpose as making the student a more valuable factor of production. He denounced "the permissive education which fails to pass on the burden of culture."[215]

Hayek is, however, correct that productivity is indeed morally urgent "at this moment, when the greater part of mankind has only just awakened to the possibility of abolishing starvation, filth, and disease; when it has just been touched by the expanding wave of modern technology after centuries or millennia of relative stability."[216] When Jesus of Nazareth remarked that you will always have the poor with you, he was making a sound inference from the data then available. Free markets beget economic growth. Economic growth is a moral imperative.

Hayek's reasoning thus yields a moderate, pro-capitalism, pro-free trade philosophy that embraces the modern regulatory and welfare state so long as it does its job properly.

Recall that Hayek's appeal, for American conservatives, was that he offered a principled basis for resisting the emergence of the modern big state. If that's his attraction, though, you'll find him disappointing. His condemnation of big government is selective and nuanced, and some of his arguments, we have seen, entail a substantial regulatory apparatus.

There is another, deeper problem with Hayek. He's a bit of a mess as a political philosopher. On the fundamental question of the criterion for a good government, he is pulled in several directions. He does not appear to be aware of the tensions within his own thought. He has no account of what our rights are, or why we have rights in the first place.

One claim to which he is often drawn (citing Kant's philosophy) is that the test of the justice of a law is that it apply to everyone: "The justification of our subjective feeling that some rule is just must be that we are prepared to commit ourselves to apply it universally."[217] He was particularly worried about administrative discretion, the power of bureaucrats to make arbitrary decisions about people's lives. Individuals are only free to make their own plans in a context of fixed rules. The rule of law aims "merely to prevent as much as possible, by drawing boundaries, the actions of different individuals from interfering with each other."[218]

Universal applicability may be necessary to the rule of law, but it can't be sufficient. Rothbard pounced on this claim, accurately observing that it would be satisfied "if everyone knew in advance that he would be tortured and enslaved one year out of every three."[219]

Hayek also sometimes sounds like a conservative. He argues that social orders aren't intentionally created but emerge spontaneously, and he distrusts those who would remake society in the name of some ideal of social justice. What makes cooperation possible is traditions of behavior whose rationale may not be articulable. This attachment to tradition can lead, and for many conservatives has led, to quietism and stagnation. Rothbard complained, again reasonably, that Hayek "believes we must blindly follow traditions even if we can't defend them."[220]

Hayek declared that he was not a conservative, because he thought it important to ask not only "how fast or how far we should move, but where we should move."[221] The spontaneous forces of society should be deliberately unleashed to promote progress: "There is, in particular, all the difference between deliberately creating a system within which competition will work as beneficially as possible, and passively accepting institutions as they are. Probably nothing has done so much harm to the liberal cause as the wooden insistence of some liberals on certain rough rules of thumb, above all the principle of *laissez-faire*."[222]

The progress he envisions is, of course, one that produces constant upheaval. So he simultaneously embraces tradition and radical change.

He needs some account of how to address the inevitable, frequent conflicts between them.

Finally, his emphasis on consequences has led some readers to deem him a utilitarian—one who regards the appropriate aim of policy as the greatest happiness of the greatest number. But Hayek rejects utilitarianism, because he doesn't think one can rationally compare states of affairs.

There's not much to like about this unstable hodgepodge.[223] Most important, Hayek has no clear account of rights.[224] That may be the main reason why he has been displaced by a more uncompromising, rights-based libertarianism. America was founded on a philosophy of individual rights. Most modern libertarians claim to be following that philosophy to its logical conclusions. Are they?

To answer that question, we must look back, centuries before Hayek.

2

RIGHTS

> Nobody can be a great economist who is only an economist—and I am even tempted to add that the economist who is only an economist is likely to become a nuisance if not a positive danger.
>
> —Friedrich Hayek[1]

Perhaps the most powerful moral basis of libertarianism is what I'll call the commonsensical property story. People work. What they own is the product of their work. They have a right to what is theirs. We enter into a social contract to protect our persons and property. If government tries to do anything else—say, imposing regulations on what people do with their own things, or taking some people's money and giving it to others—it is abusing its powers.

The commonsensical property story isn't about the consequences of this or that policy. It is about rights. Even if there are important tasks that only governments can do, or can do better than anyone else—disaster relief, or cancer research, or guaranteeing everyone decent medical care and a secure retirement—it would still be wrong to do them. You must not spend money that's not yours. If this is correct, it straightaway entails that most of what government does is illegitimate.

That story has some unpleasant entailments. Let's imagine a homeless man with a pregnant wife who is about to go into labor. He needs food, housing, and possibly medical care. If those things aren't made available, they may have to deliver the baby in whatever shelter they can find—perhaps a barn or a manger. Call him Joseph.[2] Unless someone lets Joseph's family enter their land, they won't even be able to get into the manger. This is tough luck for them, but they must respect other people's property rights.

This is the moral core of much modern libertarianism. It is a philosophical claim, and assessing it is a philosophical task. So this unavoidably will be the densest chapter in the book. We will have to unpack the argument and see if it holds together.

The commonsensical story has the enormous advantages of simplicity and easy comprehensibility. That doesn't mean it is right. There are many stories like that, such as the notion that a heavy object must fall faster than a light one, or that a pound of lead must be heavier than a pound of feathers.

When libertarians defend the commonsensical property story, they almost always use some version of arguments devised by a seventeenth-century English philosopher named John Locke. In 2017, for example, Senator Rand Paul and House Freedom Caucus chair Mark Meadows explained that they wanted to abolish the subsidies that were providing health insurance to more than twenty million people, because it was being paid for with "other people's money."[3] To understand libertarian conceptions of rights, we must begin by examining Locke's reasoning in some detail. It will turn out that he has important things to say about rights. But he's no libertarian. Libertarianism doesn't follow from Lockean premises. In Locke's world, Joseph and his family would at least be decently provided for.

Liberalism, the philosophy that values individual liberty, is an innovation of the past few centuries. It was once something new, a radical idea in a world of divine right of kings, feudal lords, and religious repression. It was a movement with ideologists. Locke was perhaps the most influential.[4] Libertarians rely on an interpretation of Locke when they claim that the United States was founded on their principles, and that its original vision has since been betrayed by the steady growth of government power.

Even if you never heard of Locke, you have probably encountered his ideas. For instance, you probably read this sometime: "We hold these truths to be self-evident, that all men are created equal, that they are endowed by their Creator with certain unalienable Rights, that among these are Life, Liberty and the pursuit of Happiness.—That to secure these rights, Governments are instituted among Men, deriving their just powers from the consent of the governed." The "self-evident" truths of the Declaration of Independence are a superbly compressed précis of Locke, whom the Declaration's author, Thomas Jefferson, called one of the "greatest men that have ever lived."[5] It should be easy to see how one could read the founding document's account of the purpose of government—"to secure these rights"—to support the commonsensical property story.[6]

Libertarianism consists in large part of selective adaptations of ideas from Locke's writings. Rothbard, Nozick, and Rand resist the transfer payments that are part of the modern welfare state, because any redistribution violates Lockean property rights. (Their arguments against regulation are cruder and less reliant on Locke.)

Is the commonsensical property story the idea that the country was founded upon? Do America's defining commitments entail libertarianism? In order to answer that question, we need to go back to the source—to look at what Locke actually wrote.

This chapter will examine Locke's arguments. He makes two claims that are important to libertarians. First, people are entitled to be rewarded for their work. Second, the institution of property, even though it produces inequalities, is good for everyone, even destitute people like Joseph.[7]

These arguments are powerful. They do not, however, demand a minimal state. They rather imply precisely the kind of state responsibilities that Hayek embraced, and which many libertarians want to categorically bar. One may perhaps be able to build a libertarian argument from Lockean materials, but if so, one must supply arguments not found in Locke himself. We will consider those additional arguments in subsequent chapters.

A leading villain in the libertarian pantheon is the twentieth-century philosopher John Rawls, who developed the most sophisticated version of the social contract theory that Locke pioneered. Rawls defended a social contract in which any inequality had to benefit the least advantaged, by redistribution when necessary. His fundamental ambition was to devise principles for a society in which the most prosperous people could justify their situations to those on the bottom, like Joseph. He is excoriated by libertarians for failing to respect property rights. Rawls, however, is right that Locke's social contract theory understates the claims of the worst-off members of society. Rawls's arguments for eliminating large concentrations of wealth are less persuasive. Hayek shows why a system that encourages wealth is likely to benefit the poorest members of society. Hayek has something to say to Joseph, something that Rawls doesn't fully appreciate.

Why think that Locke embraced the commonsensical property story?

Locke was born in England in 1632, in the reign of Charles I, who believed in and fought for absolute royal power. He wrote the *Two Treatises of Government* in 1679–80 to justify resistance to the king. His faction prevailed in the revolution of 1688, but he evidently never felt confident that the old, absolutist regime would not be restored. He dared not acknowledge his authorship until he was on his deathbed. After he died in 1704, his influence continued to spread, notably to colonial America.[8]

Locke began with the premise that there is no natural "Subordination or Subjection" among persons.[9] People are perfectly free "to order their Actions, and dispose of their Possessions, and Persons as they think fit . . . without asking leave, or depending upon the Will of any other Man."[10] The only limitation on their freedom is that "being all equal and independent, no one ought to harm another in his Life, Health, Liberty, or Possessions."[11] Those possessions are part of oneself: "Though the Earth, and all inferior Creatures be common to all Men, yet every Man has a *Property* in his own *Person*. This no Body has any Right to but himself. The *Labour* of his Body, and the *Work* of his hands, we may say, are properly his. Whatsoever then he removes out of the State that Nature hath provided, and left it in, he hath mixed his *Labour* with, and joyned to it something that is his own, and thereby makes it his *Property*."[12]

States exist to protect life and possessions. "The great and *chief end* therefore, of Mens uniting into Commonwealths, and putting themselves under government, *is the preservation of their property*."[13] Mutual protection is necessary, "the pravity of Mankind being such, that they had rather injuriously prey upon the Fruits of other Mens Labours, than take pains to provide for themselves."[14]

Thus far, we have a more elaborate version of the story that Jefferson tells in the Declaration of Independence. People agree "to joyn and unite into a Community, for their comfortable, safe, and peaceable living one amongst another, in a secure Enjoyment of their Properties."[15]

Many libertarians read these passages as arguments for unlimited property rights, categorically immune from redistribution regardless of anyone's needs. Thus Murray Rothbard, whose own philosophy we will consider in chapter 3:

> In Locke's brilliant and very sensible theory . . . two axioms: self-ownership of each person, and the first use, or 'homesteading', of natural resources, establishes the 'naturalness', the morality, and the property rights underlying the entire free market economy. For if a man justly owns material property he has settled in and worked on, he has the deduced right to exchange those property titles for the property someone else has settled in and worked on with *his* labour. For if someone owns property, he has a right to exchange it for someone else's property, or to give that property away to a willing recipient. This chain of deduction establishes the right of free exchange and free contract, and the right of bequest, and hence the entire property rights structure of the market economy.[16]

Rothbard infers "the absolute right to private property of every man."[17] He goes further, to conclusions that Locke did not endorse, but Rothbard thinks he should have: that "the State is a group of plunderers"[18] and that "Taxation is Robbery."[19]

If this is correct, then some familiar aspects of modern American politics follow. It is morally imperative to slash taxes and shrink the size of government, since every penny of that taxation is wrongfully taken. All redistribution, and much regulation, is categorically wrongful.

There is, however, a puzzle in this reading of Locke. *How can it generate property rights that everyone is obligated to respect?* What can Locke tell Joseph?

It's sometimes said that property is a relation between a person and a thing, but that's confused. Property rights are relations between people. If I legitimately own something (rather than merely possessing it, as might be true of stolen goods), everyone else on the planet has an obligation to keep their hands off it. If that's going to be true, then there has to be some reasonable basis for thinking that they have that obligation.

For Rothbard, if A has the only oasis in a desert and refuses to share his water, and B will die of thirst unless he takes some of it, B has a moral duty to die (and watch his children die) rather than violate A's property rights.[20] Joseph is obligated to starve and let his infant endure exposure to the elements if the owner of the manger doesn't feel like letting them in. The commonsensical property story here begins to look less commonsensical. What could justify such suicidal duties? Do they follow from Locke's theory of rights?

Locke's primary task was to show that the English had rights against the king. In order to do that, he needed to show that property could be justified as something other than the gift of the king. No one in his audience doubted the legitimacy of existing property rights. Literate people tended to have money. He needed to show that one could resist royal absolutism without undermining the basis of one's own property claims. He draws on arguments from nature, reason, theology, and the Bible, often leaving in doubt which of these is most important.

Locke posited that people have a right to self-preservation. Reason and religion agreed about that. So they have a right to whatever they need to keep themselves alive, specifically a right to lay claim to resources in nature and make them their own.

God has given the earth "to Mankind in common."[21] Every individual can legitimately appropriate some part of the earth by improving and using it. If he needed everyone else's permission before appropriating anything, "Man had starved, notwithstanding the Plenty God had given him."[22]

This leads Locke to the idea that we come to own things by mixing our labor with them. Most of his argument about property is presented in three crucial sentences. Here is the first of them: "Whatsoever then [someone] removes out of the State that Nature hath provided, and left it in, he hath mixed his *Labour* with, and joyned to it something that is his own, and thereby makes it his *Property*."[23] There is something about mixing labor with an object that confers ownership.

Ownership, thus understood, implies a right to exclude other people, people who did not do the work. That's the claim of the remaining two sentences: "It being by him removed from the common state Nature placed it in, it hath by this *labour* something annexed to it, that excludes the common right of other Men. For this *Labour* being the unquestionable Property of the Labourer, no Man but he can have a right to what that is once joyned to, at least where there is enough, and as good left in common for others."[24]

Thus the familiar libertarian idea that people are entitled to keep what they have worked for.

But there's a problem here. Locke's notion of mixing your labor with objects, which you then own, has become so familiar that it makes intuitive sense to many. It doesn't hold up well under analysis. Jeremy Waldron asks: "How can a series of actions be mixed with a physical object?"[25] They aren't the kind of things that can be mixed. It's like blending Beethoven with orange juice.

There is an answer. But it won't lead to Rothbardian property absolutism. It will in fact reject it, for much the same reason that Locke rejected royal absolutism. Locke's labor-mixing claim is best understood as a metaphor. A metaphor for what, though?

Locke's argument begins with the need for survival. Even if (as Locke thought) the world belongs to everyone in common, some private appropriation must be legitimate. If one imagines a "state of nature," a primitive condition without law or property rights, it must be morally permissible there to take exclusive possession of things. Otherwise, no one could even eat.

People can't leave the world alone. Life is interaction with things outside oneself. Those things become part of my life. Their improvement is the physical manifestation of my efforts. "Nature furnishes us only with the material, for the most part rough and unfitted for our use; it requires labour, art and thought, to suit them to our occasions."[26] Raw kernels of wheat aren't edible until they are cooked or ground into flour.

A. John Simmons explains that Locke understands labor to be "a kind of purposive activity aimed at satisfying needs or supplying the conveniences of life." This can be mixed with external things straightforwardly: "As we think about, choose, or carry out various aspects of our life plans (our projects and pursuits), external things are often central to them." When I work to improve an object or a piece of land, it is "brought within my life and plans."[27] It is part of me and my agency.

That generates obligations for other people. They need to keep their hands off the stuff I've worked on, for the same reasons that they need to keep their hands off my body. Their right to the products of their own labor implies an obligation to respect what's mine.[28] Locke writes that anyone who meddles with things that have been improved by another person's labor "desired the benefit of another's Pains, which he had no right to."[29]

With the advent of the convention of money, enormous inequalities become possible. These are legitimate because they have been consented to. "Men have agreed to disproportionate and unequal Possession of the Earth, they having by a tacit and voluntary consent found out a way, how a man may fairly possess more land than he himself can use the product of."[30] When Locke puts it this way, he highlights the question of what men in fact have agreed upon, and (more pertinently, since there never was any actual agreement) what it would be reasonable for them to agree upon. Eric Mack observes that Locke's argument becomes stronger if we focus on their reasons for agreeing: "All individuals will at least reasonably expect to be net gainers because of the vast expansion of productive economic activity that comes in the wake of the introduction of money."[31]

Inequality happens because some people work harder than others: "Different degrees of Industry were apt to give Men Possessions in different Proportions."[32] (Here he parts company with Hayek, who understands that industry is not invariably successful.) Those who end up with less are not entitled to take what has been created by those who end up with more. "God gave the World . . . to the use of the Industrious and Rational, (and *Labour* was to be *his Title* to it;) not to the Fancy or Covetousness of the Quarrelsom and Contentious."[33]

In short, people are entitled to what they have worked to produce. That is what the labor-mixing metaphor shows us. Those who are "Industrious and Rational" ought to be rewarded. "*Justice* gives every Man a Title to the product of his honest Industry."[34]

At this point, one is tempted to say that the industrious person deserves that product. Whatever the merits of that view, it is not Locke's. His argument does not depend on desert. But he is sometimes read that way (and so many libertarians infer that any redistributive taxation is unjust, because it takes from the deserving and gives to the undeserving). That interpretation has intuitive attractions. George Sher explains why ideas of deserving emerge naturally out of respect for people's choices. If a person's power to choose is worth anything, that value carries over to the intended and reasonably anticipated consequences of her choices: "It would be quite arbitrary to say that it is good that the agent perform the act he has chosen, but not good that he enjoy or suffer that act's predictable consequences." The consequences "are part of what the agent has chosen."[35] (Criminal law almost always follows similar logic: you're punished only if you intended, or at least were culpably reckless about, the harm you caused.) If I'm going to have a life, then I have to be able to act on the world, which will normally respond in the way I reasonably expected. Hard work should be rewarded. Sometimes honest and intelligent effort is thwarted, but this is just to say that people don't always get what they deserve.

Thus far we get property rights. But one can draw more radical implications. If the defense of property depends on the idea that people should be able to achieve what they work for, then institutions should be created capable of making that happen. The idea of freedom upon which Locke is relying is not simply freedom from state oppression. That flavor of freedom is available in conditions of chaotic civil war. Freedom consists in people actually being able to decide what to do with their lives. The character of the state and of property rights thus should be determined by investigating what specifications of each are most likely to make people genuinely free.

The freedom to enter into economic transactions is an element of Lockean liberty. "For many people," John Tomasi observes, "commercial activity in a competitive marketplace is a deeply meaningful aspect of their lives."[36]

The idea that work should be rewarded cannot, however, justify any particular distribution. It provides no basis for the magnitude of any specific reward for any specific effort. It does not even say which efforts ought to be rewarded: What about the hard work of someone who connives his way into a comfortable sinecure in a kleptocracy? It certainly does not entail that people are entitled to their pretax income, which, as Hayek emphasizes, is contingent on market conditions over which the worker has no control. That income is created jointly by the worker's efforts and fortunate background conditions, in proportions that can't even be estimated. The deepest Lockean commitment is to a world in which the "Industrious and Rational" are rewarded for their pains. When state intervention is necessary in order to make that happen, Lockeanism militates against unregulated markets.

Locke had a second, distinct argument: the institution of property is good for everyone, even those with the least amount of it. In America, where there are no clear property rights, "a King of a large and fruitful Territory there feeds, lodges and is clad worse than a day Labourer in *England*."[37] This is his answer to our hypothetical, homeless Joseph.

There is, of course, the familiar objection that property rights leave some people worse off. In the state of nature, one could take and farm unclaimed land "where there is enough, and as good, left in common for others." Once civilization has developed, however, there is no unclaimed land left, and a newcomer has to subject himself to someone else's authority: "The law compels him to starve if he has no wages, and compels him to go without wages unless he obeys the behests of some employer."[38] Property rights generate relations of authority, and the destitute laborer never agreed to that.

Lockeans have an answer: that newcomer is likely to be economically a lot better off, and to have far better opportunities, than the people who first broke ground in the unclaimed wilderness.[39] A market also limits the abuse of authority. Robert Jackson, associate justice of the Supreme Court, wrote in 1944 that "in general the defense against oppressive hours, pay, working conditions, or treatment is the right to change employers."[40]

Locke argues that private property creates wealth, which in the long run is good for everyone: "He who appropriates land to himself by his labour, does not lessen, but increase the common stock of mankind . . . he, that incloses Land and has a greater plenty of the conveniencys of life from ten acres, than he could have from an hundred left to Nature, may truly be said, to give ninety acres to Mankind. For his labour now supplys him with provisions out of ten acres, which were but the product of an hundred lying in common."[41]

As a general matter, Locke was right. Living among rich people is better than living among poor people, even if there's no more open land to claim.

The claim that property makes everyone better off raises the question, compared to what? Life in the state of nature is so wretched that one can be mighty poor, in a rich society, and still be better off than *that*. Should homeless people who sleep under bridges be grateful to live in a society that has bridges to sleep under? Should Joseph's wife be glad that she at least gets to deliver her baby indoors in a manger? Locke took for granted that the day laborers of England were "living generally but from hand to mouth."[42]

But he never went so far as Rothbard. Not only does Locke offer no support for Rothbard's extreme property rights. He gives compelling reasons for rejecting them. The claims that people are entitled to what they work for, and that property benefits everyone, imply that everyone has a reason to embrace the system of property. For Rothbard, on the other hand, property rights may create an obligation to die.

Locke explicitly rejected a conception of property rights so strong that they allowed some people to starve or oppress others: "God hath not left one Man so to the Mercy of another, that he may starve him if he please."[43] No social contract could entail this: "No rational Creature can be supposed to change his condition with an intention to be worse."[44] Inequality that produces the functional equivalent of slavery can't be legitimate: one may not "justly make use of another's necessity, to force him to become his Vassal."[45]

Lockean property rights came with a proviso that everyone's basic needs would have to be provided for[46]—the proviso that Justice Scalia denied in the Obamacare oral argument. Everyone has a right to the means of survival, and that implies not only a right to appropriate but also "a Title to so much out of another's Plenty, as will keep him from extream want, where he has no means to subsist otherwise."[47] The refusal to provide others what they need is tantamount to murder.[48] A needy person has "a Right to the Surplusage of [another's] Goods; so that it cannot justly be denyed him, when his pressing Wants call for it."[49] Joseph has a *right* to shelter, food, and other urgent needs, such as assistance when his wife delivers their child. The proviso was a severely limited one: it applied only to those with "no means to subsist otherwise"; the destitute could be forced to work; the work wouldn't pay much.[50] Still, Locke's property rights weren't Rothbard's.

Rothbard's conception, so far from being Locke's, is rather that of Locke's adversary, Robert Filmer. Locke wrote his work on government to rebut Filmer's defense of absolute monarchy. Filmer thought that the absolute power of the king was derived from that of Adam. Adam held a "natural and private dominion" over everything, and so "none of his posterity had any right to possess anything but by his grant or permission, or by succession from him."[51] Locke rejected the notion that anyone should have "an Absolute, Arbitrary, Unlimited, and Unlimitable Power, over the Lives, Liberties, and Estates of his Children and Subjects."[52] If one accepted the notion that property need only reflect the unbounded will of the owner, it would be hard to sustain Locke's and later Jefferson's resistance to royal power.[53]

What Rothbard aspires to isn't liberalism but feudalism: for both, Samuel Freeman observes, political power is conceived as "a system of personal political dependence grounded in a network of private contractual relations."[54] The ultimate value that undergirds the system is not liberty but property, and liberty can freely be sacrificed for the sake of property. For Rothbard, there is not even a right to the necessary means of survival. Joseph is out of luck. In a free market in modern conditions, it is concededly unlikely that he will have to enslave himself or his family to avoid starvation. On the other hand, sometimes survival is pricey: lifesaving medical care can be far more expensive than Locke could have imagined (and he was a doctor!)—sometimes costing hundreds of thousands of dollars for one patient.[55] Suppose you are an impecunious, attractive woman with a very sick father. In order to keep Dad alive, you may be obliged to become a prostitute. Locke would not have tolerated a social contract that presented people with such choices.[56] Would you?

While Locke was prepared to guarantee only bare survival, with no prospect of upward mobility, the system of property rights has turned out to be more generous than he was. The effects of the Enrichment have spread worldwide. As the global economic system has become more integrated, the proportion of the world population living in desperate poverty has plunged. That fact is largely the result of the development of legal systems that reliably protect property and enforce contracts.

Some are troubled by Locke's defense of unbridled acquisitiveness.[57] Older political views that aimed to create a virtuous citizenry, whether conceived in religious, military-heroic, or civic-republican terms, are set aside in favor of the pursuit of wealth. "The satisfaction of wants" in Locke, Leo Strauss complained, is "no longer limited by the demands of the good life but becomes aimless"; what Locke envisions is "the joyless quest for joy."[58] On the other hand, in the traditional societies for which Strauss is nostalgic, the pursuit of the good life was available only to a few, because most people's desperate poverty made that impossible.

Locke's observation is pertinent: "Riches may be instrumental to so many good purposes, that it is, I think, vanity rather than religion or philosophy to pretend to contemn them."[59] He did in fact expressly answer the claim that the state should demand Christian virtue. He retorted that the state wasn't actually likely to be much help: "The one only narrow way which leads to Heaven is not better known to the Magistrate than to private Persons, and therefore I cannot safely take him for my Guide, who may probably be as ignorant of the way as my self, and who certainly is less concerned for my Salvation than I my self am."[60] He thus anticipated Hayek's claim that we are so opaque to one another that we are best served by all-purpose means to our various ends, which the state cannot know. Locke is not oblivious to humanity's deepest aspirations. He simply claims that they are best pursued freely, without manipulation by the government.

Locke's second, property-benefits-everyone argument is related to his first, labor-mixing claim. The power to realize one's intentions, to control a bit of the world, is precisely what wealth is. Economic growth means that more people have more of that power. The English day laborer can more easily control his physical environment than the king in America, as evidenced by the fact that he "feeds, lodges and is clad" better. Locke has, at least, a plausible story to tell to Joseph. Both arguments point to a world in which the "Industrious and Rational" are rewarded for their pains. Both defend markets to the extent that they bring that world into existence. But that standard also gives us a criterion to determine when markets fail.

Locke's theory legitimates markets, not necessarily everything that actually happens in market economies. These have well-known pathologies—pathologies that count as such even within the terms of Locke's theory.

Some consensual transactions can have nasty effects on third parties. My factory can prosper while it dumps runoff that poisons the neighborhood children. Pollution is the tip of a large iceberg. Moreover, thriving markets do not guarantee that Lockean rights will be respected. They have functioned very efficiently when rights violations were ubiquitous.[61] Consumers tend to focus on price and quality. They generally don't know or care how goods and services are produced. The antebellum American South's slave-labor economy boomed as a supplier of cotton to the English textile industry, and was so important to it that the Confederacy hoped that it could use England's dependence to extort political and perhaps even military support. (In the event, during the Civil War, the English deficit was closed by increasing cotton production in India.) The logic of the market, which tends to produce goods in the smallest lots that consumers want, made slavery *more* brutal, by encouraging the breaking up of slave families. Free markets have also supported extractive kleptocracies, such as Zaire under Mobutu: selling natural resources is a reliable way for thugs to support their armies.

Markets can also generate inequalities of information that undermine Lockean rights. The authority relations that markets engender are ameliorated by the right to change jobs, but that presumes that the workers actually understand and consent to the terms of employment. The contracts between large sophisticated producers and individual proletarians typically involve huge asymmetries of information, and so facilitate agreements predicated on fraud. (When we hired you, we forgot to mention the odorless toxic fumes you'd breathe every day.[62])

Locke assumes a government that protects everyone's person and property. When government is too beholden to rich interests, it tends to look the other way when rights are violated. Locke demands respect for those rights, but does not contemplate an institutional mechanism adequate to guarantee them.[63]

His defense of inequality is underdeveloped. When he cites examples of property justly acquired, he includes "the Turfs my Servant has cut."[64] He thinks that you mix your labor with an object, and are entitled to the product of that labor, even if the actual work is done by your hired employee. One can easily draw different conclusions from his premises. Early-nineteenth-century radicals argued that Lockean natural right demanded the nationalization of land and the redistribution of wealth.[65] If the turf-cutter demands that the state increase the minimum wage, it's hard to say that he "desire[s] the benefit of another's Pains, which he had no right to."[66] On the contrary, Alan Ryan observes, in Locke "it seems that the landlord owns without working while his laborers work without owning."[67]

In a society with a division of labor, most of what each laborer transforms has already been worked on by others. That is not the case in Locke's fantasy of the state of nature, where the solitary individual clears some forest and starts farming it. Someone may have planted and weeded what the turf-cutter is cutting. When so many people have mixed their labor with the object, the labor-mixing argument doesn't tell us how much of the gain each of them is entitled to.[68]

So what is a fair distribution of the wealth created by a complex, cooperative system of production? A prominent response, given its classic formulation in 1899 by the economist John Bates Clark, is to "give to every agent of production the amount of wealth which that agent creates."[69] By this he means that each person should be paid the market value of his work, what economists call its marginal product. Paying that amount—pretax wages—will channel labor to its most highly valued employment, the same way that market prices will direct any resource to those willing to pay the most for it. Rawls observed that Clark's argument "appeals to a traditional idea of the natural right of property in the fruits of our labor."[70] Clark's argument may be taken to support the claim of his contemporary William Graham Sumner, that the distribution of wealth in a market "is right just because it will produce unequal results—that is, results which shall be proportioned to the merits of individuals."[71]

To see what's wrong with Clark's theory, it's necessary to clarify some economic terms. People who produce for a market normally do not in fact receive all the wealth that they create. If I grow my own carrots, then I'll keep producing them to the point at which I'm tired of eating carrots. I'll consume every bit of the value I produce. But in a market, some of the people who buy my carrots would have been willing to pay more than the market price: some people *really* like carrots. When I sell to them, I get some of the wealth I created, but they get some of it too. In competitive conditions, they get most of it, since I have to set my prices low enough to get someone to buy the last carrot I need to sell. This difference between market price and what consumers are willing to pay is what economists call *consumer surplus*.

Markets inevitably generate a lot of consumer surplus, because sellers don't know enough about each individual buyer to charge the exact amount that each buyer is willing to pay. Even if they did know that, competition would drive prices down toward the cost of production. The result is that consumers tend to capture most of the wealth created by competitive markets.

The production of consumer surplus is in fact what's terrific about market competition. It makes ordinary folk richer, by forcing producers to sell them high-quality goods at low prices. Clark's criterion thus can never be satisfied. No producer gets all the wealth she creates.

Moreover, no producer creates the market value of what she produces. That value depends on the environment she happens to occupy. Your matchless ability to play professional basketball commands a high price only because you were lucky enough to be born into a world in which that skill happened to be wanted (and in which most others happened to lack your aptitude). That added value thus is not attributable to you alone. It is a social product, based on the contingent scarcity of your contribution to the division of labor. It is largely an accidental monopoly, like being the owner of the only oasis in a desert.

Similarly if your wage collapses because of some technological innovation, the introduction of competing sources of labor, or an economic contraction. You did not suddenly become less deserving. Thus Rawls's answer to Clark: "The marginal product of labor depends on supply and demand."[72] It has nothing to do with justice.[73]

Clark opposes redistribution, which "would violate what is

ordinarily regarded as a property right" because it "would require the taking from some men of a part of their product, in order to bestow it on others who might be more necessitous."[74] (Clark is no friend of Joseph.) But, again, this presupposes that our pretax income is "our own property by right of creation."[75]

"Taxation of earnings from labor is on a par with forced labor," writes Nozick.[76] He thinks that, when income is taxed, the worker is to that extent forced to work for someone else, because the fruit of a proportional part of her labor is taken from her against her will. A 25 percent tax on an eight-hour workday means that the worker is enslaved for two hours a day. If the individual owns herself, then that self-ownership is violated when she must labor for someone else's purposes. The fact that taxation is the product of democratic processes does not redeem it; it merely implies "ownership of the people, by the people, and for the people."[77] This talk of "forced labor" is calculated to bring to mind Stalin's gulags, with conditions that don't much resemble what happens when taxes are withheld from a business executive's handsome paycheck.[78] But there is also a deeper philosophical problem.

Nozick presupposes that pretax income has moral significance—in other words, that Clark is right and there is a fundamental right to one's marginal product, or at least to the full value of the product to prospective purchasers. But that confuses efficiency with justice.

The deepest error in Clark's notion is the idea that the worker's contribution to a joint product is quantifiable. The model is one in which the laborer sells his labor for a wage and thus abandons all claim to the product beyond that wage. But in fact responsible agency is inalienable. A master and servant who participate in a crime are both criminally liable. When they jointly produce a good or service, the division of its value must be settled by convention. It cannot arise out of the transaction, because the product itself is jointly produced. Among the available conventions, the price system has obvious advantages, but that is not because it captures each person's contribution. The indispensable role of the laborer is the basis of the bitter 1915 trade union anthem, "Solidarity Forever":

> It is we who plowed the prairies; built the cities where they trade;
> Dug the mines and built the workshops, endless miles of railroad laid;
> Now we stand outcast and starving midst the wonders we have made . . .

It is efficient to pay people their marginal product. Milton Friedman claims that "unless an individual receives the whole of what he adds to the product, he will enter into exchanges on the basis of what he can receive rather than what he can produce."[79] But what this logic really demands is that there be some differential between labor with higher and lower levels of marginal product. People should have incentives to move from labor with lower market value to labor with higher market value. If you improve your productivity, your earnings should rise. But that is not the same as paying you what the market would give you.

To see why the difference between entitlement and incentive matters, consider the Earned Income Tax Credit (EITC). The program supports low-and moderate-income working parents by subsidizing their wages up to a maximum, phasing out with each dollar of income above that level. It is designed so that the worker benefits from each additional dollar of earned income, so the program does not diminish the incentive to work more hours or get a better job. Rather, that incentive is increased, because the worker is paid more than the market would pay her. She has more reason to get a job in the first place, which is precisely what the program aims at. (Taxation of high incomes similarly leaves untouched the incentive to shift human and other capital to its most productive uses.[80])

The EITC has pulled millions of working poor families out of poverty. The positive effects on the children of families who receive the EITC are particularly pronounced: they are healthier from infancy onward, stay in school longer and get better grades, and as adults they work more hours, have higher earnings, are more likely to attend college, and (because they contribute more to Social Security) will have more retirement income.[81] It is one of the most successful antipoverty programs ever devised.

On the other hand, it violates Clark's principle of distributive justice. It taxes those with high wages and gives part of their marginal product to the working poor. The Rawlsian response to Clark is that there is no injustice here, nor in other programs that ameliorate the inequalities generated by the market, because the marginal product of high earners is the consequence of facts that they did not cause: the vagaries of supply and demand and the dependence of their productivity on their place within a complex division of labor.[82]

In the argument that crushed his principal adversary, Locke relied precisely on this division of labor objection. Filmer claimed that Adam had created the human race by begetting them, that he therefore owned his progeny, and that by a line of succession the King is the owner of his people, with the rights that a master has over slaves. (One might say that Filmer anticipated Clark.) Locke responded that parents do not make the child, which they often do not even intend to create. Procreation happens as a by-product of desires that God implanted in them. "To give Life to that which has yet no being . . . to frame and make a living Creature, fashion the parts, and mould and suit them to their uses; and having proportion'd and fitted them together, to put into them a living Soul" is one of "the Incomprehensible Works of the Almighty."[83]

That same objection to unlimited private property is available whenever we shift our focus from the solitary farmer in the state of nature to an advanced industrial society. Any agent in a complex division of labor is in the same position, working with materials he did not make and could not have made himself. So one can turn the same objection back onto Locke. Why is the last human maker (or his employer) the exclusive owner in the one case but not the other?[84]

A related problem is that Locke's conception of the social contract allowed those with more property to exercise an unfair degree of power over those with less. Notably, his conception may be consistent with a property qualification for voting. In easily imaginable circumstances, it could be rational for the poor to bargain away their civil liberties when entering into a social contract.[85] Joseph was entitled to a job, not necessarily to the franchise. The fact that everyone is better off leaving the state of nature does not show that all deals that take us out of that deplorable situation are just. Even if there must be private property, that doesn't entail any specific distribution. The fact that private property is justified "does nothing to explain why the particular people who are the least well-off occupy the positions in society that they do."[86]

Finally, the deepest problem is that both of Locke's arguments, that one is entitled to what one produces and that the institution of property benefits everyone, are hostage to the contingencies of the market. If the justification for the system is that it rewards everyone's efforts and gives them a reasonable opportunity to prosper, then that justification fails if conditions happen to be such that those efforts chronically fail.

All these objections come together in the work of Rawls, the most important modern social contract theorist, who published from 1951 until his death in 2002.

Rawls led a privileged life, with much less drama than Locke's. He held a series of comfortable professorships at Princeton, Cornell, MIT, and (for most of his career) Harvard. For decades he was the object of near-universal adulation. Everyone knew he was the greatest living political philosopher. While I was a visiting fellow at Harvard in 1994–95, I became friendly with him by talking to him while he stood alone at receptions. Everyone else was too intimidated to approach him. He was obviously embarrassed by his godlike status. His interest in fairness, and discomfort with his own privileges, had roots in bitter personal experience.

When he was a child, two of his younger brothers died, at least one of them from disease contracted from him. When he was seven years old, he became seriously ill. Bobby, twenty-one months younger, had been told not to enter Jack's room, but sneaked in to keep him company. Soon Bobby caught Jack's diphtheria. Jack recovered. Bobby did not. The next winter, Jack contracted pneumonia, which soon thereafter killed two-year-old Tommy.[87] "Rawls later admitted that this tragedy had contributed to the development of a severe stutter, which afflicted him for the rest of his life."[88] It is perhaps unsurprising that the central theme of his life's work was arbitrary injustice. He writes in a bland, dispassionate style, but the passion is there if you look for it.

Rawls thought that the problem with Locke's imagined social

contract was that it gave excessive weight to morally irrelevant considerations: "The result [of Locke's procedure] is that persons enter the compact situation not solely as free and equal, reasonable and rational, but also as in this or that situation with this or that amount of property. Their legitimate interests are shaped accordingly and may set them at odds. If we want to work out a political conception in which the terms of social cooperation and the form of regime are independent of such contingencies, we must find a way to revise the social contract view."[89]

Rawls agreed with Locke that labor produces entitlement. He insisted, however, that the wealth of an industrialized society is the product of joint activity rather than of solitary producers in the state of nature.[90] Our whole society produced this wealth together.[91] Moreover, however it was produced, our society generates the specific rules of property law. Laws must be such that everyone has a reason to consent to them.

Rawls proposed that society should be understood as a scheme of cooperation among equals. In order for the social contract to be fair, its terms should be devised without any of the parties relying upon their position in society, most relevantly whether they would be rich or poor. In a hypothetical situation with their information thus restricted, the parties would agree to what he calls "the difference principle": inequalities are acceptable only to the extent that "they are to be to the greatest benefit of the least advantaged members of society."[92] Any inequalities must be arranged in such a way that the poor are better off than they would be under any alternative scheme of cooperation.[93] Locke, on the contrary, had argued only that in a fair social contract, the poorest people are better off than they would be if there were no government at all. Their poverty did not itself arise out of the social contract.

Locke imagines property rights being acquired by individuals before they ever enter into society. For Rawls, such rights themselves must be the objects of agreement. And that means that the agreement needs to somehow take account of inequalities that arise out of those rights. The basic idea, as Rawls's colleague T. M. Scanlon has put it, is that "an institution is unfair if it produces significant differences in income and wealth for which no sufficient reason can be given."[94]

If there is to be a basic structure of property rights that generates such differences, Scanlon writes, that structure is acceptable only if one of two conditions is met: either they "could not be eliminated without infringing important personal liberties," or "they are required in order for the economic system to function in a way that benefits all."[95] The first is irrelevant because, unlike in Locke, property rights are not prepolitical but created by law. The state can impose provisos on property without violating rights. But the second is important: free markets inevitably generate inequalities, but they also produce wealth that tends to improve the condition of those on the bottom.

In some of his statements of the difference principle, Rawls offers a less demanding formulation: "The social order is not to establish and secure the more attractive prospects of those better off unless doing so is to the advantage of those less fortunate."[96] That principle is not far from Hayek's proposal that "we should regard as the most desirable order of society one which we would choose if we knew that our initial position in it would be decided purely by chance."[97]

If in fact the inequalities engendered by free markets—and there is no way to know in advance how great those inequalities will be, because it is impossible to predict the magnitude of the opportunities at the top—produce economic growth that tends to benefit the worst off, then Rawls's principle of avoiding "outcomes that one can hardly accept" has real power here. It means that it is morally urgent to bring about growth that benefits the world's poorest people. And that means accepting the concomitant inequalities.

Even Marxists should accept inequalities that are entailed by a fair social contract. Marx wrote: "The life-process of society, which is based on the process of material production, does not strip off its mystical veil until it is treated as production by freely associated men, and is consciously regulated by them in accordance with a settled plan."[98] Conscious regulation needn't mean leveling or Leninist central planning unless these benefit the worst off, which they manifestly do not. Marx carefully avoids speculating about what "freely associated men" will decide to do with their freedom. Their "settled plan" might be (though this would have surprised Marx) to enrich everyone with property rights, free markets, and a generous welfare state.

Libertarians have tended to reject the difference principle because they think it entails taxation that violates property rights, and is insensitive to the possibility that some people deserve more because they have worked harder. As we have seen, Rawls can easily answer those objections. What libertarians have, for the most part, failed to see is that the basic principles of property and contract are not inconsistent with the difference principle, and may in fact be demanded by it. Once more, the disagreement is less deep than it seems.

The fundamental idea is to devise terms of social cooperation that can be accepted, freely and without resentment, by those who are worst off. Rawls aims to say to those people, you are richer than you would be in a more equal society. Those terms of cooperation will include the familiar freedoms of religion, speech, and so forth. Persons must be free to choose their own jobs and workplaces, and that limits central direction of the economy. But neither property rights nor rights to one's marginal product can be comparably strong.

In a just, prosperous society, wealth would have to be shared with the poor. Much of this has in fact happened through economic growth. But a free market economy distributes its benefits unevenly and unpredictably, and so if the poorest are to be guaranteed a fair share, it is unlikely to reach them by any means other than taxation and spending. Rawls eventually concluded that this would mean, for example, a right to health care.[99] His reasons were roughly analogous to Locke's justification for a right to the means of subsistence. Who could possibly agree to a social contract in which property rights were distributed in a way that might leave her without the resources she needs to stay alive? Rawls became known as the preeminent philosophical defender of the welfare state.[100]

Rawls's Harvard colleague Nozick, expressly relying on Locke's arguments, offered what has become the standard libertarian objection:

Rawls was insufficiently respectful of liberty and property. Rawls would continually meddle with free agreements among citizens in order to support a preconceived pattern of distribution. Any claim for such a pattern "ignores the question of where the things or actions to be allocated and distributed come from." Those things may already belong to "people who therefore may decide for themselves to whom they will give the thing and on what grounds."[101] A state should protect citizens from force and fraud, enforce contracts (perhaps even contracts to sell oneself into slavery), and do nothing more. Under no circumstances should it interfere with the existing distribution of property except to rectify past violations of property rights. So, as in Rothbard, our homeless friend Joseph is again out of luck.

Nozick's criticism rests on a fundamental misunderstanding of Rawls, who is asking what property rights there ought to be to begin with. Nozick presupposes that we already know which existing property holdings are morally justified.[102] He stipulates, without argument, that the "central core of the notion of a property right in X, relative to which other parts of the notion are to be explained, is the right to determine what shall be done with X."[103] (He was influenced by Rothbard, and misunderstood Locke in the same way.)

Rawls makes no such assumption. His claim is that institutions such as property are conventions, and should be designed with their likely distributional consequences in mind.[104] "Redistribution" mislabels what Rawls is proposing. His claim is that institutions that guarantee a fair share for the least well-off, such as taxation to support free public schools, are properly part of—not an exception to—the system of property rights.

For Rawls, property rights are not facts of nature but socially constructed. They are not really facts of nature in Locke, either; they reflect the will of God that humans be able to sustain themselves. Even in Locke, the basis of property rights entails obligations. "Since [for Locke] a person has a property for the sake of preserving himself and others," James Tully explains, "once his preservation is secured, any further use for enjoyment is conditional on the preservation of others."[105] Nozick doubts "the claim that society (that is, each of us acting together in some organized fashion) should make provision for the important needs of all its members."[106] That claim (with the proviso that "important" means "most urgent") is however built into Locke's account of rights, and Rawls reasonably asks why anyone would agree to a social contract that did not incorporate such a commitment.

Nozick objects to any idea of justice that holds that goods should be distributed according to any pattern, such as maximizing the position of the least advantaged.[107] No patterned principle of justice "can be continuously realized without continuous interference with people's lives."[108] If a "pattern" refers to a specific overall distribution, then he is correct. But he extends his claim to any system of redistribution through taxation. Such a system does not impose an overall pattern. It simply guarantees a minimum at the bottom, with no limit on the top. In welfare states with high levels of taxation, it has remained possible to become a billionaire, and in fact billionaires have proliferated.

Nozick concedes: "One might try to squeeze a patterned conception into the framework of the entitlement conception, by formulating a gimmicky obligatory 'principle of transfer' that would lead to the pattern."[109] He responds that "no principle of transfer in a free society will be like this."[110] Assuming that a welfare state is a kind of patterned distribution, the gimmick he describes is, however, already present in Locke, in the proviso that one leave "enough and as good" for others.[111] And in property rights in all existing regimes, since they are subject to some redistributive taxation (if only to provide free police protection for those too poor to pay taxes). It is even part of Nozick's own theory, since he has his own version of the "enough and as good" proviso: property rights must not make people worse off than they would have been in a state of nature.[112]

The fact that people have inherited such gimmicky rights, and have built their lives in reliance on them—presuming, for example, that they could rely on Social Security and Medicare in their old age—raises a different difficulty for Nozick. If we were today to reconceptualize existing property rights so that they were as absolute as Nozick contemplates, this would itself be a massive redistribution, transferring entitlements from the beneficiaries of these gimmicks to the holders of the pertinent (previously encumbered) titles. Those entitlements, we saw in chapter 1, are themselves a kind of property, much like an annuity: a future stream of income that the recipients will be able to dispose of without having to justify their actions to anyone else.

Nozick's dismissive talk of gimmicks show that he doesn't understand property rights—what they consist in and how they operate in the world. The actual positive law of property is not so wooden as he imagines. We saw that Hayek had the same problem. It is a chronic flaw in libertarian theory. Property is its central idea, and libertarians are tenaciously attached to property rights. Yet they don't know what property is. They don't understand all the forms it can and does take.

Let's take a step back and consider why social contract theory is attractive at all. That theory aims to justify political power—and property rights, enforced by the state, are a kind of political power—by showing that political institutions are, or have been, or ought to be unanimously agreed to. This elicits the obvious objection, raised by David Hume in 1748, that there never was any such agreement.[113]

A defense of social contract theory appropriately proceeds through two stages.

The first of these is what Jeremy Waldron calls "negative hypothetical contractarianism": we can *rule out* some principles of justice using a contractarian approach. One can "show that a suggested principle of justice is *un*acceptable by showing that there is no remotely plausible or coherent counterfactual hypothesis under which the principle would command the universal consent of citizens."[114] The nastiest principles are instantly excluded: slavery, hereditary aristocracy, the sort of utilitarianism that would impose enormous pain on some in order to make everyone else a little happier. And certain formulations of libertarianism.

No one could sanely agree to Rothbard's notion of an obligation to starve if one has no money for food.[115] "Time and again, Locke argues (against various permutations of royal absolutism) *not* that the people have not in fact consented to these arrangements, but rather that the arrangements are such that rational consent to them is *unthinkable*."[116]

The second stage is trickier: the proponent of the social contract must persuade *you*, the reader, the audience for political philosophy, to consent to the institutions of a just society. That is the real source of social contract theory's continuing appeal. Once we stop believing that the holders of political power are ordained by God, legitimate authority must come from ourselves somehow, if it is to come from anywhere. We have to agree to it. Hume is right that you haven't in fact agreed. Implied or tacit consent won't do. If political legitimacy depends on agreement, then the agreement has to be real. *But you can make it real.* Perhaps you *should* now agree to certain terms of political life. Two types of reasons are familiar: agreement might be in your interest, or you might have a moral duty to agree.[117] Both are in fact pretty compelling. A world without legal obligations is a mighty scary place, and you don't want to live there. We owe it to one another to bring a lawful world into existence.

If society rests on this combination of interest and moral duty, then property rights rest on the same foundations. Similarly with the provisos attached to those rights, such as taxation.

On Rawls's view, taxes are not, strictly speaking, the government taking your money. They are part of a system of property rights in which some subset of the social output is allocated for collective rather than individual determination of the use to which it will be put. Rawls does not think that there is any uniquely justified specification of that subset's size or use. Private property has no meaning outside that total system, which includes taxation. Political life did not begin after I was already sitting in the state of nature with my brokerage account.[118] In a market economy, no one can possibly have a right to any particular level of income from her labor, since, as we already noted, that income depends on market conditions that have little moral significance. Redistributive taxation doesn't thwart anyone's expectations, since that practice has existed since before any of us was born.[119] The actual structure of property rights comes with a proviso that resembles the "rake" in a casino poker game: players know when they start the game that the house will take a percentage of each pot. Since those are the rules, announced in advance, they do not violate justice in acquisition.

(Locke did not contemplate such taxation, but nor did he think that the wealthy were entitled to keep all their holdings; they had individual duties of charity.) Rawls's proviso that inequalities must benefit the worst off is, to use Nozick's language, "internal to the theory of property itself, to its theory of acquisition and appropriation."[120]

Many Americans (and if they live to retirement age, all Americans) depend, not merely on traditional forms of property, but on institutional guarantees, often supported by taxation. They regard such guarantees as *theirs*, and thus inarticulately partake of the more sophisticated, Rawlsian understanding. This is evident even when they oppose reform: consider the infamous warning to a Congressman to "keep your government hands off my Medicare."[121] Part of the justification for today's system of property rights is that it gets Joseph's wife out of the manger and into the maternity ward.

There is room in Rawls for the Lockean idea that labor should be rewarded. In a scheme of cooperative work, those who contribute to the social product deserve to gain from their contributions.[122] They are also entitled to have their legitimate expectations satisfied.[123] But that tells us nothing about what those expectations should be.

> Now it is true that given a just system of cooperation as a framework of public rules, and the expectations set up by it, those who, with the prospect of improving their condition, have done what the system announces it will reward are entitled to have their expectations met. In this sense the more fortunate have title to their better situation; their claims are legitimate expectations established by social institutions and the community is obligated to fulfill them. But this sense of desert is that of entitlement. It presupposes the existence of an ongoing cooperative scheme.[124]

The fact that the social surplus is the product of cooperation means that there are many possible allocations that would make cooperation worthwhile for all concerned. No one is entitled to any particular scheme, such as awarding each person the marginal market value of their contribution.

We are back to claims about what producers deserve. "In order to serve as a distinctive basis for assessing institutions," Scanlon observes, "desert claims need to be distinct from claims of institutional entitlement or legitimate expectations."[125] Very few desert claims are "pure," that is, grounding claims of appropriate treatment "*simply* by facts about what a person is like or has done."[126] Examples include "claims regarding expressions of praise, admiration, gratitude, blame, or condemnation."[127] A praiseworthy action deserves praise regardless of the effects of that response. But this is not true of tangible rewards. "The fact that a person has played a particular role in a productive economic process may be grounds for admiration or gratitude. But this does not, in itself, make any particular level of monetary award appropriate."[128]

Rawls's difference principle, that inequalities are acceptable only if they benefit the least advantaged, does not say how much inequality it will justify, whether it demands, permits, or prohibits a capitalist economy, or whether it requires ongoing equalization. The principle is controversial. Some philosophers claim that it is too focused on the needs of those on the bottom, neglecting the value of income-stabilizing programs such as Social Security and unemployment insurance that benefit the middle class.[129] Some argue that those at the bottom should demand only that they have enough to satisfy their needs: not equality but sufficiency.[130] All these views exclude a position like Rothbard's, in which market outcomes are sacrosanct and the worst off are entitled to nothing at all. We are also a long way from delivering any plausibly adequate minimum, however specified. (Rawls once asked rhetorically, "Can anyone seriously believe that the inequalities of our society work out to the best advantage of the least favored, or that they nearly do so?"[131]) The question of what to do when we surpass it is unlikely to arise soon.

Rawls was ambivalent about capitalism, and was perennially attracted to alternative schemes such as liberal socialism. He never discusses the critical literature on socialism, or the Hayekian claim that it would inevitably be wasteful and tyrannical. He never engages with the evidence that capitalism is indispensable to democracy. He thinks that the state should intervene "gradually and continually to correct the distribution of wealth," for example through "inheritance and gift taxes" and "restrictions on the rights of bequest."[132]

Would that kind of redistribution, constantly breaking up concentrations of wealth, benefit the least advantaged? Rawls thought that it obviously would. Hayek challenged that claim.

Hayek did not really disagree with Rawls's difference principle, that inequalities must operate to the benefit of the least advantaged. In fact, he embraced something like it: "We should regard as the most desirable order of society one which we would choose if we knew that our initial position in it would be decided purely by chance."[133] He cheerfully took on the Rawlsian burden of showing that a free market, with the inequalities it engenders, benefits even the least advantaged members of society.[134] He argued that what "has contributed most during the last two hundred years to increase not only the absolute but also the relative position of those in the lowest income groups has been the general growth of wealth which has tended to raise the income of the lowest groups more than the relatively higher ones."[135] (He did not consider the possibility of an economy like that of the contemporary United States, where the gains pool at the top.)

Hayek declared that there was no necessary inconsistency between his view and that of Rawls.[136] He quoted with approval Rawls's claim that "principles of justice define the crucial constraints which institutions and joint activities must satisfy if persons engaging in them are to have no complaints about them. If these constraints are satisfied, the resulting distribution, whatever it is, may be accepted as just (or at least not unjust)."[137] Hayek wrote that this was "more or less what I have been trying to argue."[138] He offered Rawlsian reasons why those at the bottom ought to accept a lot more inequality than Rawls had in mind.

Hayek recalled how he had once been placed in a dreadful Rawlsian choice situation. In London in 1940, anticipating that the city would soon be devastated by Nazi bombing, he "received offers from several neutral countries to place my then small children with some unknown family with whom they would presumably remain if I did not survive the war. I had thus to consider the relative attractiveness of social orders as different as those of the USA, Argentine and Sweden." Any decision "would have had to be made in consideration of the particular environment in which chance was likely to place them in one of those countries. For the sake of my children who still had to develop their personalities, then, I felt that the very absence in the USA of the sharp social distinctions which would favour me in the Old World should make me decide for them in favour of the former." He sardonically noted the limits of opportunity in 1940s America: "I should perhaps add that this was based on the tacit assumption that my children would there be placed with a white and not with a coloured family."[139]

Locke's justification for the inequalities that a free market produces is underdeveloped. Hayek offers a better answer to Rawls's demand for constant redistribution. He also presents a distinctive perspective on regulation that interferes with markets—a perspective that has largely been absorbed by the American Democratic Party, though not many libertarians have noticed that.

Hayek never makes anything like Locke's labor-mixing claim. Nor does he think that free markets give people what they deserve. Desert is in part the fulfillment of reasonable expectations. Precisely by promoting innovations that make society richer, markets sometimes disappoint those expectations.

Hayek puts his entire weight on Locke's other claim, that markets benefit the worst-off members of society. What people need is not a just allocation of goods but clear rules so that they can pursue their welfare in their own way. Since he doesn't rule out redistribution, justice as he understands it does not demand Joseph's homelessness and destitution.

As we've seen, Locke's claim that markets benefit the worst off is on the whole true. Hayek thought that free markets had created and would expand the Great Enrichment. He was right. He was even right about why.

Hayek did not so much dispute Rawls's difference principle as claim that capitalism satisfies it. Inequalities in a free market, even massive inequalities of wealth, benefit the least advantaged.[140] Inequality is useful for the same reason markets are useful: it is a way of making use of more information than any central authority can know. Large concentrations of capital are tools for discovering new technologies of production, which in the long run will benefit the poorest. The pain of low wages and unemployment directs labor toward its most productive uses. Property rights are not immune from redistribution and regulation. But he insisted that a market that operates for the most part without state manipulation of wages and prices is the only way to deliver on the Rawlsian promise.

3

TYRANNY

> Contradictions do not exist. Whenever you think you are facing a contradiction, check your premises. You will find that one of them is wrong.
>
> —Ayn Rand[1]

One day in 1969, Senator Barry Goldwater was walking through a group of antiwar protesters near the Capitol when a policeman told him, "Say, Senator, there's a former aide of yours here." He recognized and walked up to one of the protesters—a bearded man in a field jacket. "Karl, where the hell have you been? I haven't seen you for months." The protester, Karl Hess, explained that he didn't think Goldwater's staff would appreciate having a shaggy hippie in his office. "Piss on them," Goldwater replied. "You're my friend. Give me a call as soon as you're free."[2]

Hess had been a conservative activist as early as 1944, when he wrote speeches for the Republican National Committee. In 1954, he was fired from a staff job at *Newsweek* magazine because of his excessive enthusiasm for the demagogic Senator Joseph McCarthy. He helped write the 1960 and 1964 Republican platforms, and was a speechwriter for Goldwater's 1964 presidential campaign.

After Goldwater's defeat, Hess became disillusioned with the Republican Party. He read and then had long conversations with Murray Rothbard, who showed him that there was a link between his earlier conservatism and the New Left he was now drawn to. He became a prominent advocate for anarcho-capitalism: the philosophy that, if the state were abolished, all its functions would be better accomplished by private contracts. (We'll examine it shortly, when we consider Rothbard.) He published a defense of that philosophy in *Playboy* magazine, and was profiled at length in the Sunday magazines of the *New York Times* and the *Washington Post*. The *Post* reporter declared, with some hyperbole, that "after switching from Old Right to New Left, from business suits to Levis, Hess is still the same man—dead-set on his same libertarian cause—the old Karl Hess and the new Karl Hess are one and the same."[3]

Hess's transformation bespeaks the transformation of libertarianism as a political philosophy. Until the mid-1960s, it was a movement of laissez-faire businessmen seeking to spread the Hayekian gospel. It focused on economic liberty. During the next ten years, the libertarian movement incorporated ideals of personal liberation that were reshaping American culture more generally, defending sexual freedom, the legalization of marijuana, the abolition of the military draft. It came to stand for a general right to be weird.

The metamorphosis of the sixties is reflected in the Libertarian Party's 2020 platform. "We defend each person's right to engage in any activity that is peaceful and honest, and welcome the diversity that freedom brings." The platform stands for economic liberty: "All efforts by government to redistribute wealth, or to control or manage trade, are improper in a free society." But the principle of liberty also has implications for drug policy: "Individuals have the freedom and responsibility to decide what they knowingly and voluntarily consume." And sex: "Consenting adults should be free to choose their own sexual practices and personal relationships." At the core is a romanticism one never finds in Hayek: "The world we seek to build is one where individuals are free to follow their own dreams in their own ways, without interference from government or any authoritarian power."[4]

That romantic aspiration captures something that's missing from Hayek, though his program facilitates it. People need all-purpose means to pursue their own aspirations. If they have those means, then they don't need to justify themselves to anyone else. They are free to develop what they regard as best in themselves. This ideal of authenticity is common ground between large parts of both the political left and right. Our disagreements turn on how to realize it. That insistence on personal autonomy translates easily into rights talk—a kind of discourse that Hayek has no interest in.

Hayekian libertarianism, which aims to reduce government intervention in the economy in order to promote growth, is fundamentally about consequences. But modern libertarianism is not only based on claims about good consequences. It also insists on individual rights. Hayek's lack of interest in rights talk helps to explain why he has had less appeal than the philosophers I'll consider in this chapter. Another reason why his more sober reflections have been left behind by modern libertarianism is that he was never a completely comfortable ally of that anti-New Deal business movement. His views were too contingent on facts. Those facts, we saw in chapter 1, might turn out to justify regulations that are inconvenient for industry. The businessmen were, and some continue to be, driven by nostalgia for an age when one didn't need to worry about all those regulations. Libertarianism presents itself as a timeless political philosophy, but in fact it is a peculiar cultural formation, like hip-hop, French impressionism, and summer blockbuster movies: a manifestation of a particular moment. (Which is not necessarily a criticism: some such formations have enduring value.)

Here it will be helpful to clarify the definition of libertarianism. We said at the outset that it was the idea that liberty will be promoted by limiting government to the protection of person and property. Hayek is the founder of modern libertarianism, but it should be clear by now that he doesn't exactly fit this mold. As I said at the beginning, his work isn't well understood even by avowed libertarians, who claim him as one of their own.

Those who share his views often say that they aren't libertarians, but more precisely *classical liberals*: as Richard Epstein defines it, they embrace "the protection of liberty and private property under a system of limited government."[5] This description is vague enough—and classical liberalism is indeterminate enough—to encompass views that are as open to regulation and redistribution as Hayek's. (And, in a different way, Epstein's.) Libertarianism, however, is commonly associated with a much stricter view, one that categorically bars these. Here we will consider the most influential formulations of *that* view.

The commonsensical property story can't be inferred from Locke. But a lot of people still believe it. Rothbard, who tried to get it out of Locke, had views of his own. He is not nearly so well known as Rand, the bestselling author, or Nozick, the prominent philosopher. But in his own way, he may be more influential. His libertarianism mirrors fairly exactly the view that so many people share. Neither Hayek nor Epstein would let Cranick's house burn down. Rothbard would.

In this chapter, we will survey the philosophies of Rothbard, Nozick, and Rand, all of whom replace Hayek's concern for consequences with a rigid insistence on the sanctity of property rights. They fall into two camps. Nozick and Rand are minimal-state libertarians. They want the state to prevent force and fraud but do nothing else. Rothbard is an anarcho-capitalist. He wants to do away with the state altogether.

Some self-identified libertarians with whom I have discussed this book, who work at intellectually serious policy-wonk institutions such as George Mason University and the Cato Institute, have suggested that I omit this chapter. They tend to be neo-Hayekians, skeptical of government but open to evidence, and are offended if you confuse their views with Rothbard's or Rand's. But they underestimate the influence of these writers' romantic absolutism. It is not merely that extreme libertarianism is more common in popular culture. It is more influential in politics. In chapter 6, I will examine the revealing fight over Obamacare. Hayekian proposals to use market mechanisms to deliver health care more efficiently found no traction in the Republican Party. When it regained power in 2017, it was in this respect Rothbardian, supporting draconian measures that would have taken health insurance away from at least twenty million people. With climate change and COVID, too, the party embraces a catastrophic program that could make sense only in a Rothbardian framework.

The Libertarian Party's present platform, and the thinking of many libertarians who don't belong to the party, owe something to Hayek, but much more to Rothbard. When the party was founded, he had been developing libertarian arguments for decades. He joined it shortly after it was founded and soon became its intellectual leader. Ron Paul called him "the founder of the modern libertarian movement."[6] Most libertarians don't know how much they owe him.

Rothbard was born in 1926 to Jewish immigrants from Poland and Russia. He received his BA and PhD from Columbia University, and while a student attended the NYU seminar of Ludwig von Mises, who many years earlier had been Hayek's teacher. He was a smart economist, and turned out to be prodigiously productive. Rather than pursue an academic position, he became an analyst for the Volker Fund, an anti-New Deal think tank that had also funded Mises at NYU and Hayek at the University of Chicago. The fund collapsed because of internal disagreements in 1962. In 1966, at age forty, Rothbard became a part-time teacher of economics to engineering students of the Brooklyn Polytechnic Institute. In 1986, he joined the economics faculty at the University of Nevada at Las Vegas. He died in 1995.

He produced a large body of writings, but was also a tireless political advocate. An anarchist from an early age, he embraced a variety of political positions that might seem inconsistent. The consistency was that they all opposed the state and the elites in power. He thought the Constitution should not have been ratified. He lamented the South's defeat in the Civil War. He supported Senator Joseph McCarthy (because he was disruptive), Adlai Stevenson (because his foreign policy would have been less aggressive than Eisenhower's), Ross Perot and Pat Buchanan (because they were populist). He embraced Black nationalism and the racist David Duke. In fusing libertarianism and racism—he understood the value of racist ideas for defending the unequal division of property in America and concomitant poverty of Black Americans—he anticipated the alt-right and Donald Trump.[7]

He wrote about economics, politics, American history, and political philosophy. His knowledge was immense, and his judgments sometimes shrewd. At a time when almost everyone believed that the Soviet Union could persist indefinitely as a great power, he concluded that its system was doomed, and that its ambitions of promoting revolution abroad would inevitably wane. After the revolution, "there is only one way a man can rise above the slave level and make any sort of career for himself: to join the Communist Party." Thus "we may confidently expect that as time goes on, and the old revolutionary generation dies out, their successors will more and more be simple careerists, and not dedicated Communists at all."[8]

He was a marginal figure until the late 1960s, without much of an audience. Most Americans had faith in the state and were untroubled by its aggressive foreign policy and its alliance with large corporate interests. The economy boomed after World War II. Then Vietnam, Watergate, and the stagflation of the 1970s created a new skepticism about government, culminating in the election of Ronald Reagan in 1980.

Rothbard was one of the first to see the political possibilities. In a 1968 essay in *Ramparts*, the leading magazine of the New Left, titled "Confessions of a Right-Wing Liberal," he wryly noted:

> Twenty years ago, I was an extreme right-wing Republican, a young and lone "Neanderthal" (as the liberals used to call us) who believed, as one friend pungently put it, that "Senator Taft had sold out to the socialists." Today, I am most likely to be called an extreme leftist, since I favor immediate withdrawal from Vietnam, denounce U.S. imperialism, advocate Black Power, and have just joined the new Peace and Freedom Party. And yet my basic political views have not changed by a single iota in these two decades![9]

Libertarianism broke through to the mainstream media in 1971. Articles covering the movement appeared in *Newsweek*, *Time*, *Playboy*, *Esquire*, the *Wall Street Journal*, the *Washington Post*, and the *Nation*. Rothbard placed two pieces on the *New York Times* opinion page and began appearing on television. Macmillan solicited a book manuscript, his best-known work, *For a New Liberty*.[10] That same year, he joined the newly formed Libertarian Party, and became its most articulate voice.

In 1976, long conversations with Rothbard helped persuade industrialist Charles Koch to create the Cato Institute, a new libertarian think tank.[11] One scholar who attended a 1979 program recalls that the institute "was at its inception distinctly Rothbardian in orientation," and that "most of the lecturers were committed Rothbardians."[12] Eventually, Rothbard split with Koch over policy differences, and helped found the Mises Institute, which continues to be the central bastion of anarcho-libertarianism. He helped write Ron Paul's newsletter, which began the increasingly potent fusion of libertarianism with racism, but his own philosophy, as we shall see, did not depend on racist arguments. He was willing to enlist any allies against the state, including some pretty nasty ones. He was an equal opportunity opportunist.

Rothbard takes the libertarian's hatred of state oppression to its maximum. He demands a world with no government at all, in which the market rules everything. Even police and legal services should be offered by competing entrepreneurs. Others had made these arguments before him. His philosophy resembles that of the nineteenth-century abolitionist Lysander Spooner, whom Rothbard admired intensely. But Spooner never attracted the kind of following that Rothbard got. The culture had become more receptive to such views.

The core moral principle upon which Rothbard founds his philosophy is nonaggression: "No man or group of men may aggress against the person or property of anyone else."[13] If one combines this with a right to private property, one can logically infer "the right of free exchange and free contract . . . the right of bequest, and . . . the entire property rights structure of the market economy."[14] (As we saw in chapter 2, he purports to be elaborating upon the work of Locke, but there is no nonaggression principle in Locke.[15])

The nonaggression principle entails anarchy. States use force to impose taxes. The use of force to seize property is barred by the principle. It's that simple.

Why believe in the principle? Rothbard posits that "each man may only live and prosper as he exercises his natural freedom of choice, adopts values, learns how to achieve them, etc."[16] (This is not universally true; some people are coddled by others all their lives and like it.) From this he infers that "if someone aggresses against him to change his freely-selected course, this violates his nature; it violates the way he must function."[17]

That doesn't sound nice, but it's not clear why it would be categorically wrong. My natural freedom of choice is blocked when I'm not allowed to drive through a red light, but coercive enforcement of traffic laws might, on the whole, facilitate my capacity to live as I like. Coercion always needs justification, but that doesn't mean that the justification will never be forthcoming.

Rothbard tries to root his ethics in human nature. Arguments of that kind present well-known difficulties, arising from David Hume's famous argument that one cannot infer conclusions about what ought to be done from premises that merely state what is the case.[18] The point is a simple one of logic: unless there's a normative premise, you can't deduce a normative conclusion. As it is familiarly put: you can't derive an ought from an is. But even if one rejects this claim (Rothbard does),[19] *he* hasn't stated premises from which his conclusions follow.

He has a second, independent argument for strong property rights. He claims that there are only three possible views to take on the issue of self-ownership. Either each person owns his body and what he produces, or each of us equally owns everyone else's body, or one group owns themselves and everyone else.[20] Matt Zwolinski explains the error here:

> Rothbard's argument "works" by wrongly claiming that there are only three possibilities regarding self-ownership, two of which are obviously insane, and therefore his position wins by default. But if there are infinitely many possibilities, this victory-by-elimination strategy won't work. The libertarian position of full self-ownership, just like every other conceptually possible position one might take on the issue of self-ownership, stands in need of independent moral argument.[21]

Rothbard appears to be ignorant of all the ways that the existing property rights he is so keen to defend are already encumbered.

Ownership of land, for instance, involves a huge range of duties to maintain it. Mere possession of title will sometimes cost the owner money.[22]

We already saw this mistake in chapter 2, where Nozick dismissed as "gimmicky" the idea of property rights that are subject to the possibility of redistributive taxation. Our response was that all existing property rights are already subject to this proviso. For Rothbard, too, the libertarian notion of absolute property rights rests on a confused understanding of its own central concept. Property rights are subject to a broader range of specifications than Nozick or Rothbard imagine.[23]

Rothbard's nonaggression principle is supposed to protect property, but what counts as aggression depends on the specification of property rights. Is it aggression against you if I hot-wire your car and drive it away? If you forcibly try to stop me, which of us is the aggressor? To return to the story with which this book began: Is it unjust aggression to use tax money to support a fire department? One can lay down as a rule, "Don't hurt people and don't take their stuff," but one must then know what counts as their stuff.[24]

Rothbard's answer relies on Locke's account of property rights. He offers the example of a "sculptor fashioning a work of art out of clay and other materials." He interprets Locke's labor-mixing metaphor as we did: "Surely, if every man has the right to own his own body, and if he must grapple with the material objects of the world in order to survive, then the sculptor has the right to own the product he has made, by his energy and effort, a veritable extension of his own personality."[25] That is the foundation of the entire theory. "The central core of the libertarian creed, then, is to establish the absolute right to private property of every man: first, in his own body, and second, in the previously unused natural resources which he first transforms by his labor."[26] From this absolute right Rothbard infers the "central axiom" that "no man or group of men may aggress against the person or property of anyone else."[27]

That axiom entails anarchism: "While opposing any and all private or group aggression against the rights of person and property, the libertarian sees that throughout history and into the present day, there has been one central, dominant, and overriding aggressor upon all of these rights: the State."[28] Because the state characteristically uses force, in fact is defined by its monopoly of force over its territory, the state is inherently rights-violating: "Taxation is Robbery."[29]

Anarchy is not commonly a term of admiration, and Rothbard understands that the proposal to abolish the state is likely to frighten many of his readers. Nonetheless, he insists that "whatever services the government actually performs could be supplied far more efficiently and far more morally by private and cooperative enterprise."[30] He would privatize not only roads and bridges but also police and courts. In a free market, individuals will hire private contractors to protect them from violence. That would produce multiple private police forces, with no central authority over them. Peace and prosperity would follow, because it is not in the interests of repeat players to seek short-term gains at the cost of long-term conflict. Absolute property rights will mean that some people are destitute, but this would merely be justice. In a free market, or even in the somewhat unfree markets of modern society, Rothbard thinks, the poor tend to be responsible for their own poverty because they do not take advantage of the opportunities they have.

Rothbard cites some societies, such as medieval Iceland, in which he claims that custom-based private dispute resolution worked. These societies, however, were small, everyone was a repeat player, and norms were widely shared. Informal cooperation is harder in a complex society of millions of strangers.

It is not as though anarchy has never been tried. The human race has plenty of experience of multiple armed factions trying to exercise control over the same geographical area. They are colloquially known as warlords. Jeffrey Winters surveys such arrangements—prehistoric societies and medieval Europe are his principal illustrations—and finds that the effect is a chronic state of warfare, in which any peace is fragile and temporary. There are few examples from advanced industrial countries. One is the mid-twentieth-century Mafia Commission in the United States. It was predicated on the value of cooperation, which promised and often delivered huge financial benefits for all participants, but its equilibrium was punctuated by frequent wars and assassinations.[31] And that's in a world of repeat players: the gangsters who killed one another sometimes had known each other for decades.

The modern state actually did begin as a coalition of armed associations, but with different consequences than Rothbard imagines. Warlords do indeed have an incentive to cooperate. That does not mean establishing a free market with low barriers to entry that encourages competition and innovation, or providing equal protection of the law to those who are not armed. They are generally more interested in maintaining their status and passing it on to their heirs. A leading study of state development reports that, in political orders that are made of such coalitions, "the key link that constrains military power is embedding the individuals who direct military power in a network of privileges. By manipulating privilege, interests are created that limit violence."[32] What actually emerges from networks of protective associations, all over the world, is some variety of hereditary aristocracy. The need to buy off powerful stakeholders constrains the ability of leaders to take steps that would improve the wealth of the elites taken as a whole. "Elite bargains that fail to allocate policy benefits and privileges in rough accord with underlying violence potential cannot be sustained."[33] Political manipulation of the economy is, in many countries, a means for avoiding civil war: "Economics is politics by other means."[34]

No society has ever transcended this condition without consolidated government control of the military.[35] Only then is it possible to create the impersonal rule of law. The powerful state that Rothbard loathes is the indispensable precondition of the robust capitalism that he idolizes. (His proposal to privatize the state, because then markets will work better, is like someone who has had a very productive month deciding to do even better the following month by giving up food and sleep.) It is also the context in which the honest and trustworthy security companies he has in mind have come into existence. If any of those companies today were to act toward civilians as fourteenth-century English nobility did, the police would show up in a hurry.

A major cause of the Great Enrichment is the proliferation of transactions among people who don't know each other, never meet each other, and often don't even speak the same language. That happens because there is an impersonal institution ready to enforce their contracts and maintain the peace.

Of course, as we saw in chapter 2, there never was a social contract. Political order, Mancur Olsen observes, emerges when roving bandits are replaced by stationary bandits, who exert a monopoly of force over a given geographical area and so have an incentive to protect persons and property for the sake of more tax revenue in the future.[36] But whatever the nasty origins of the state, a flourishing human life is impossible without it.

Rothbard also extended his libertarianism to foreign policy: he wanted the United States to retreat from its international commitments. The attractions of that view during the Vietnam era were clear. But the bigger picture is that the value of a strong state abroad mirrors that of a strong state at home. The United States really has been the world's policeman since World War II, and (clumsy disasters such as Vietnam, Iraq, and Afghanistan notwithstanding) that is a major reason why free trade has boomed and wars have been contained.[37]

However, all the optimistic projections about anarchism are in some ways beside the point. Rothbard thinks that the nonaggression principle is categorical: political authority is illegitimate regardless of the consequences.

Those consequences can be pretty bad. Rothbard doesn't care. He thought that there are no positive obligations, even of parents to children. The parent "does not have the right to aggress against his children, but also the parent should not have a legal obligation to feed, clothe, or educate his children, since such obligations would entail positive acts coerced upon the parent and depriving the parent of his rights. The parent therefore may not murder or mutilate his child . . . but the parent should have the legal right not to feed his child, i.e., to allow it to die."[38] This would be immoral, Rothbard cheerfully conceded. But one should have a legal right to do immoral things.

Redistribution is categorically barred, because it violates property rights. Rothbard, we saw, took Locke's labor-mixing justification for

property to an extreme that would have astonished Locke. Why would one construe property rights in such absolute terms? Rawls would ask, why would anyone agree to such categorical rights, which could doom some citizens to avoidable starvation? A further complication is that many existing property titles are the product of historical injustices, rather than the energy and effort of their present possessors. Rothbard acknowledges this; he thinks that the emancipated slaves were entitled to compensation for their forced labor, a measure that would have transferred Southern plantations to them. In the present, however, Rothbard summarily dismisses the problem: "Where we are not sure about a title but it cannot be clearly identified as criminally derived, then the title properly and legitimately reverts to its present possessor."[39]

Rothbard's attachment to property rights is tenacious. Hayek suggested that if a monopolist controlled a commodity indispensable to some people's existence—if, for instance, all sources of water except one were to dry up, so that people "had no choice but to do whatever the owner of the spring demanded of them if they were to survive," then state intervention would be appropriate.[40] Rothbard retorted that the owner of the oasis "is responsible only for the existence of his own actions and his own property." Denying access to the water, even if the neighbors will die of thirst—perhaps he regards the spring as sacred and will not sell the water at any price—is "within his rights as a free man and as a just property owner."[41] (Is it even necessary to say tha Rothbard wanted to abolish all of antitrust law, and would have see nothing wrong with today's competition-stifling monopolies?[42])

Rothbard's nonaggression principle is even more stringent than comprehends. He thinks that it prohibits fraud. But fraud is not agg sion, and he is committed to the idea that individuals are respon for their own welfare. One of the pertinent responsibilities is d mining whether to believe the information one receives. Fraud, appears to be permissible in Rothbard's world.[43]

What about regulation? Hayek, we saw, thought that in order to prosperity, a state must do more than protect persons and pr

also has to regulate in order to prevent negative externalities. How does Rothbard propose to address pollution and the like?

A fundamental objection to regulation, Rothbard thought, is that government lacks enough information to know where the unjustified externalities are or what level of regulation is optimal. He radicalizes Hayek's claim that we are opaque to one another. Cost-benefit analysis is impossible: "Costs are purely subjective and not measurable in monetary terms."[44] Without the information supplied by markets, we can't tell how people price their utilities, and any cost–benefit analysis is guesswork.[45] The argument is clever but perverse. Must we allow factory smoke to shorten the lives of thousands of children in the neighborhood, because there's no market to tell us how much the children's lives are worth, to them or anyone else? It may be difficult to assess the human costs of pollution, but the answer that is sure to be wrong is zero.[46]

Rothbard struggled with the pollution question. He oscillated between two solutions, both so extreme as to be unworkable. He ended up embracing unlimited environmental destruction.

At first, Rothbard saw that his extreme vision of property rights entailed that pollution is a kind of trespassing. Like Mises, he thought that courts could issue injunctions against it. "The polluter sends unwanted and unbidden pollutants—from smoke to nuclear fallout to sulfur oxides—*through* the air and into the lungs of innocent victims, as well as onto their material property. . . . Air pollution that injures others is aggression pure and simple."[47] Property rights were the answer to the pollution problem. "If a private firm owned Lake Erie . . . then anyone dumping garbage in the lake would be promptly sued in the [privatized] courts for their aggression."[48] Class action suits could be deployed "to enjoin anyone from injecting pollutants into the air."[49] He acknowledges that there would be social costs to outlawing the internal combustion engine. But all will be well: "If air pollution is allowed to proceed with impunity, there continues to be no economic incentive to develop a technology that will *not* pollute."[50]

That's simple enough. It's *too* simple. Matt Zwolinski observes that

"the libertarian commitment to property rights is so absolute, and so far-reaching in its implications," that it may make impossible demands.[51] Set aside the problem that technological alternatives to fossil fuels could not instantly be called into existence. Carbon dioxide is a pollutant. Another libertarian, David Friedman (son of Milton), observed that "If I have no right to impose a single molecule of pollution on anyone else's property, then I must get the permission of all my neighbors to breathe. Unless I promise not to exhale."[52]

Rothbard eventually revisited the pollution question, and qualified his response in a way that drove him to the opposite extreme, relaxing the ban on harming others. "Air pollution . . . of gases or particles that are invisible or undetectable by the senses should not constitute aggression per se, because being insensible they do not interfere with the owner's possession or use."[53] Such pollution may be harmful, but the victims "must assent uncomplainingly" to the harm unless they can prove "beyond a reasonable doubt" that there is "strict causality from the actions of the defendant to the victimization of the plaintiff."[54] Polluters should have the equivalent of an accused criminal's presumption of innocence: "It is far better to let an aggressive act slip through than to impose coercion and commit aggression ourselves."[55] On this basis, he denounced the Clean Air Act of 1970.[56]

The environmental laws of that time were enacted because in some cities, the air was becoming dangerous to breathe and the river water toxic. Acid rain was destroying forests. Absent regulation, some cities surrounded by mountains, such as Los Angeles and Denver, might now be uninhabitable. If the harm to persons doesn't matter, what about the damage to property values?

Consider one type of pollution that has now been banned: the use of lead additives in gasoline. Ingestion of lead damages the kidneys and raises the blood pressure. It is particularly devastating to the brains and nervous systems of children. Reagan came into office skeptical of claims that lead was harmful. He cut the EPA's budget and nearly eliminated its enforcement division. When one oil refiner complained about the cost of compliance with existing regulations, Reagan's EPA administrator, Anne Gorsuch, assured them that the law would soon be changed and wouldn't be enforced. "I can't tell your client to break the law," she said after the meeting, "but I hope they got the message." Once EPA officials had studied the science, and learned that relaxing the rules would poison two hundred thousand children, they enacted even stricter rules than the Carter administration had proposed.[57] Reagan was a sincere Hayekian, and that is what Hayekian environmental policy looks like. Between 1976 and 1991, the average American child's blood lead level dropped by more than 75 percent.

There is now evidence that leaded gasoline emissions are even more harmful than was then understood. In multiple countries, the rise and fall of the use of leaded gasoline correlated with increases in violent crime. Researchers hypothesize that the brain damage in urban children made them more prone to violence. There is an impressive correlation with the crime wave of the 1960s and 1970s. When the lead was restricted, the crime tapered off.[58] This meant fewer rights violations—but it is still not clear that the regulations can be justified within Rothbard's framework. Rights violations aren't permissible even to prevent others from committing rights violations.[59] Rothbard's demand for strict proof of causality means that we must tolerate all of this.

Not everyone is convinced by the lead-crime connection. But what's relevant for us is that, for Rothbard, it doesn't matter. If nonaggressive individual activities bring about a state of affairs in which the basic libertarian rights, security of person and property, are insecure, if they make violent death more likely, regulation remains impermissible. You will have the consolation of knowing that what killed you and your family wasn't the state.

Rothbard's principles, properly interpreted, do not in fact license these harms. His flat ban on *visible* invasions of property, and indifference to *invisible* invasions, is peculiarly ad hoc and impossible to reconcile with his nonaggression principle. If you are damaging my body and property, why does it matter that I can't detect the damage as it's happening? The nonaggression principle prohibits poisoning as well as assault.[60]

Rothbard is thus torn between prohibiting everything and leaving industry free to gas its neighbors. The only constant is that, either way, you can't breathe. A theory that promises clear boundaries between one person's liberties and another's is unable to address this crucial boundary question in a sane way.[61]

Property rights have never been so absolute as Rothbard imagines. The law of nuisance is more nuanced. Neighbors must put up with minor unwanted noises, smells, and other small annoyances. "The reciprocal nature of the gains and losses," Richard Epstein explains, "make it likely that most individuals will benefit from the increased liberty of action more than they will suffer from the additional disruption in their daily lives."[62] Epstein observes that courts will enjoin nuisances only when the harms are nonreciprocal and severe. Nuisance litigation can't succeed when the harms are cumulative, the consequence of small actions by many polluters. In such cases, Epstein observes, there is no workable alternative to regulation. Rothbard doesn't grasp any of this. Once more, he does not understand property.

In chapter 6, we will consider the way in which contemporary libertarians such as Charles Koch deal with the challenge of climate change. Their response is remarkably similar to Rothbard's. His evasive discomfort with the fact of pollution is one of his most enduring and dangerous legacies.

Recall that Hayek's deepest tension is his simultaneous conservative attachment to traditional social forms, without which markets cannot function, and his desire to abolish all limits on capitalism's creative destruction. Rothbard has no such problem, because he sees no value in inherited social forms. Let them be swept away. We will surely be freer, because the state will no longer push us around.

The anarchic planet for which Rothbard yearns is an exciting and adventurous place.[63] Hello, cruel world! It is, however, unlikely to be conducive to the gains from trade that have constituted the Great Enrichment. The likely transaction costs are evident in the post-apocalyptic vision of the libertarian science fiction novelist Robert Heinlein:

FARNHAM'S FREEHOLD
TRADING POST & RESTAURANT BAR

American Vodka
Corn Liquor
Applejack
Pure Spring Water
Grade "A" Milk
Corned Beef & Potatoes
Steak & Fried Potatoes
Butter & some days Bread
Smoked Bear Meat
Jerked Quisling (*by the neck*)
Crepes Suzettes to order

!!!Any BOOK Accepted as Cash!!!
DAY NURSERY

!!FREE KITTENS!!

Blacksmithing, Machine Shop, Sheet Metal Work-
You Supply the Metal

FARNHAM SCHOOL OF CONTRACT BRIDGE
Lessons by Arrangement
Social Evening Every Wednesday

WARNING!!!
Ring bell. Wait. Advance with your Hands *Up*. Stay on path, avoid mines. We lost three customers last week. We can't afford to lose YOU. No sales tax.[64]

Robert Nozick's *Anarchy, State, and Utopia* is the most important scholarly work of libertarian philosophy. Published just three years after Rawls's *Theory of Justice*, it appeared at an opportune political moment. It immediately attained an academic respect that Rothbard never got, and became the most prominent foil to Rawls. It is beautifully written and fun to read. Its style is exciting and digressive, constantly darting off on interesting tangents. Nozick must have been marvelous in the classroom. His work was an immense gift to libertarians. E. J. Dionne observes: "Welfare staters and libertarians each had their own Harvard philosopher. . . . Within the world of politics, libertarians could rest secure that their own genius had thought matters through to first principles and had come out just where they were."[65]

It is not generally understood how much Nozick owes to Rothbard. Nozick was a social democrat when he began graduate study in philosophy at Princeton in 1959. A fellow student introduced him to libertarianism, and one evening took him to one of the many discussion sessions in Rothbard's Manhattan apartment.[66] The encounter made a huge impression, and continued to shape Nozick's work after he joined the Harvard philosophy department. *Anarchy, State, and Utopia* made him famous. But he did not continue his work in political philosophy. Instead, he focused on a range of other philosophical problems, leaving this book to speak for itself. He died in 2002.

Anarchy, State, and Utopia is in large part an attempt to stipulate Rothbard's premises and then avoid his anarchistic conclusions, by showing how a (minimal!) state can be justified on Rothbard's terms. It is best read as an extended footnote to Rothbard. As such, it is a complex, fascinating flop. Nozick's argument fails on multiple levels: it does not rehabilitate the inadequately defended nonaggression principle, it does not refute the anarchist inference from that principle, and (as we saw in chapter 2) it does not justify its conception of property.

Rothbard, we saw, offered little basis for his nonaggression principle. That was one of many reasons why professional philosophers have never taken him seriously. Nozick evidently saw the problem, because he started from scratch with an entirely different foundation. He proposed to base the principle on Immanuel Kant's dictum that people should always be treated as ends in themselves, never as mere means. Kant notoriously is often difficult to read, but the core of his ethical philosophy is straightforward and familiar: people must be treated with respect. (Friedrich Nietzsche remarked that "Kant wanted to prove, in a way that would dumbfound the common man, that the common man was right."[67]) From the Kantian premise that "there are different individuals with separate lives and so no one may be sacrificed for others," Nozick infers a "constraint that prohibits aggression against another."[68]

Paraphrasing Rothbard without attribution, Nozick addresses the hypothesis that taxation, even to support minimal police protection, arguably violates rights: "When the state threatens someone with punishment if he does not contribute to the protection of another, it violates (and its officials violate) his rights."[69] Taxation, Nozick thinks, is a kind of forced labor, compelling citizens to work for the state.

Thus far, as in Rothbard, the implication appears to be anarchism. Nozick, however, thinks that he can show that a legitimate state could arise without violating anyone's rights.

Recall that Rothbard thinks that in conditions of anarchy, people would voluntarily form mutual-protection associations that guard the members' persons and property. Nozick proposes that a state could evolve out of this world of protective associations. He doesn't try to defend Rothbard's optimism about anarchy. Instead, he aims to show that Rothbard's world leads to a minimal state:

> If one could show that the state would be superior even to this most favored situation of anarchy, the best that realistically can be hoped for, or would arise by a process involving no morally impermissible steps or would be an improvement if it arose, this would provide a rationale for the state's existence; it would justify the state.[70]

To summarize a complex set of steps very briefly, one of those associations is likely to eventually dominate the others, because people will rationally flock to the biggest and most powerful such association. That association, however, cannot guarantee its members the promised security if there are some hard-to-identify nonmembers interspersed among the population. Thus it must forcibly bring them into the association, but must compensate them by providing them with protection as well.

Protection is, however, all that the state is authorized to provide.

It "may not use its coercive apparatus for the purpose of getting some citizens to aid others."[71] Redistribution, even to prevent starvation, is categorically prohibited.

That led many readers to conclude that Nozick was opposed to the American welfare state. In an often-neglected passage, however, he declares that "one cannot use the analysis and theory presented here to condemn any particular scheme of transfer payments, unless it is clear that no considerations of rectification of injustice could apply to justify it." In a condition where "the least well-off group in the society have the highest probabilities of being the (descendants of) victims of the most serious injustice who are owed compensation . . . past injustices might be so great as to make necessary in the short run a more extensive state in order to rectify them."[72] He then cites a book arguing for Black reparations.[73] He resists easy categorization as an opponent of all redistribution.

Nozick did not say much about regulation, but he thought that a society should "permit those polluting activities whose benefits are greater than their costs."[74] That sounds a lot like the Hayekian case for regulation. It avoids the binary extremisms of Rothbard. Zwolinski observes, however, that it does this at the cost of "abandoning the moral core of libertarianism."[75] How can polluters be entitled to injure others whenever the benefits exceed the costs? Nozick has embraced Rothbard's crude understanding of property rights, which has no way to think about pollution.

Undertaking the requisite cost-benefit analysis, in cases not addressed by nuisance law (such as pollution with major cumulative effects), will require a far bigger state apparatus than Nozick contemplates. The relevant facts are complex. Pollution involves a huge number of chemicals interacting with the environment, and with the bodies of human beings, in a huge number of ways. The Environmental Protection Agency has an immense, expensive staff to sort out these facts. It has to. Nozick's premises imply that this is part of the state's legitimate job. He is a minimalist only with respect to redistribution. His position on regulation is essentially Hayek's and Epstein's.

Rothbard promptly answered Nozick. Nozick, he observed, did not deny that compelling people to join the state and pay taxes violates the nonaggression principle. Compensation does not make this acceptable. Violations of rights are not excused when the transgressor is willing to pay for his fun. (Rothbard's response is structurally identical to the Republican complaint against Obamacare—you can't force someone to buy an unwanted product—but it was better reasoned than that complaint, because it was a sound inference from the nonaggression principle. That principle is obviously not part of the US Constitution, which was enacted to prevent rather than to produce anarchy.[76]) So Nozick has not refuted Rothbard's claim that the nonaggression principle entails anarchism. Anyway, absent a market to set prices, there is no way to determine what the compensation for nonmembers should be.[77] There are many criticisms of Nozick,[78] but this most devastating one is not well known, because political philosophers are unfamiliar with Rothbard and tend not to see how much Nozick depends on Rothbard's implausible premises, or how unpersuasive are his inferences from those premises.[79]

A deeper problem, if libertarianism relies on a Kantian foundation, is that Kant's moral theory doesn't support the nonaggression principle or anarchism. Nozick is hardly the first philosopher to try to work out a Kantian political philosophy. Someone else got there first. His name was Immanuel Kant. Kant reached the opposite conclusion: it was anarchy that failed to treat people with dignity.

Like Locke, Kant was a social contract theorist. Unlike Locke, however, he did not think that the social contract was based on the interests of the contractors. It was based on their moral duties.

Kant's core commitment is that people have an obligation to treat one another with respect—as ends in themselves rather than as mere means. Kant thought that this is impossible in conditions of anarchy. If I claim any rights that can coercively be enforced, I have to point to some shared source of authority.

Explaining Kant's argument, Christine Korsgaard offers the example of property rights:

> To claim a right to property is to make a kind of law; for it is to lay it down that all others must refrain from using the object or land in

> question without my permission. But to view my claim as a *law* I must view it as the object of a contract between us, a contract in which we reciprocally commit ourselves to guaranteeing each other's rights. It is this fact that leads us to enter—or, more precisely, to view ourselves as already having entered—political society.[80]

Even if I succeed in enforcing my rights, unless there is some source of law outside my own will, this is mere brute force. If I'm going to claim a right, then I've already assumed that people can have rights—that it's possible for others to have rights against me. "It is a duty of justice to live in political society. That is to say, others have the right to require this of you, because that is the form that their authority to enforce their own rights takes."[81] If rights are going to be enforceable, then there must be some authority with the competence to enforce them. "Justice, which is the condition in which we have guaranteed one another our rights, exists only where there is government."[82] People in a state of anarchy thus have an obligation to form a government and thereby bring themselves under the sway of law.

There are, of course, many unjust governments. Kant agreed with Rothbard about that. But Kant thought that since no perfectly just government is possible, we have an obligation to treat existing governments as though they were legitimate. (Kantians have since pointed out that this won't justify obedience to a state that attacks the very idea of human dignity, as Nazi Germany or antebellum slaveholding America did.) Similarly with property claims. Respectful relations are impossible unless people have secure property titles. Therefore, absent convincing evidence to the contrary, we should treat what people have now as their property. The precise contours of property rights—and the appropriate level and objects of taxation—are appropriately left to the state to determine.[83] So the state is entitled to the aggressive behaviors that trouble Rothbard, such as the coercive collection of taxes.

The state does not, however, have unlimited discretion to craft property rights in any way it likes. Certain arrangements are barred by the logic of Kantian respect. One of the prohibited specifications is the absolute property rights that Nozick advocates, because they jeopardize the liberty that property rights are supposed to protect.[84] It is impermissible for the state to create a system of property rights that leave some people utterly at the mercy of the will of others for their survival. One could not consent to such relations of domination, any more than one could consent to slavery. Property exists for the sake of liberty. Liberty does not exist for the sake of property.

Kant thus thought that government is "authorized to constrain the wealthy to provide the means of sustenance to those who are unable to provide for even their most necessary natural needs."[85] Kant does what Nozick thinks cannot be done: he can "accept the strongly put root idea about the separateness of individuals and yet claim that initiating aggression [by collecting taxes] is compatible with this root idea."[86] If one wants a more detailed account of what kinds of property rights are just, then one must consider what terms of social cooperation would be agreed to under fair bargaining conditions. That takes us back to Rawls.[87]

One of the most memorable passages in Ayn Rand's novel *The Fountainhead* describes the cluster of vacation homes that Howard Roark has designed in Monadnock Valley. A young cyclist is surprised to discover them:

> There were small houses on the ledges of the hill before him, flowing down to the bottom. He knew that the ledges had not been touched, that no artifice had altered the unplanned beauty of the graded steps. Yet some power had known how to build on these ledges in such a way that the houses became inevitable, and one could no longer imagine the hills as beautiful without them—as if the centuries and the series of chances that produced these ledges in the struggle of great blind forces had waited for their final expression, had been only a road to a goal—and the goal was these buildings, part of the hills, shaped by the hills, yet ruling them by giving them meaning.[88]

Roark was given the opportunity to construct this masterpiece by a group of investors who did not care that his work had been condemned by all the most influential critics. It turns out that they were swindlers who sold 200 percent of the stock, expecting and hoping it would fail. They are shocked to learn that there is a market for the homes—that a previously unknown population of individuals see the value of Roark's work. The crooks go to prison, but the project prospers.

The Fountainhead can be read as a Hayekian parable. Capitalism does not reward virtue.[89] Mediocrities like Peter Keating prosper by flattering the powerful. Panderers like the newspaper publisher Gail Wynand become fabulously rich by appealing to consumers' lowest instincts. (One of capitalism's greatest virtues, its responsiveness to what people want, is a matter of ambivalence for Rand, who despises the masses.) Geniuses like the visionary architect Henry Cameron are neglected and die in poverty. But there is room for brilliance to be rewarded. Because control of capital is decentralized, individuals are free to take reckless risks. The world is unpredictable: even schemes that seemed doomed, that *aimed* at doom, sometimes succeed. Experimentation and discovery can happen. Free markets cannot, however, be relied on to give people what they deserve.

Rand's later and more politically influential novel, *Atlas Shrugged*, offers a far cruder picture. There, a character who clearly is speaking for Rand herself declares that "when men live by trade—with reason, not force, as their final arbiter—it is the best product that wins, the best performance, the man of best judgment and highest ability—and the degree of a man's productiveness is the degree of his reward."[90] It is that vision of capitalism, in which markets give people exactly what they deserve and any redistribution is unjust, that she elaborates in her later writings and is best known for.

Her novels have introduced more people to libertarianism than any nonfiction writer, herself included. Roy Childs wrote that "to attempt the task of identifying her effect" on the libertarian movement "is rather like trying to sort out the effects of Christianity on Western Civilization."[91] House Speaker Paul Ryan said that her work was "the reason I got involved in public service." He gave his staff copies of *Atlas Shrugged*.[92] A 1991 Library of Congress–Book of the Month Club survey found that more Americans cited *Atlas Shrugged* as the book that had most influenced their lives than any other book except the Bible.[93] Glenn Beck and Rush Limbaugh embraced her ideas. The BB&T banking corporation provided more than sixty colleges with funding for programs in the "moral foundations of capitalism" that require students to read Rand.[94] Gary Johnson, who received 4.4 million votes as the 2016 Libertarian candidate for president—the most that any of the party's candidates have ever received—said that "I view big government in the same way that the novelist and philosopher Ayn Rand did—that it really oppresses those that create, if you will, and tries to take away from those that produce and give to the non-producers."[95] From 2009 to 2014, *Atlas Shrugged* sold 2.25 million copies (although much of that is bulk purchases by foundations that give free copies to students).[96] Donald Trump admired *The Fountainhead*: "It relates to business (and) beauty (and) life and inner emotions. That book relates to . . . everything." Trump identified with Howard Roark.[97]

Rand was born as Alisa Rosenbaum in Russia in 1905. When she was a child, the Red Guard nationalized her father's chemistry shop, and her once prosperous family became desperately poor. Faced with the incompetence and tyranny of the Soviet authorities, she escaped to America in 1926. *The Fountainhead*, published in 1943, made her famous. *Atlas Shrugged* followed in 1957. She wrote no more fiction after that, but focused on philosophical work until she died in 1982.

Rand is a novelist first and a philosopher second. Her moral vision is vividly presented in her fiction. We will begin by considering that vision.

Here is the story of *Atlas Shrugged*:

The novel's protagonist, Dagny Taggart, is a railroad company heiress who keeps her company solvent in the face of irrational interference from rapacious officials. She notices that America's leading industrialists have been mysteriously disappearing, and that the economy is increasingly dysfunctional. As the story develops, she gradually becomes aware that these developments are connected. The captains of industry have gone on strike in protest, leaving the country to be led by incompetents. By the end, she has joined them.

John Galt, who leads the strike and explains its moral basis, declares that under capitalism, "The man at the top of the intellectual pyramid contributes the most to all those below him, but gets nothing except his material payment. . . . The man at the bottom who, left to himself, would starve in his hopeless ineptitude, contributes nothing to those above him."[98]

Rand's core idea is that the productive elite, who are the source of wealth, are being parasitized by government transfer programs that benefit the lazy and undeserving. "Money is *made*—before it can be looted or mooched—made by the effort of every honest man, each to the extent of his ability. An honest man is one who knows that he can't consume more than he has produced."[99] Any redistribution is inherently evil: "It means the right of the incompetent to own their betters and to use them as productive cattle."[100]

The principle for which Rand's heroes stand is "that men who wish to deal with one another must deal by trade and give value for value. Money is not the tool of the moochers, who claim your product by tears, or of the looters, who take it from you by force. Money is made possible only by the men who produce."[101]

The Fountainhead similarly portrays a solitary genius maintaining his integrity against a mob of mediocrities. The time-servers constantly try to destroy Roark, but he is sublimely indifferent, and ultimately he triumphs.

At the center of Rand's moral universe is the brilliant individual who transforms the world. It is an intoxicating vision. Brian Doherty, the principal historian of libertarianism, observes that this is the source of Rand's appeal: "*Fountainhead* lovers don't just want to hiss at [the book's villain] Toohey—they want to *be* Roark. And despite cavils about his 'unrealism' or 'inhumanity,' a man of consummate skill, bursting creativity, and unyielding integrity is a man eminently worth being."[102]

Producers, looters, moochers: the human race naturally falls into neat divisions, like the sections of an orange. Taxation for any purpose other than the protection of property is theft: "The man who produces while others dispose of his product, is a slave."[103]

The producer-moocher dichotomy has a prominent place in contemporary American politics. Consider Paul Ryan's "Roadmap for America's Future":

> growing numbers have come to rely on government, not themselves, for growing shares of their income and assets. By this means, government increasingly dictates how Americans live their lives; they are not only wards of the state, but also its subjects, increasingly directed in their behavior by the government's "compassion." But dependency drains individual character, which in turn weakens American society. The process suffocates individual initiative and transforms self-reliance into a vice and government dependency into a virtue. The Nation becomes a sort of vast Potemkin Village in which the most important elements—its people—are depleted by a government that increasingly "takes care" of them, and makes ever more of their decisions for them. They take more from society than they provide for themselves, which corrodes society itself, from the inside out.[104]

Mitt Romney similarly channeled Rand when he denounced 47 percent of Americans "who are dependent upon government, who believe that they are victims, who believe the government has a responsibility to care for them, who believe that they are entitled to health care, to food, to housing, to you-name-it—that that's an entitlement." Such people cannot be convinced to "take personal responsibility and care for their lives."[105]

An obvious problem with this picture, one that we already considered in chapter 2, is the difficulty of assessing each person's contribution in a complex economy. Is a professional who received a government-subsidized education, or a retiree who subsists on Social Security, one of Romney's 47 percent? It depends on whether they have taken more than they have contributed. That question is unanswerable. Certainly the market value of their receipts and product, which depend on the contingencies of supply and demand, cannot answer it. "Rand advocated a reverse Marxism," Jonathan Chait observes. "In the Marxist analysis, workers produce all the value, and capitalists merely leech off their labor. Rand posited the opposite."[106] The fundamental flaw in Marx's analysis is that it is impossible to quantify the contribution of labor to value in the way that he posited. Rand makes the same mistake.

Rand's vision also depends on an account of property. Before you can know who the moochers and looters are, you have to know what people are entitled to. Chapter 2 examined Locke's and Rawls's answers to that question. We found that at the deepest level, Hayek was consistent with Rawls and even with Obama. Hayek did not rule out redistribution or regulation, but laid down strict conditions for both. The Galts and Roarks ought to be encouraged and protected, but they're not entitled to be free from regulation or taxation. For Rand, however, the very state measures that Hayek thought necessary were the motivation for the strikers in *Atlas Shrugged*.

Hayek and Rand were both passionate opponents of Soviet communism. Both thought that free markets were an indispensable condition of political liberty. Both defended the inequalities that markets inevitably generate. Both saw what centralized economic control did to their own countries. Yet their accounts of what is valuable about free markets were radically different.

The fundamental divide between them, the divide that still matters today, concerns the question of whether the distributions that unregulated markets create are just. A second disagreement is whether markets can legitimately be regulated when they fail.

Rand is furious at those who take what they're not entitled to. To know whether she's right to be angry, we need to know what people are entitled to—in other words, we need what neither Hayek nor Rand can offer, a philosophical account of property rights. Before you get mad about having your things taken, you need to know that they are really yours. Southern slaveholders fought the Civil War because they wanted to protect their property. It turned out that *they* were the looters and moochers.

Rand's understanding of property rights is not well developed in her fiction, so we turn to her philosophical writings. There she argues that, from basic facts of human nature, she can infer the necessity of "a full, pure, uncontrolled, unregulated laissez-faire capitalism," which "has never yet existed, not even in America."[107] Rand advocates a minimal state, in which the only legitimate function of government is to protect property and enforce contracts.[108] In that state, there would be no compulsory taxation; government would be supported by voluntary contributions.[109] (Good luck with that.) But unlike Rothbard, she is happy to let the state coercively enforce rights.

In Rand, as in Locke, there's a right to appropriate. But unlike in Locke, there are no obligations at all to anyone else, and no justification of the basic structure, which is taken to be a fact of nature. Recall that one difficulty for Locke is that, if people own whatever they produce, then they own their children. Locke's response, that the father does not fashion every detail of the child, vitiates that theory of ownership in any context involving a division of labor. Yet in Rand, the old socialist objection, that one is working on material that is already the product of the work of others in a social division of labor, isn't even considered.

At one point in *Atlas Shrugged*, Hank Reardon, one of the novel's heroes, "remembered the time when, aged fourteen, faint with hunger, he would not steal fruit from a sidewalk stand."[110] Rawls, of course, would ask why anyone would accept Rand's absolutist conception of property rights. Why should we think that property rights are such that Reardon had an obligation to starve? Rand not only did not engage with Rawls but proudly announced that she did not intend to read him.[111] She did read Hayek—with loathing.[112] She regarded him as "an ass, with no conception of a free society at all." Reading his defense of inequality, she wrote: "Why call it 'inequality'? Poverty for a man who isn't worth much is not *inequality*. Unearned payment would be."[113] Both Rawls and Hayek would ask why starvation is the appropriate fate of a person whose labor "isn't worth much" in the market—worth that is contingent on forces he had no control over.

Rand expects a remarkable degree of docility and deference from the losers. The protagonist of *Atlas Shrugged*, Dagny Taggart, is a railroad company heiress who keeps the company solvent in the face of irrational opposition from her incompetent brother and rapacious government officials. Dagny's faithful assistant, Eddie Willers, is described in oddly feudal terms: "He had spent most of his childhood with the Taggart children, and now he worked for them, as his father and grandfather had worked for their father and grandfather."[114] This natural and unchallenged hierarchy also extends to the sexual realm. In the course of the story, Dagny passes through the beds of three titans of capitalism, each more of an alpha male than his predecessor. Each of the men yields her to his successor with implausible good grace. Rand fails to grasp at least one aspect of human possessiveness, the possibility that Atlas might not take it well if a woman leaves him for another man.[115] A novelist ought to understand psychology better than that.

Locke bases his theory of property on man's right to preserve himself. For Locke that is only relevant in the state of nature, but Rand raises the stakes so that survival is in some sense threatened whenever property rights as she conceives them are not respected. "*Rights* are conditions of existence required by man's nature for his proper survival."[116] She is not always precise about this,[117] but sometimes she makes clear that she is focusing not on bare biological survival—obviously the human race survived before she came along, and it was continuing to survive even in the Soviet Union—but on "that which is required for man's survival *qua* man."[118]

The sense of danger is suffocating. "Man has to work and produce in order to support his life. He has to support his life by his own effort and by the guidance of his own mind. If he cannot dispose of the product of his effort, he cannot dispose of his effort; if he cannot dispose of his effort, he cannot dispose of his life."[119] Reviewing Nozick, George Kateb wrote: "I find it impossible to conceive of us as having nerve endings in every dollar of our estate."[120] For Rand, on the other hand, any claim on any part of the market return on one's labor is a mortal threat.

"Man's survival qua man" turns out then to be an ideal of personal flourishing: prosperity in a pitiless capitalist economy.[121] Humans have intrinsic purposes, and the goal of life is to realize those purposes. This was the view of the ancient Greek philosopher Aristotle, whom Rand admired intensely. Aristotelian approaches to ethics continue to have a large following, notably in Catholic natural law theory.

Aristotle's ethics, however, raise a familiar problem. Aristotle thought that one could discern purposes in nature. Modern science, on the other hand, starts from the premise of purposeless brute matter, and holds humans to be made of such matter. On this account, no human purposes can be inferred from the bare fact of human rationality.[122] We get to decide what our purposes are.

To see the problem, consider the debate over the moral status of homosexuality. The traditional condemnation was fundamentally Aristotelian: the sexual faculty has an intrinsic purpose, which is related to reproduction. The response that won the argument was that sex serves lots of purposes, and happiness is evidently one of them.[123] Religious traditionalists don't get to tell us what our fundamental purposes are. Neither does Rand.

Modern philosophers have offered various accounts of human flourishing. All of them have tried to account, in various ways, for something that Aristotle never worried about: there evidently are quite a lot of ways to flourish as a human being. Much modern liberal theory begins from that premise, and radicalizes Hayek's insight that in many ways we are opaque to one another. What's good for me is not necessarily good for you. The most sophisticated theorists have aimed to give people a set of capabilities that are elements of many different kinds of life that people have found desirable. That view has Rawlsian implications: property rights should be allocated in a way that ensures that everyone is able to exercise those capabilities.[124]

Rand has a very different vision. Her ideal of uninhibited self-seeking is a personal one, unburdened by obligations to others. It has had attractions for many. But why should anyone accept Rand's account of human flourishing if they are attracted to a different one? Even if Rand has described the best kind of life, that doesn't say anything about the just distribution of property, or what should be the fate of those who can't or don't want to live up to Rand's ideal. The ethic she offers is not merely a personal one. She proposes it as a just basis for society.

Even if man has certain tendencies qua man, Rand needs to show why one ought to preserve those in all persons, or why all persons have a right to them. We are back to Hume's argument that you can't derive an ought from an is.[125] Rand is fundamentally confused about what a right is: "If man is to live on earth, it is *right* for him to use his mind, it is *right* to act on his own free judgment, it is *right* to work for his values and to keep the product of his work. If life on earth is his purpose, he has a *right* to live as a rational being: nature forbids him the irrational. Any group, any gang, any nation that attempts to negate man's rights, is *wrong*, which means: is evil, which means: is anti-life."[126]

The word *right* is italicized four times in the passage just quoted. Matt Zwolinski points out that the first three uses of the word describe what is morally permissible, perhaps obligatory, for a person to do. In the fourth, "he has a *right*," she is describing a claim he has against others. Rand does not explain the basis of that claim. She doesn't notice that she's relying on an ambiguity in the meaning of the word *right*." The foundation of Rand's ethical theory is thus a semantic error. "In order to remain consistent with egoism, it seems that Rand must claim that *A*'s right against *B* must be grounded not in *A*'s interests, but in *B*'s. In other words, *B* only has an obligation to refrain from interfering with *A* if it is good for *B* to do so."[127]

So even if you stipulate that Rand's egoistic ethical premise is correct, it doesn't entail *any* interpersonal obligations—not even the obligation, on which she insists, to refrain from initiating force against another. "How does the rightness *for Jones* of his using his own mind support the claim that it would be wrong *for Smith* to impede Jones's use of his own mind?"[128] These empirical facts about Jones somehow are supposed to create an obligation in Smith, but Rand never shows how this is possible. People engage in force and fraud for self-interested reasons, and they sometimes achieve their ends by doing so. Locke, responding to the egoistic ethic of Thomas Hobbes, raised the same objection: "An Hobbist, with his principle of self-preservation, whereof himself is to be judge, will not easily admit a great many plain duties of morality."[129]

Sophisticated libertarian philosophers have carefully analyzed Rand's theory of rights, and find with evident frustration and disappointment that there's nothing there except undefended assumptions and circular arguments.[130] (It is educational malpractice to require students to read her work as if it were an example of serious philosophy.)

Rand has her own labor-mixing theory. Workers produce and have a right to what they produce. Any transfer by any means other than trade is looting. "The principle of trade is the only rational ethical principle for all human relationships, personal and social, private and public, spiritual and material."[131] She acknowledges the division of labor, but its only significance is that "it enables a man to devote his effort to a particular field of work and to trade with others who specialize in other fields."[132]

Here she is on to something. She has in fact captured an important ethical ideal: the value of interpersonal respect between "men who do not desire the unearned, who do not make sacrifices nor accept them, who deal with one another as *traders*, giving value for value."[133] Such relationships, based on independence, are "the only form of brotherhood and mutual respect possible between men."[134]

At Rand's core is, not a theory of property rights, but an ideal of reciprocity. That ideal is attractive. It is, I suspect, the source of her rhetorical power. It corresponds with an important part of the experience of anyone who has been paid for useful work.

The pitiless anonymity of a market is one of the best things about it. It makes it possible for a person to know that his work is valued and rewarded by people who don't know him and don't care about him. The only possible explanation is that the work is good! Success in that tough arena proves that he really has something of value to offer the world, that the world is somehow better off because he exists.

Reciprocity is distinct from deserving.[135] I may deserve success, and that success may have been thwarted by forces no one could have prevented, such as accident or disease (Hayek's point), and insurance may even replace my lost income on a dollar-for-dollar basis. I'm still in a bad situation. The fact that I'm getting what I deserve is not sufficient for a satisfactory life. My life is still missing the crucial element of reciprocity. Kant talks about the importance of treating people as ends, but it is also important to most of us to be a means—to be useful to other people.[136]

This is a crucial constraint upon redistribution. People need not only to earn an income but to know that they matter. They need jobs. Which work fits which person is a question that can't be answered by any central planner. With respect to that, you really are on your own. One of the great strengths of the Earned Income Tax Credit is that, unlike work requirements for welfare, it does not subject individuals to state monitoring and tutelage. It merely rewards work, work that someone values and is willing to pay for.

On the other hand, even though markets are often occasions of reciprocity, they are not the only such occasions. The police live off the public fisc and are supported by compulsory taxation. Rand does not claim that they are moochers. And what Rand offers is not really reciprocity but mutual advantage, which can happen without the relations of respect to which she appeals. If I agree to feed your starving family if you all agree to be my slaves, mutual advantage has been achieved, but not mutual respect. Rand appeals to "brotherhood and mutual respect" in contexts in which they do not and cannot exist. Her defense of capitalism relies on principles to which she is not entitled.[137]

Like Locke, Rand thinks that labor deserves to be rewarded. People have a right to what they produce—which is to say, they have a right to whatever price they can demand for their work. If basketball surges in popularity, then the spike in the incomes of talented basketball players belongs to them as a matter of right, and it would be wrong to tax any of it for the benefit of anyone else. Virtue is "the consciously chosen pursuit of a productive career, in any line of rational endeavor, great or modest, on any level of ability. It is not the degree of a man's ability nor the scale of his work that is ethically relevant here, but the fullest and most purposeful use of his mind."[138]

As Hayek saw, however, economic value is not intrinsic. Supply and demand are, in the aggregate, arbitrarily unpredictable. Work that is valuable one day becomes worthless the next, for reasons no one could have foreseen. As I noted in the introduction, millions of middle-aged American workers, who have faithfully done their jobs for decades, are suddenly discovering that machines have replaced them. Now they face economic catastrophe. They don't see better opportunities for the next generation, either. A 2016 poll found that 56 percent of Americans think their children will have a lower standard of living than they do.[139] Rand will say that if they now get less, that shows that they deserve less. Rawls would ask why anyone would agree to terms of cooperation that produce such results, in a country that grows steadily richer. Rand thinks that "the degree of a man's independence, initiative and personal love for his work determines his talent as a worker and his worth as a man."[140] One's compensation in the market does not, however, correspond to these virtues. (Rand implicitly acknowledges this in *The Fountainhead*, where the brilliant architect Henry Cameron dies frustrated and the yellow journalist Gail Wynand becomes rich—while the meddling government bureaucrats of *Atlas Shrugged* are nowhere to be seen. The tension between that earlier novel and the later market-worship of *Atlas Shrugged* and her nonfiction writings is too little noticed.)

Hayek and Rawls both understand that markets don't and can't give people what they deserve, according to standards of reciprocity or any other standards. Reciprocity is, in a way, at the heart of Rawls's theory of justice. His fundamental disagreement with Rand is over the meaning of reciprocity.

The closest Rand comes to noticing that there is a problem here is her short essay on patents and copyrights. Patents, she claims, are "the heart and core of property rights," and "once they are destroyed, the destruction of all other rights will follow automatically, as a brief postscript."[141] Why? Because a mind has a right to "that which it has brought into existence." Intellectual property is "the legal implementation of the base of all property rights: a man's right to the product of his mind."

Rand thinks that, unlike other forms of property, intellectual property must have a time limit. Real property "can be left to heirs, but it cannot remain in their effortless possession in perpetuity: the heirs can consume it or must earn its continued possession by their own productive effort." In contrast, "intellectual property cannot be consumed. If it were held in perpetuity, it would lead to the opposite of the very principle on which it is based: it would lead, not to the earned reward of achievement, but to the unearned support of parasitism."[142] Recall that Locke worried about those who "desired the benefit of another's Pains, which he had no right to,"[143] "the pravity of Mankind being such, that they had rather injuriously prey upon the Fruits of other Mens Labours, than take pains to provide for themselves."[144] But he never suggested that those with inherited property were among those undeserving parasites.

Can't other forms of property similarly support parasitism? Rand thinks that this is impossible: "In a free, competitive society, no one could long retain the ownership of a factory or of a tract of land without exercising a commensurate effort." The entire universe of inherited stocks and tenant farming vanishes by assumption. So does the possibility, clearly delineated by Hayek, that any of the financial rewards allocated by markets merely reflect dumb luck.

Rand's difficulty in theorizing intellectual property arises because this kind of property is manifestly a social creation, designed to produce incentives for desired behavior. The US Constitution grants Congress the power "To promote the progress of science and useful arts, by securing for limited times to authors and inventors the exclusive right to their respective writings and discoveries."[145] The purpose and the limitation go together. Like other libertarians, Rand doesn't understand the concept of property.

Reliance on government as a source of income is a poor proxy for the debilitating effects of dependence. A legally guaranteed income is a source of *independence*. There is, of course, a serious question of reciprocity if the income is simply a dole, though this can also be said of inheritance. One response is to make good use of one's undeserved capital, to show that one deserves to have received this gift.[146] (In *Atlas Shrugged*, the Taggart siblings are heirs to a railroad empire. Dagny is a shrewd and hardworking manager, while her brother, James, is a useless fool.) Some of those who get government checks, such as retirees or wounded veterans, can invoke reciprocity as well. Rand thought Social Security unjust, but as we noted in chapter 1, the relations of dependence that existed between parents and children before the program was created, when most parents depended on their children's support in old age, had their own corrosive effects on reciprocity.

Hayek shows why Rand's vision isn't even fair to the entrepreneurs. It understates their courage. Running a business is hazardous. Unforeseeable events constantly threaten ruin. "The attempt to achieve a valuable result may be highly meritorious but a complete failure, and full success may be entirely the result of accident and thus without merit."[147] This is why a minimal capitalist economy can't possibly provide security to everyone. Its inevitable precariousness, Hayek shrewdly observed, is poorly understood by those who have lived their lives as employees, whose security is guaranteed by the successful risk-taking of someone else.[148] That someone else, however, lives with constant danger. If the market reliably rewarded effort, it wouldn't be so scary.

This brings us to the last large difference between Rand and Hayek. It is the subtlest, but perhaps most important: a difference of affect. Hayek always writes in tones of benevolent concern: the market is good because it "brings about a greater satisfaction of human desires than any deliberate human organization could achieve."[149] He genuinely cares about people on the bottom. His frustration with systems of centralized control is rooted in the conviction that those systems hurt the very people they purport to protect.

Rand, on the other hand, is a hot ball of rage. Her hero John Galt's fifty-six-page speech at the end of *Atlas Shrugged* declares that any redistribution of income benefits only "the weakling, the fool, the rotter, the liar, the failure, the coward, the fraud."[150] Rand's attitude toward the weak was nicely summarized in 1957 by her disciple, Alan Greenspan, later Federal Reserve chairman: "Parasites who persistently avoid either purpose or reason perish as they should."[151] (Paul Ryan has said that as a Christian he repudiates her atheism. It is this pitiless contempt for the weak, not atheism, that is Rand's deepest inconsistency with Christianity.)

In one nasty passage in *Atlas Shrugged*, the foolish arrogance of those who won't let the capitalists do their jobs produces a dreadful train accident. Hundreds of passengers are killed. The reader is surprised to learn that all the victims deserved to die.[152] The gleeful enumeration includes "a professor of economics who advocated the abolition of private property, explaining that intelligence plays no part in industrial production, that man's mind is conditioned by material tools, that anybody can run a factory or a railroad and it's only a matter of seizing the machinery," and "a sniveling little neurotic who wrote cheap little plays into which, as a social message, he inserted cowardly little obscenities to the effect that all businessmen were scoundrels."[153] This literary style, combining didacticism and homicidal fury, is reminiscent of the writings of the Marquis de Sade: *Justine lay bound, naked, spread-eagled on the floor. The Baron stood over her. Gleefully he brandished his whip. And he lectured her for seventeen pages.*

Rand was entitled to her bitterness. Escaping Communist Russia, she found that she could not get American intellectuals to believe her stories of what she had seen there, because they were so entranced with Stalinist claptrap.[154] The leftists of *Atlas Shrugged* seem implausibly stupid, but when one reads Rand's biography, one learns that she was honestly reporting her personal experience. One biographer observes that the novel's "failure of the transportation system, the collectivization of industries, and the resulting economic atavism all broadly reproduce the Russian transition period under Lenin."[155]

But this does not justify her extrapolations from that experience. She thought that the New Deal would lead to "a Totalitarian America, a world of slavery, of concentration camps and firing squads."[156] If Roosevelt were reelected in 1940, she thought there might never be another federal election.[157] More than twenty years later, she believed that John F. Kennedy was a fascist.[158]

How can one explain the continuing popularity of this flavor of delusional grievance, particularly among billionaires? Some people take a childish pleasure in being told that they are beings of a superior order, but even that isn't necessarily bundled with anger and disdain for other people's needs. Part of the explanation may be that today's business class tends to be more educated than earlier elites. They know that academic intellectuals tend to despise those who get rich by producing goods and services.[159] The best writing in *Atlas Shrugged* is the triumphant procession of a train roaring up and down mountains on superstrong tracks made of a newly engineered metal. Rand's anger here is overwhelmed by her infectious joy in the power of human ingenuity. The passage is genuinely inspiring, an eloquent panegyric to capitalist achievement.

Few novelists appreciate the work of business as Rand does. Resentment is inevitable. It's *justified*. You smug intellectuals sit at your reliable word processors, in your houses whose roofs don't leak, surrounded by modern affluence, and sneer at the hardworking people who make it possible? The hell with you![160] But it's possible to take this to extremes: "The American businessmen, as a class, have demonstrated the greatest productive genius and the most spectacular achievements ever recorded in the economic history of mankind. What reward did they receive from our culture and its intellectuals? The position of a hated, persecuted minority."[161]

What about pollution? In *The Road to Serfdom*, Hayek wrote that the market would not prevent "the harmful effects of deforestation, of some methods of farming, or of the smoke and noise of factories."[162] Some regulation would be necessary. In her copy of the book, Rand wrote: "The God damn fool! Who decides all that? By what standard? The fool is so saturated with all the bromides of collectivism that it is terrifying!"[163] She never engaged the problem in any detail. The closest she came was an essay that denounced environmentalism for its hostility to technology and progress. She did acknowledge the legitimacy of laws "prohibiting some kinds of pollution, such as the dumping of industrial wastes into rivers," because they involved "specifically *defined* and *proved* harm, physical harm, to person or property."[164] Her demands for proof seem less exacting than Rothbard's. No individual could prove that any particular dumping of waste had harmed him—that's why Rothbard (in one of his moods) thinks the pollution must be tolerated—yet she thinks it can be outlawed. The statement of her position is so brief that it is impossible to know her reasoning.

In Rand's map of the moral universe, there are two alternatives, egoism and altruism. Her definition of altruism is idiosyncratic: "Altruism declares that any action taken for the benefit of others is good, and any action taken for one's own benefit is evil. Thus the *beneficiary* of an action is the only criterion of moral value—and so long as that *beneficiary* is anybody other than oneself, anything goes."[165]

It is possible that, somewhere on earth, a few religious ascetics adhere to altruism thus defined. (She may also be parodying the rhetoric of the Soviet Union.) Most people think it is appropriate to tend primarily to one's own wants, but that the needs of others count for *something*: prudence is a virtue, but so is charity. Rand finds that idea profoundly threatening. There is in her writing a persistent sense of being overwhelmed by the demands of others: if I give them anything at all, they will devour me. "If you own a bottle of milk and give it to your starving child, it is *not* a sacrifice; if you give it to your neighbor's child and let your own die, it *is*."[166] Might you, however, have more milk than your child needs?

Sometimes Rand is in a mellower mood. She despises those who are "totally indifferent to anything living and would not lift a finger to help a man or a dog left mangled by a hit-and-run driver."[167] She thinks it appropriate to help a neighbor who is in financial straits, if we can afford to and he deserves it. She thinks that people who cannot work must rely on voluntary charity, thus implying that charity is appropriate.[168] Her deepest objection to institutionalized charity is that it is disrespectful, regarding "mankind as a herd of doomed beggars crying for someone's help."[169] Such help must be the exception and not the rule. It cannot be demanded because of normal and predictable misfortunes such as "poverty, ignorance, illness and other problems of that kind."[170]

These passages suggest the possibility of (partial) convergence with Hayek, who likewise would allow the state only to "assist the individual in providing for those common hazards of life against which, because of their uncertainty, few individuals can make adequate provision."[171] But there are important differences. Hayek includes "sickness and accident"[172] among the hazards he would provide for, while Rand expressly excludes "illness."

Not even Rawls wants people to be moochers. In his first book, he defined "a conception of justice as providing in the first instance a standard whereby the distributive aspects of the basic structure of society are to be assessed."[173] This pays too much attention to the distribution of things and too little to social relations. In particular, it overlooks the destructive effects of marginalization—exclusion from the economic life of the community. There are people whom the economic system will not use, often racially marked. "Even if marginals were provided a comfortable material life within institutions that respected their freedom and dignity," Iris Marion Young objected, "injustices of marginality would remain in the form of uselessness, boredom, and lack of self-respect."[174] Rawls eventually came to share this concern: "Given the lack of background justice and inequalities in income and wealth, there may develop a discouraged and depressed underclass many of whose members are chronically dependent on welfare. This underclass feels left out and does not participate in the public political culture."[175] Reciprocity matters. A fair social contract would avoid the development of such an underclass.

Rand thinks that charity can be an appropriate remedy. But the state can do nothing, because that would violate rights. The argument is essentially the same as Rothbard's.

Rand envisions an individual free from human dependency. It is an illusion. We cannot be free without the necessary external conditions. Rand cited her own success as a penniless immigrant: "I had a difficult struggle, earning my living at odd jobs, until I could make a financial success of my writing. No one helped me, nor did I think at any time that it was anyone's duty to help me."[176] It wasn't true. Relatives in Chicago took her in and lent her money. She never paid it back, even after she was rich.[177] Rand's affinity for the philosopher Friedrich Nietzsche is ironic. He understood vengeful rage masquerading as principle. And distorted personal history: "'I have done that,' says my memory. 'I cannot have done that,' says my pride, and remains inexorable. Eventually—memory yields."[178] It is worth noting here that self-identified libertarians are disproportionately male, and that libertarians tend to exhibit a relative deficit of empathy.[179] Blindness to the facts of human interdependence is a pathology to which men are disproportionately prone.

Rand acknowledged that human beings are social animals. But she hated that fact: "For instance, when discussing the social instinct—does it matter whether it had existed in the early savages? . . . Supposing men were born social (and even that is a question)—does it mean that they have to remain so? . . . If man started as a social animal—isn't all progress and civilization directed toward making him *an individual*? Isn't that the only possible progress? If men are the highest of animals, isn't *man* the next step?"[180]

It is not clear how her aspirations can be reconciled with the facts of infancy and old age. She seems impelled to wish them away. This relentless denial of human vulnerability has costs of its own. In Rand's case, it led her to drive away nearly everyone she had been close to (including Rothbard, as it happens). When she died, the only one at her bedside was a paid nurse.

The most attractive aspiration in Rand is the independence of judgment, and faith in oneself, displayed by Roark, the hero of *The Fountainhead*. The book has surely helped many young people with its message that they should pursue their own deepest aspirations, and not care about impressing others.[181] But even Roark has preconditions. We're told that he worked his way through college, but could he exhibit the same fierce independence today if he were saddled with $150,000 in student loans? Might not state-funded financial aid help produce more Roarks than we could otherwise have?

We've now surveyed the three most important thinkers who took libertarianism beyond Hayek's consequentialism to a more absolute conception of property rights and the minimal or nonexistent state.

Of these, the most influential political philosopher is Rothbard. The leading history of libertarian thought observes that he is the writer "whose influence explains most about what makes the ideas, behavior, and general flavor of American libertarianism unique."[182] Nozick is more philosophically rigorous, but he does little to work out the practical implications of his view. His main accomplishment was to make a Rothbardian position philosophically respectable.[183] Rand can't really be called a philosopher at all, since there's so little distance between her premises and her conclusions. She matters because she gives emotional weight to an ideal that is more fully worked out by others. The current Libertarian Party platform mirrors Rothbard's views fairly precisely.

The yearning for human freedom has always been utopian. The world we find ourselves in is full of obstacles. Libertarianism envisions a radically different one, in which people no longer need to use force against one another, but can nonetheless cooperate and trade.

Ideals are an indispensable element of political philosophy. You can reason as much as you like, but reasoning has to start somewhere: speaker and listener have to agree on some goal worth pursuing. Nietzsche wrote that every philosophy is "a desire of the heart that has been filtered and made abstract."[184] The desire that underlies both Locke and Rawls is a vision of universal independence and power in conditions of peace and prosperity. It is an inspiring vision.

Without fantasy, there would be no progress. We need to imagine a different world before we can escape what's dreadful about this one. But aspirations can conflict. Some of them are unrealistic or unworthy.

Libertarians have been drawn away from the unsentimental Hayek to more melodramatic visions. It is hard not to contemplate those visions with some affection.[185] But that affection must be tempered when government is induced to act on the basis of fantasy.

4

NANNY

> Any approach . . . which in effect starts from the assumption that people's *knowledge* corresponds with the objective *facts* of the situation, systematically leaves out what is our main task to explain.
>
> —Friedrich Hayek[1]

As I said in the introduction, when I first encountered libertarianism, my two big problems with it were that it would legalize all drugs and invalidate all antidiscrimination laws. I suspect I'm not alone. In the next two chapters, I address those concerns.

We have not yet discussed a tenet of libertarianism that is, for many people, its most attractive quality—one that is common ground among Hayek, Rothbard, Nozick, and Rand. It rejects, as a matter of principle, restricting people's liberty for their own good.

The point is often sound, but it is overstated. In a world with no such restrictions, people can find that they are unable to live the lives that they themselves think best. This can happen in two ways. First, cognitive limitations that are very common can lead people to make disastrously bad decisions. And second, predatory businesses can—indeed, have a financial incentive to—take advantage of those cognitive limitations in order to exploit and defraud their customers. Sometimes paternalism makes us freer. I'll begin by focusing on drug laws. Then I will consider all the ways in which the state protects us from being misled in commercial transactions, notably with workplace safety, consumer protection, drug effectiveness, and financial protection.

Libertarian notions have weakened these protections, most dramatically by licensing the abuse of arbitration clauses in contracts.

The classic libertarian anti-paternalist formulation is that of John Stuart Mill: "The only purpose for which power can be rightfully exercised over any member of a civilized community, against his will, is to prevent harm to others. His own good, either physical or moral, is not a sufficient warrant."[2] Hayek agrees: "Individuals should be allowed, within defined limits, to follow their own values and preferences rather than somebody else's . . . within these spheres the individual's system of ends should be supreme and not subject to any dictation by others."[3] Thus he opposed prohibition of homosexual conduct, because "where private practices cannot affect anybody but the voluntary adult actors, the mere dislike of what is being done by others, or even the knowledge that others harm themselves by what they do, provides no legitimate ground for coercion."[4] And Rothbard: "What [the libertarian] wants for everyone is freedom, the freedom to act morally or immorally, as each man shall decide."[5] David Boaz, vice president of the Cato Institute, puts the point pithily: "Conservatives want to be your daddy, telling you what to do and what not to do. Liberals want to be your mommy, feeding you, tucking you in, and wiping your nose. Libertarians want to treat you as an adult."[6]

Mill's principle is very widely believed. Each year at least one of my law students recites it as if it were part of the Constitution (it isn't), and everyone else in the room nods with approval.

But they don't really believe it. I show them this by asking them whether they think heroin, cocaine, or methamphetamine should be available in convenience stores. The Libertarian Party platform is uncompromising. It declares that "Individuals have the freedom and responsibility to decide what they knowingly and voluntarily consume."[7]

There's an important idea here: most people use illegal drugs responsibly, and the law's interference with them is pointless. But these drugs also do so much harm that most people are willing to make at least this exception to Mill's principle. A principle is weak if it comes with the vague proviso "except sometimes." Drawing the line with more precision necessarily involves approving a limited kind of paternalism. America's war on drugs has been so destructive that there is a serious case to be made for complete legalization. That case, however, can be persuasive only if it engages with the inevitable human costs, which disappear from the Libertarian Party's crude analysis. That has implications that go beyond the drug case.

I said in chapter 1 that libertarianism is a variety of liberalism, the political philosophy that—unlike older ideologies, aimed at military or religious virtue—aims at creating conditions in which people are free to live as they like. Liberalism's rivals each have their own ideal of what a person should be: the loyal servant of the king, the self-denying religious ascetic. At the center of the liberal ideal is the free, self-determining individual.

That individual may be imagined to be entirely self-sufficient. Libertarianism, particularly of the Rothbard–Rand variety, holds that the way to bring such individuals into existence is to minimize state power. But Howard Roark was somebody's baby once. Free people don't just happen. They have to be brought into existence. That's why parenting is so hard, and perhaps harder in a free society, where young people have so many opportunities to make irreversible mistakes. In a variety of ways, the creation of free people requires an active state. In some cases, it requires that the state engineer the environment of choice for people's own good.

The liberal ideal implies limits on paternalism, but they are nuanced. Sarah Conly has offered this careful formulation: "Legislation should intervene when people are likely to make decisions that seriously and irrevocably interfere with their ability to reach their goals, and when legislation can reliably prevent them from making those bad decisions, and where legislation is the least costly thing that can reliably prevent them from making these bad decisions. The majority of decisions we make do not meet these conditions."[8]

Her concluding point—that these conditions are usually not satisfied—is the real principled limitation on paternalism. But the conditions *are* satisfied often enough that a bar on paternalism would actually, in many cases, deprive people of control over their own lives.

I'll begin by considering the drug question in some detail.[9] The libertarian position deserves to be taken seriously. There is no reason to think that a self-governing person will entirely abstain from psychoactive drugs. Each of us sometimes finds our mental state to be bad in itself or an obstacle to our goals or both. Sometimes we just feel that a buzz would be fun. The ordinary citizen is made better off by her morning coffee and evening beer. Every drug, even the most dangerous ones such as heroin and cocaine, is consumed responsibly by most users: less than 20 percent of those who try cocaine or heroin become dependent.[10] Some drug use aims at deep spiritual ends.[11] In short, when the law denies rational persons the right thus to chemically control their internal states, it perversely harms those it purports to want to help.

On the other hand, the illegality of these drugs prevents some people, who are now living largely autonomous and self-determining lives, from trapping themselves in destructive addictions. In 1830s China, there were between four million and twelve million opium addicts.[12] No one knows what would happen in the United States if those drugs were legalized.[13]

Libertarians correctly point out that many of the pathologies of drug use are artifacts of illegality. Many drug consumers in contemporary America are in wretched health, undernourished and sickly, sometimes infected with AIDS as a result of shared hypodermics. They often steal to support their habits, and the drug trade produces enormous violence and corruption. If drugs were legal and cheap, these people would be able to get their supply with no danger to their health, and needle sharing would disappear. Drug addicts could live more comfortably than they do now, albeit in some cases at the margins of society. Purveyors of alcohol today do not engage in gang wars, and most alcoholics are not criminals.[14]

Yet even discounting these effects, the obsessive addict's (or the alcoholic's) life can be a pretty terrible one, sometimes cut off from most of the goods that make life worthwhile. That's why so many addicts work so hard to get themselves off the stuff, and bitterly regret that they ever tried it.

Recall from chapter 1 the idea, which does so much work for Hayek, that our preferences are radically opaque to one another. The limits of our understanding of each other's concerns are a reason not to demand explanations from one another, or to be too ready to paternalistically interfere. Deirdre McCloskey, a sophisticated economist and a transgender woman, is understandably impatient when asked to explain her own transition from male to female:

> a demand for an answer to why carries with it in our medicalized culture an agenda of treatment. . . . I say in response to your question of why?, "Can't I just be?" You, dear reader, are. No one gets indignant if you have no answer to why you are an optimist or why you like peach ice cream. These days most people will grant you an exemption from the why question if you are gay. In 1960 they would not and were therefore eager to do things to you, many of them nasty. I want the courtesy and the safety of a whyless treatment extended to gender crossers.[15]

She is right, of course. But it is excessive to infer, as some liberal political philosophers have, that the state should be absolutely neutral toward all conceptions of what counts as a good life.[16] The drug case shows the limits of that notion. Distraction from human goods is part of the *concept* of drug abuse. Drug use is abusive if and only if the user cannot integrate chronic drug use with other goals.

Rothbard takes it as axiomatic that *every* market transaction is beneficial: "The fact that both parties chose the exchange demonstrates that they both benefit."[17] The addiction case puts some pressure on that axiom. In a similar spirit, economist Gary Becker: "People often become addicted precisely because they are unhappy. However, they would be even more unhappy if they were prevented from consuming the addictive goods."[18] On this model, one does a young person a kindness by introducing her to heroin, since that enlarges her store of information.

Addiction is itself an obstacle to human freedom. In the episode of the country of the Lotus-Eaters in the *Odyssey*, we are told that the sailors who ate lotus "wanted to stay there with the lotus-eating people, feeding on lotus, and forget the way home."[19] When Odysseus "took these men back weeping, by force, to where the ships were," his primary concern was for himself: he needed their help. But was it perhaps bad for the men themselves to want to forget the way home? Would it have been more respectful to leave them there? Would that have promoted their liberty? "It is not disrespectful," Conly observes, "to accurately estimate someone's abilities, and to respond to those appropriately."[20]

People have second-order preferences. They want to want some things, and not to want other things. They want to become certain kinds of people, the sort of people who can carry out long-term projects like success in a career and being a good parent. Many of us are more likely to succeed in governing ourselves if we are not incessantly subjected to certain temptations.

The task of an intelligent libertarian policy would be to maximize liberty—to get out of the way of drug users who know what they're doing, while minimizing the number who drift into abuse and helping addicts to free themselves. This would be very much in the spirit of Hayek. The great virtue of markets is that consensual transactions make both parties better off. The way we know that is that both parties have rationally decided to make the deal. If there's a deficit of rationality on one side, then we can no longer be sure that everyone's situation has been improved. The heroin dealer sometimes does his customers no favors. The law should be allowed to know that.

There is a lot of middle ground between absolute legalization and the disaster that is contemporary drug policy.

Mark Kleiman argues that even a liberal framework that seeks to maximize people's ability to control their own lives should have room in it for the regulation of "vice," which he defines as any "activity voluntarily engaged in that risks damage and threatens self-command."[21] While vice legislation often reflects social prejudice and exhibits excesses of its own, there may sometimes be good reason to interfere with certain vices—most important, "that many of its participants regret their initial choice to adopt it."[22] The mechanisms by which the vices do this include addiction, intoxication, temporal myopia, irrationality in the management of risk, routine, and the effects of fashion (which takes the form of both peer pressure and favorable word of mouth about new drugs whose harms are not yet understood).[23] These mechanisms confound the assumption of ordinary economic analysis that the consumer is a reliable judge of her own interests.[24]

He proposes what he calls "grudging toleration." It has three elements: (1) Teach people better decision skills and impulse control; make them more aware of self-command as a problem and the specific threats to it. (2) Create conditions that discourage use of vicious goods and services, by making them expensive or hard to obtain, and restrict promotional messages for those vices. (This is the part libertarians find hardest to swallow.) (3) Temper the bad results: make it safer to perform vices, make it easier to quit, and target for special regulation those whose vices are a problem for others. The goal ought to be to maximize conscious choice and to minimize impulsive mistakes. (It is worth noting that a minimal state such as Nozick and Rand advocate would even rule out subsidized treatment for drug addicts.)

Grudging toleration is not a universal panacea. Kleiman thinks that the worst drugs, such as cocaine, are so dangerous that grudging toleration is too weak a policy. On the other hand, grudging toleration has much to recommend it as a policy, not only for presently illegal drugs such as marijuana and LSD but also for legal but harmful substances such as alcohol and tobacco, and other dangerous vices such as gambling.[25] (In some ways, gambling is worse than heroin. A heroin addict can have a family, a job, and even some property; a gambling addict will burn through those assets.)

Libertarians must reject Kleiman's approach. Making drugs hard to get is better than banning them altogether, but it still interferes with liberty. Subsidized drug rehabilitation programs redistribute wealth well beyond Hayek's social minimum. They are explicitly designed to rescue people from their own bad decisions.

People, libertarians typically argue, have a right to endanger themselves. Even if the number of cocaine abusers were to rise a hundredfold, this would simply be the result of individuals' free decisions, and so would not properly be the law's concern. (In some formulations, this is accompanied by a Randian joy in cruelty: those who are weak enough to destroy themselves get what they deserve.)

This rights-based argument relies on a peculiar understanding of liberty. Many chronic drug abusers are not now choosing the lives they lead, and they never did choose them. Paternalism may be insulting, but so is regarding a crack-addicted prostitute as if she had decided after reflective deliberation that this would be an attractive career option. It is a perversion of liberal ideals to respect whims and impulses that yank a subject around like a marionette.

Another libertarian response is that we have to tolerate this damage, because unless paternalistic legislation is absolutely prohibited, we are on the slippery slope to tyranny. But all slippery slope arguments depend on a prediction that doing the right thing in the instant case will, in fact, increase the likelihood of doing the wrong thing in some future danger case.[26] In fact, America has been an unusually free society while it has been restricting opiates. Present drug policy is cruel and racist, but there are many forms of restriction, such as Kleiman's, that need not be. It is possible to restrict substances without today's orgy of mass incarceration. If the aim is reducing consumption, diminishing returns set in very quickly. During Prohibition, alcohol consumption dropped by between 33 and 50 percent,[27] even though nearly nothing was spent on enforcement.[28] It was enough that the stuff couldn't be openly marketed. We could radically reduce the billions we spend on the drug war without moving all the way to full legalization.

Mill writes that "the strongest of all the arguments against the interference of the public with purely personal conduct is that, when it does interfere, the odds are that it interferes wrongly and in the wrong place."[29] Liberty demands that it interfere rightly and in the right place.

Let's go a little deeper, and consider the appropriate role of paternalism in a free society.

All liberals, libertarians and Rawlsians alike, think that we each have the right to direct our own lives, and that we have a duty to respect one another by not interfering in others' choices about what ends to pursue. The ideal is powerful and attractive. Its possibility depends, however, on the existence of selves of the right kind: self-governing agents who really do make choices about what ends to pursue. When a person is incapable of making such choices, such non-manipulative relations are impossible. That is why it is appropriate to paternalize children.[30] Since the purpose of liberal rights is to allow persons to exercise their moral and rational powers, liberalism requires that persons develop those powers to some minimum degree.

Liberty is not just free movement in a world without obstacles. That is what we would encounter in the vacuum of outer space, where we would die within seconds. Freedom requires both internal and external conditions.

The self-governing self does not just materialize in the world. It has to be constructed, and there are typical pitfalls in the process of construction. The most potent grassroots political force in the formulation of drug policy is parents who are concerned that their children will be seduced by the lure of drug use.[31] These parents are not crazy. They are trying to make their children into autonomous people who are capable of choosing and pursuing real goods, and they are trying to ward off real hazards that can frustrate these goals.

Outlawing the ingestion of certain chemicals is a clumsy strategy for constructing the liberal self, however. There is no one-to-one relationship between any chemical and any behavior. The danger that any drug presents to the liberal self depends on the norms that surround its use.

The same drug can be harmless in one society and disastrous in another, or even in different situations in the same society. Consumption of alcohol was not generally regarded as a social problem at all in colonial America, when Americans annually consumed more than seven gallons of absolute alcohol per capita. The Puritans did backbreaking labor on their farms, and regular shots of beer, cider, or spirits helped get through the day. Drunkenness was stigmatized and rare. Alcohol became regarded as a problem in the late nineteenth and early twentieth centuries, when per capita annual consumption was approximately two gallons, but intoxication and dissipation were common.[32]

The goal of policy should be to minimize not drug use but a certain kind of destructive drug use, and to construct and reinforce social norms of appropriate behavior toward drugs. Many drug users have the capacity to consume responsibly. This skill set should be more widely available. But we should also acknowledge the limitations of what can be accomplished in this regard. The substances that give Kleiman pause, whose allure he thinks too powerful for grudging toleration to work, suggest that there are fields in which paternalism is unavoidable. Some situations overwhelm our capacity for self-government. All government can do when confronted with such cases is keep us from hurting ourselves.

Libertarianism aims for a society of rational, self-governing agents. But we know that, a lot of the time, people do not and cannot measure up to this ideal. People are imperfectly rational. They are subject to systemic emotional and cognitive biases: overconfidence, poor risk assessment, inertia. A lot of decisions are the product not of rational deliberation but of default rules, framing effects, and other ways in which the human mind arrives at decisions unconsciously. There have been huge strides in the scientific understanding of these processes.[33]

In such cases, Cass Sunstein and Richard Thaler have argued, policy should "influence choices in a way that will make choosers better off, *as judged by themselves.*" The decisions that are blocked are "decisions they would not have made if they had paid full attention and possessed complete information, unlimited cognitive abilities, and complete self-control." [34]

One easy example, they think, is the construction of default rules. Participation rates in employee pension programs depend heavily on whether one must opt in or opt out: if enrollment is automatic, participation rises dramatically.[35] People mean to save for retirement. Many don't. Appropriate default rules make it more likely that they will do what they want to do.[36]

One typical libertarian response to Sunstein and Thaler is to acknowledge these failures of rationality but to aim to encourage "greater reflection and deliberation, with the aim of shifting persons from an intuitive into a more analytical mindset that will cause them to examine choices more closely."[37] With respect to a great many decisions that affect our lives, we do not *want* to engage in greater reflection. That demands time that we can't spare. We want to pursue the projects that matter most to us, and delegate other decisions to someone else.[38] Forcing us to deliberate about everything (or more precisely, attempting to force the impossible) is its own form of officious paternalism. It is in fact totalitarian: rather than block a single option, which would be bad enough, it dictates how we are to spend our time and direct our attention.

Another rejoinder is to argue that what appear to be failures of rationality may simply be the process of ordinary learning: "An important part of rationality is experimenting with different choices, discovering one's preferences over time, learning from one's mistakes, structuring one's environment, adopting strategies for self-control."[39] But sometimes the experimentation in question leads to catastrophic and irreversible harm. We shouldn't mourn the fact that Social Security has prevented destitution among the elderly, thereby denying them valuable lessons in the importance of saving.

It is also true that government decision makers are subject to their own biases and distortions of judgment.[40] But this is not a complaint specifically about paternalism. It is an argument against any legislation at all.[41]

Paternalistic regulation offends libertarian sensibilities. But our rationality is bounded. We are more likely to live the lives we actually want if we are sometimes paternalized. Rejecting paternalistic regulation, because you hate the idea that your competence is limited, is like attacking the practice of medicine because you hate the idea of being vulnerable to illness.

There are many other contexts in which paternalism makes people freer. Consider again a piece of New Deal legislation that libertarians have been attacking for more than half a century: Social Security. The day after Franklin Roosevelt proposed it, the Chamber of Commerce's board of directors authorized a committee "to determine whether such legislation may be demonstrated as leading definitely to the complete socialization of the United States."[42] We examined Hayek's skepticism about the program in chapter 1. If you look at libertarian writings from any decade since it was founded, you will find confident, gleeful predictions that it is on the verge of collapse.

Most Americans do not save enough for their old age. When Social Security was enacted, most of the elderly lived in some kind of economic dependency, too poor to support themselves.[43] After benefits were raised in the 1960s, the poverty rate among the elderly fell from 35.2 percent in 1959 to 15.3 percent by 1975. Today, not counting earned income and other government transfers such as veterans benefits, Social Security benefits constitute 94 percent of income for retirees in the bottom fifth of income, and 92 percent in the next fifth. It is less than half only for the top fifth, for whom it is still 31 percent. Absent Social Security, the poverty rate for Americans over sixty-five would leap from 9 percent to 44 percent.[44] Nearly half of American families have no retirement savings at all. Not only is financial expertise scarce; so is skill at picking reliable private sector financial advisors. It is rational for most people to hire the state to manage their retirement assets. Social Security is the single most effective antipoverty program in the United States.[45]

In 2004, the George W. Bush administration proposed a libertarian, anti-paternalist reform: to partially privatize Social Security savings, and to allow people to invest that money on their own, paying back upon retirement what they took out of their account. This was, two Nobel Prize-winning economists observe, "like giving the most vulnerable part of the population a loan to speculate in the stock market, or the bond market, with government money—with payback on this loan beginning, at quite a high rate of interest, at the date of retirement."[46] There was a substantial danger of catastrophic loss. But Bush was fixated on the idea of shifting risk to individuals. His conception of liberty, in practice, would have meant that some sophisticated retirees would have been wealthier. Unsophisticated ones would subsist on dog food. The proposal collapsed when it proved extremely unpopular.

That suggests that paternalism is tolerable to most Americans when their necks are on the line.

Libertarians tend to offer two responses to this situation. One is to boldly predict (as Hayek did) that, if the safety net were cut off, that would induce people to save more prudently. The other is that people justly bear the consequences of failure to provide for their retirement. These claims sometimes come paraded together—both were offered in behalf of the Bush plan—but the tension between them is obvious. One can't simultaneously say "Don't worry, you'll be fine" and "Tough luck, you'll have the life crushed out of you, but that's okay, because you will deserve to be punished."

Paternalism sometimes facilitates people's ability to live the lives they want. That modest conclusion undergirds familiar interventions to guarantee workplace safety, consumer protection, drug effectiveness, and sound banking. None of these fields of regulation would be necessary if people were perfectly rational. In each, libertarian rhetoric is constantly being used to denounce regulation.

Quite a lot of regulation involves cognitive failures of this kind. Consider the application of consumer protection law to product safety. If people were perfectly rational, then it would be appropriate to regard safety as a good with a price, subject to normal consumer choice: those who value safety more will pay extra to get it. But in fact choice doesn't work that way. This is a field characterized by inevitable myopia and asymmetrical information.

A rational consumer will accept some dangers in products, since some risks are worth it: automobiles kill, but they're a lot better than walking. If she had infinite information and cognitive capacity, she would make her own cost-benefit analyses. But, of course, that doesn't happen. So regulators must do the job.

We observed in chapter 1 that the Obama administration subjected its regulations to cost-benefit analysis as a check on unnecessary regulation. The quantification is imprecise. One can't know the value of innovations that never happen because of regulatory burdens. The benefits are likewise difficult to quantify, especially when a regulation prevents injury or death. At some point, qualitative judgments are unavoidable.

For instance, in 2010, the Department of Transportation proposed to require rearview cameras in new cars. The annual cost would exceed $2 billion, and that number exceeded the quantifiable benefits of avoiding backover deaths and injuries. But the Department noted that more than 40 percent of the victims were children under the age of five, and the "qualitatively distinct risk . . . of directly causing or contributing to the death or injury of one's own child."[47] You could say that consumers ought to think about that when they buy cars. They won't. The fact that they won't reveals nothing about their attitudes toward mortal dangers to their children. They just can't think of everything. The market won't supply the optimal level of safety.

Freedom isn't the absence of regulation. It is the capacity to construct one's life as one likes. That means the capacity to focus on what matters to us, in reasonable security that we will not be blindsided by all the matters we inevitably neglect. Some paternalistic intervention is merely a collective delegation of certain decisions to the state, in the way that one delegates responsibilities to any professional. I'm not competent to decide what toxins are unsafe to inhale at the workplace, but I'm sure that I don't want to leave that decision to my boss. Interference with my liberty of contract makes me freer.

The categorical libertarian bar on paternalism can also license predation masquerading as liberty.

The growth of knowledge of the ways in which people are imperfectly rational has created a situation in which businesses are under competitive pressure to manipulate and deceive their customers and employees.[48] If the market rewards dishonesty and opacity, then dishonesty and opacity are what it will deliver.[49] Paternalistic laws restrain destructive market pressures.

Consider arbitration provisions in contracts, which typically require the economically weak contracting party—the consumer or employee—to waive access to the courts for disputes that arise out of the contract. Instead, such disputes are remitted to a forum designed to the specifications of the stronger party, which drafted the provision. Should such waivers of legal rights be permitted?

Supreme Court Justice Neil Gorsuch articulates the question thus: "Should employees and employers be allowed to agree that any disputes between them will be resolved through one-on-one arbitration?" A regime in which employees' rights are nullified by boilerplate contract terms is here imagined as a new form of freedom, in which the parties commit to "individualized arbitration procedures of their own design."[50] The libertarian premises are clear: these transactions are consented to in a market, hence legitimate. And, of course, the plural in "their own design" is misleading. In the case in which these passages appear, employees were denied any effective remedy for alleged wage theft. This is typical of contemporary arbitration law.

The Supreme Court has become increasingly hospitable to the use of arbitration clauses in employment and consumer contracts. Since 1985, in more than two dozen decisions, it has relied on a dubious interpretation of the 1925 Federal Arbitration Act to expand the scope of the act beyond anything its authors contemplated, and to restrict the ability of states to protect their citizens. The consequence is that workers and consumers sign away their rights, usually without knowing that they have done so, in long boilerplate contracts.[51]

Arbitration, properly used, can be a fair way of resolving low-level disputes. In the consumer and labor contexts, however, it is heavily biased in favor of the business and the employer.

Recent studies find a huge gap in outcomes: "Plaintiffs' overall economic outcomes are on average 6.1 times better in federal court than in mandatory arbitration ($143,497 versus $23,548) and 13.9 times better in state court than in mandatory arbitration ($328,008 versus $23,548)."[52] Put another way, "Damages from arbitration are 16 percent of the average damages from federal court litigation and a mere 7 percent of the average damages in state court."[53]

The corporation that drew up the contract always gets a veto over who the arbitrator will be, so arbitrators have an incentive to please those who are repeat players. The effect is dramatic: "The first time an employer appeared before an arbitrator, the employee had a 17.9 percent chance of winning, but after the employer had four cases before the same arbitrator the employee's chance of winning dropped to 15.3 percent, and after 25 cases before the same arbitrator the employee's chance of winning dropped to only 4.5 percent."[54]

As a general matter, plaintiffs are less likely to win in arbitration.

> Employee win rates in mandatory arbitration are much lower than in either federal court or state court, with employees in mandatory arbitration winning only just about a fifth of the time (21.4 percent), which is 59 percent as often as in the federal courts and only 38 percent as often as in state courts. Differences in damages awarded are even greater, with the median or typical award in mandatory arbitration being only 21 percent of the median award in the federal courts and 43 percent of the median award in the state courts.[55]

Some arbitration clauses also require the plaintiff to pay the cost of arbitration, which can amount to thousands of dollars. The consequence is that many complaints, even ones involving aggression and theft, are never brought at all.

The law is now full of traps for the unwary. The Supreme Court voided a Montana law requiring that arbitration agreements in contracts appear on the first page of the contract in underlined capital letters. The clause buried in the contract at issue required all disputes to be arbitrated in distant Connecticut. The plaintiffs, who had lost their life savings, could not travel that far and were left with no recourse.[56]

The Supreme Court has also held that arbitration clauses can be used to eliminate the right to join a class action. The consequence is that the misbehavior that such suits target—small thefts and abuses that affect large numbers of consumers or workers, producing millions of dollars in illicit profits—is insulated from any legal remedy.[57] Justice Scalia denied that people's substantive rights were being nullified, using reasoning that approaches the mystical: "The fact that it is not worth the expense involved in *proving* a statutory remedy does not constitute the elimination of the *right to pursue* that remedy."[58]

The same logic has even been extended to personal injury suits. Contractual relationships sometimes lead to bodily harm, notably relationships "between doctors and patients, HMOs and members, landlords and tenants, employers and employees, car manufacturers and motorists, utilities and homeowners, schools and students, summer camps and campers, stores and shoppers, lawyers and clients, airlines and passengers, travel companies and travelers, and so on."[59] Arbitration has been compelled for "claims of medical malpractice, sexual harassment, hate crimes, discrimination, theft, fraud, elder abuse and wrongful death."[60] It has even been argued that employers have a right to compel arbitration if an employer's negligent supervision leads to an employee's sexual assault.[61]

In response to a *New York Times* exposé of these practices, a writer from the Garrison Center for Libertarian Advocacy Journalism declared that the source of the problem was that "most customers don't bother to read contracts pertaining to small-money matters, or have them reviewed by attorneys, before signing them. That's a choice. . . . If you don't want to commit to arbitration in general, or to individual arbitration in particular, don't sign contracts committing yourself to those things."[62] From the standpoint of Rothbard, Nozick, or Rand, that is the right answer. But it's likely bad news for markets.

Justice Gorsuch's opinion, in the decision quoted earlier, killed three class action suits brought by employees who claimed that they had been illegally underpaid. One reason employers are tempted to engage in wage theft is that the amounts, individually, often are not worth litigating about. Individuals are unlikely to risk the displeasure of their employers to recover small underpayments, and from the employer's point of view, the small wrongs can add up to a nice gain. The problem of such small cumulative wrongs is the primary justification for class action suits, in which a group of plaintiffs with similar claims can aggregate them into a single lawsuit. But the possibility of bringing such suits has been nullified by a broad reading of freedom of contract.

Is this really freedom?

The classic Hayekian complaint against government regulation is that it promotes parasitism. Unions, cartelized industries, and the like are allowed to charge consumers more than they would pay in a free market.[63] The new arbitration rules encourage a different kind of parasitism. They redistribute wealth from unorganized individuals to big businesses.[64]

Among the lawyers who devised the use of arbitration to eliminate class actions was one John G. Roberts, later chief justice of the United States. Once he was on the Supreme Court, he provided the crucial vote for a strained interpretation of the Federal Arbitration Act to shut down consumer and employment discrimination suits.

Doubtless class action suits can be a nuisance for businesses, and sometimes they're not meritorious. But when they are entirely blocked, really nasty business practices can be conducted with impunity. In one case, Sprint allegedly imposed roaming charges for customers' cell phone calls *from their homes*. If this was true, each individual suffered a roughly twenty-dollar loss, far too little to be worth suing for on an individual basis, even though it was worth quite a bit to Sprint.[65] (Sprint's successful legal argument was that it did not matter if it was true.)

In the world that the Court's arbitration jurisprudence has brought about, honesty is a competitive disadvantage. Businesses that do not swindle their customers for small sums, or routinely steal from their employees, are foolishly leaving money on the table.

Business is a good and honorable pursuit because, in a free market, you can be confident that your good or service is making your customers better off. If you weren't somehow improving the world, you wouldn't be making any money. That is Hayek's core insight. But the Court's arbitration jurisprudence has distorted incentives so that markets now sometimes reward dishonesty. This should not be a source of joy for those who believe in free markets.

"I accept the terms and conditions." Nobody reads through the text of the agreement before installing software. But if law is unwilling to paternalize, then it must say that by clicking that button, you consented to every detail of the fine print.

To see what a weird world the rejection of paternalism would lead us to, consider how libertarianism deals with the problem of fraud.

It is conventionally said that a minimal libertarian state would protect against force and fraud. Hayek, Epstein, Rothbard, Nozick, and Rand all agree about that. But this is hard to reconcile with the antipaternalist idea that individuals are responsible for themselves in a free market. People are conclusively presumed to understand and assent to every detail of the boilerplate contracts that they agree to. This can lead to the dissolution of legal protection and the creation of new forms of feudalism. Thus, once more, libertarianism risks betraying its core commitments.

Fraud is not aggression. All these writers are committed to the idea that individuals are responsible for their own welfare. One of the pertinent responsibilities is determining whether to believe the information one receives. The swindler has respected his victim's rights to personal security and to own and control property. The victim freely agreed to the transaction. Contracts are often about the allocation of risk. As a general matter, the libertarian approach to contract is caveat emptor—let the buyer beware. Libertarians reject the notion that we have affirmative duties toward one another. Yet a ban on fraud presupposes that sellers have such duties, to impart to buyers material facts about what they are offering. As a general matter, libertarians deem it inappropriately paternalistic to void contracts merely because one of the parties made a mistake. Those who carelessly agree to deals they should have rejected must take responsibility for their decisions and accept the consequences.

Fraud, then, presents a difficult case for the libertarian. Unless the presumption of competence is relaxed in at least some cases, libertarianism cannot prohibit fraud.[66]

Here is the approach that makes the most sense given Hayekian premises. Since the core virtue of markets is that each transaction makes both parties better off, the operational definition that most precisely defines what should be barred is behavior that induces one party to accept a transaction that is obviously not in his interest, because the other party has taken advantage of psychological or informational weaknesses. Markets are valuable because consensual transactions make both parties better off. That value disappears if one party agrees to a transaction only because he is misled.

That was Hayek's view. Fraud is the functional equivalent of coercion: "Where it is successful, the deceived becomes in the same manner the unwilling tool, serving another man's ends without advancing his own."[67] It warrants state intervention. "Even the most essential prerequisite of its [the market's] proper functioning, the prevention of fraud and deception (including exploitation of ignorance), provides a great and by no means fully accomplished object of legislative activity."[68]

That approach treats people as vulnerable to deception, and fails to respect all their choices. It is suspect from the perspective of Rothbard and many other libertarians. The uncertain status of fraud predisposes them not to detect it when it exists.

Here's the basic legal definition of fraud, from *Black's Law Dictionary*, the most standard of sources: "A knowing misrepresentation or knowing concealment of a material fact made to induce another to act to his or her detriment."[69] The definition assigns to the state just the sort of judgments that make libertarians itchy. The law decides which facts are material, and it decides what counts as detriment. The dictionary quotes with approval a classic definition: "any kind of artifice by which another is deceived."[70] The fact of deception is what constitutes the fraud: one has a duty not to bring about that effect. A secondary definition of fraud makes that duty clear: "A reckless misrepresentation made without justified belief in its truth to induce another person to act."[71] A deception may not be intentional, but it is still fraud if it is reckless.

The law of fraud depends on presumptions about what a reasonable person would want to know. Here lies the problem. Liberalism is from the beginning committed to the idea that people are opaque to one another. What is good for me is not necessarily what is good for you; what I care about is not necessarily what you care about. Locke thought this was true about the means of salvation. Hayek expanded the idea to all preferences: all I can know about what others want is what the price system tells me. If that is right, then Hayek has a problem: it is not possible to know that a "material" fact was not disclosed in a transaction, because outsiders can't know what facts are material. I did not mention to you that the cow I sold you was sick and dying, but how could I know that you wanted the cow for milk or meat? Maybe you just wanted to photograph it. Courts have not been impressed by such arguments. They understand that there is a limit to human opacity.

There is, of course, always doubt about whether any particular transaction depends on such weaknesses. Misleading speech is a fuzzy category: all speech misleads some people. I am probably misleading someone who is reading this. We have to decide how many misled people are too many.[72] But when we have that conversation, we are already assuming that fraud is real and that we can detect it. We are also exercising situation-specific judgment, of a kind that troubles libertarians who long for clear rules.

Markets both depend upon and facilitate trust among strangers, which in turn facilitates markets in a virtuous cycle. They have enabled a massive worldwide network of cooperation. "Trust," economist Luigi Zingales observes, "facilitates transactions because it saves the costs of monitoring and screening; it is an essential lubricant that greases the wheels of the economic system."[73]

The disappearance of social solidarity is not only a problem for democracy. It is a problem for capitalism as well. Anytime predatory behavior is rewarded, trust is damaged. People who have thus been burned, and denied any legal remedy, become cynical about markets. As I noted in the introduction, loss of faith in capitalism on the left is as big a problem in contemporary American politics as small-government fundamentalism on the right. That loss of faith is often rooted in bitter experience. Defenders of capitalism should not be working to make such experiences proliferate. Libertarianism, however, rests on a different kind of cynicism.

The rise of libertarianism, E. J. Dionne suggests, is the consequence of a loss of faith in public life after Vietnam, Watergate, and the failures of the Carter administration. "The growing popularity of the libertarian cause suggested that many Americans had given up on even the possibility of a 'common good.'"[74] Its rise is "a sign of a deep sickness in the democratic system."[75]

What's peculiar about libertarianism is that it elevates the erosion of social capital to a matter of high principle. It yearns for the complex cooperation that markets offer, but without the legal support that they need.

The categorical rejection of paternalism is yet another instance of libertarian romantic fantasy, here an infantile vision of invulnerability. "The justifiability of paternalism," Conly observes, "does suggest that we are not godlike beings, but that is because we are not godlike beings." Respect for persons does not demand that we treat them as if they were such beings. "Realism cannot be degrading, and treating people in accordance with their actual abilities is not insulting or disrespectful."[76] Libertarian anti-paternalism envisions people who do not depend on anyone, who are not vulnerable to manipulation and fraud. So the government need not protect against those wrongs. Which is great news for their perpetrators.

Under the guise of consent, the Supreme Court has created a new droit du seigneur, advertised as freedom.

5

LIBERTY

> Liberty is essential in order to leave room for the unforeseeable and unpredictable. . . . It is because every individual knows so little and, in particular, because we rarely know which of us knows best that we trust the independent and competitive efforts of many to induce the emergence of what we shall want when we see it.
>
> —Friedrich Hayek[1]

Rand Paul, perhaps the most libertarian US Senator, has a problem with the Civil Rights Act of 1964. As a candidate, he objected to the prohibition of discrimination by private businesses.

> PAUL: I like the Civil Rights Act in the sense that it ended discrimination in all public domains, and I'm all in favor of that.
>
> INTERVIEWER: But?
>
> PAUL: You had to ask me the "but." I don't like the idea of telling private business owners—I abhor racism. I think it's a bad business decision to exclude anybody from your restaurant—but, at the same time, I do believe in private ownership.

He now claims that he never opposed the act.[2] That isn't true, but he has to say it. His earlier position, the orthodox libertarian line, is politically impossible in contemporary America—almost as bad as suggesting that heroin should be available at convenience stores.

Here, too, the libertarians are partly right and partly loony.

The freedom to decline transactions for any reason, like the freedom to consume drugs, ought to be absolutely protected. Except sometimes. In both cases, neither Hayek nor Rothbard is able to specify the "sometimes."

Antidiscrimination law is another revealing window into the power and limits of libertarianism. We saw in the last chapter that in order for people to actually be free to do what they want with their lives, they need to have some capacity to control themselves.

Liberty has external as well as internal preconditions. One is not free unless one has an adequate range of transactional partners.

The right to be free from discrimination is a peculiar kind of right. Most rights prevent some kind of invasion of person or property. With antidiscrimination law, on the other hand, the state compels people to enter into contractual relations that they would prefer to avoid.

The fundamental classical liberal rights are those of bodily integrity, property, and contract. John Locke writes that "the business of Laws is not to provide for the Truth of Opinions, but for the Safety and Security of the Commonwealth and of every particular man's Goods and Person."[3] If they are respected, then conflict is easy to avoid. If all associations must be based on mutual agreement, then even in religious matters, "no man will have a Legislator imposed upon him, but whom himself has chosen."[4] Those who find one another's presence unendurable can stay apart. Discrimination thus facilitates peace and prosperity.

That kind of reasoning leads many libertarians to reject any antidiscrimination law as a matter of principle.[5] Ayn Rand despised racism but thought Congress "has no right to violate the right of private property by forbidding discrimination in privately owned establishments."[6] Murray Rothbard wrote: "'Discrimination,' in the sense of choosing favorably or unfavorably in accordance with whatever criteria a person may employ, is an integral part of freedom of choice, and hence of a free society."[7] Robert Bork complained that the Civil Rights Act presupposes "that if I find your behavior ugly by my standards, moral or aesthetic, and if you prove stubborn about adopting my view of the situation, I am justified in having the state coerce you into more righteous paths. This is itself a principle of unsurpassed ugliness."[8]

Senator Paul appears to have had this kind of consideration in mind when he initially opposed the act. He backed away from that position, but there is a valid Hayekian concern—one that does not reject all antidiscrimination laws, but supports them only when certain conditions are satisfied.

The general rule, in employment decisions, is employment at will. An employer normally has the privilege of refusing to hire, or of firing, employees for any reason or no reason. He need not justify these actions to any official. Antidiscrimination laws, such as the Civil Rights Act, are exceptions to this general rule. So long as an employer does not engage in the enumerated types of discrimination, she has the privilege of being as arbitrary as she likes. I can, for example, absolutely refuse to hire anyone whose eyebrows are not at least three inches long.

There are good Hayekian reasons for the rule of employment at will. It would be a terrible burden on the economy for government officials to have to approve every firing, much more every refusal to hire, that takes place in the private sector. Where such laws have been enacted, unemployment has predictably been higher, because employers are reluctant to hire people who will be hard to get rid of if they don't work out. Moreover, there is little reason to think that most types of arbitrary refusal to hire are likely to have much effect on anyone's opportunities. Although I may refuse to hire people with short eyebrows, other employers will compete for their services, and so will bid their wages up to pretty much the same level that they would have been if I had been willing to hire them. And the market will also punish me for my foolishly discriminatory hiring practices, since competent short-eyebrowed workers will go to work for my competitors. My tendency to discriminate means that I am turning away better workers and hiring worse ones. The overall tendency is for people like me to be driven out of the market.

In a diverse society, markets facilitate peaceful cooperation among people who radically disagree about fundamental values. The ease of refusal to deal is part of what makes that work: gains from trade are available only if one can persuade counterparties, with whom one may otherwise have almost nothing in common, to freely agree to trade. The market thus stimulates not only competition but also empathy. One must understand the desires of strangers well enough to attract their business, and transactions require the continuing unforced consent of those who participate.[9] Markets, Nathan Oman observes, "cannot be made to instantiate the norms of deep, moral recognition or equality . . . without eroding their value as a sphere in which contestation over such deep political and moral concerns is muted."[10]

Considerations of this sort led Richard Epstein to argue that the Civil Rights Act ought to be repealed.[11] In a free market, he argued, we can expect that Black Americans' wages (for instance) will be as high as they can be.[12] Shortly before the act was passed, Milton Friedman opposed it with essentially the same argument.[13]

Note the fundamentally Hayekian character of Epstein's analysis. Epstein is making a prediction based on a model of how markets work. Hayek himself may have endorsed this reasoning. He was skeptical of antidiscrimination laws, and thought that private entities should be able to discriminate on the basis of race, though governments should never do so.[14] But we don't know his reasons. A central theme of his defense of free markets is the opportunities they create for people to pursue their diverse goals. He understood the limits of America's capacity to deliver such opportunities: recall that when he decided in the 1940s that his children (if they became refugees from England) would have their best opportunities if raised by an American family, that conclusion depended on "the tacit assumption that my children would there be placed with a white and not with a coloured family."[15] He never wrote about the problem of racism.[16]

Epstein did not persuade many people. The point most commonly made by his critics was that he had not adequately acknowledged the power of racism. Some groups are subject to *pervasive* discrimination. When the Civil Rights Act was enacted, his critics argued, racism was sufficiently ubiquitous to withstand the egalitarian tendencies of a well-functioning free market.[17] In effect, it functioned like a cartel: prejudice prevented white employers from bidding up Black wages.

Antidiscrimination law can have a powerful effect on economic opportunity. We know that Black wages, for instance, went up dramatically after the act was passed. In 1964, the median income of nonwhite males was 57 percent of median white male income. By 1985, that ratio had risen to 66 percent. The proportion of Black men working as professionals or managers relative to whites rose from 32 percent to 64 percent.[18] And the most dramatic progress came in the first ten years after the act.

No law prevented law firms from employing women. Yet Sandra Day O'Connor, who would eventually serve on the Supreme Court, could not get a job at a law firm when she graduated Stanford in 1952.

Epstein does not succeed in showing that antidiscrimination law should not exist, but he does show why the burden is on those who want antidiscrimination law to be extended to new classes, and what it is that they need to show. A Hayekian framework thus helps us avoid confusion about discrimination, which is sometimes treated as though it were like an assault on a person. The case for antidiscrimination law resembles the case for regulation. It is justified only if market failure can be shown.

What, in this context, does *market failure* mean? One of the great virtues of markets is the proliferation of opportunities. Not only are employers given powerful incentives to employ the most qualified people, but they are also rewarded if they come up with new uses for human capital, new ways of taking advantage of human talents that the market is neglecting. People can start businesses of their own. There are not only many career paths but many different understandings of what counts as success. A lot of the time, what Epstein predicts does in fact happen: workers whom most employers shun find niches where their abilities are appreciated and rewarded.

But sometimes markets fail to provide such opportunities. In 1964 America, the waste of African American human capital was massive. Employers paid no price for this behavior, because their competitors were doing the same thing. There is plenty of evidence that racial discrimination persists today, in contexts in which it is difficult to prove. Repealing the Civil Rights Act, as Epstein proposes, would be a dangerous experiment.

The promise of libertarianism is that each person will be free to pursue his own path without having to answer to anyone else. Yet pervasive discrimination can confront one with roadblocks at every turn. In 1964, African Americans were formally at liberty to transact with anyone. Yet from the moment of birth, they faced a debilitating series of barriers. They face them today.[19]

This exposes a deep flaw in the libertarian conception of freedom. The lives that most of us hope for require the cooperation of others. We want to be autonomous, but we are social beings. Capitalism helps: the anonymity of the market means that we don't need to please other people or live up to their expectations, so long as we are able to sell something that they want. That's why the gay liberation movement began in cities, where most people don't know each other and it was possible to be economically, and therefore socially, autonomous.[20]

But it sometimes happens that a characteristic that we can't hide, such as our race or sex, is the object of pervasive discrimination. Then our opportunities are blocked everywhere.[21] Under those circumstances, a law prohibiting discrimination can make us freer.

This phenomenon is not unique to the United States. All over the world, some groups have conquered others, and then established patterns of domination and exclusion that persist centuries later. That is why antidiscrimination laws can likewise be found in numerous countries.[22] They are a common feature of modern capitalism.

Of course, these laws burden the liberty of prospective employers. Some have strong desires to discriminate, and philosophers disagree about whether those desires deserve any weight. But the burden is sometimes trivial.

Consider the curious case of discrimination on the basis of credit scores. There is no evidence that credit scores are a reliable indicator of job performance. But credit agencies marketed their product to employers, and a lot of employers bought it. In the age of the internet, delivering the information that the bureaus possess costs them essentially nothing, so they could provide this product at a low price. Credit checks were used by fewer than one in five employers in 1996. A majority were using them by 2010. Many people then found that, because of poor credit scores, they couldn't get a job anywhere. Several state legislatures responded with statutes banning the use of credit scores in most jobs.[23] Limited interventions in the market *in the name of liberty* are appropriate when some people are cut off from a large range of opportunities.[24]

The credit score case is an easy one, because employers weren't emotionally invested in this kind of discrimination. They were merely misled into thinking that this was a wise business practice, when they were actually wasting a small amount of their money to purchase information that was worse than useless. On the other hand, some forms of discrimination are part of American culture, preeminently discrimination on the basis of race and sex. The ban on discrimination weighs on some people heavily. They *want* to discriminate, and are frustrated because they can't. Antidiscrimination law is generally understood to be part of a larger project of cultural transformation, aiming to eradicate or marginalize prejudiced attitudes such as racism. Can that be justified in the face of the libertarian challenge?

It can. Libertarianism is fundamentally incompatible with the notion that some classes of persons are beings of an inferior order who have no rights. Such prejudices have typically meant that the law couldn't even be relied upon to protect their minimal rights of person and property. African Americans were lynched; violence against women was casually tolerated; police regarded assault on gay people with indifference and sometimes perpetrated it themselves. A guarantee of Lockean rights demands a culture that respects those rights.[25]

Pervasive prejudice has to be combated with equally strong cultural forces. This takes us into the realm of pollution and taboo. Liberal theorists are uncomfortable with the invocation of such primitive impulses, but they appear to be an ineradicable part of humanity's moral vocabulary.[26] So racism itself has come to be stigmatized as contaminating. It is so deep in American culture that this kind of counter-taboo is probably necessary. In each case, the aim is to induce citizens to regard the relevant prejudice as itself ritually unclean.

This is in some tension with liberal ideals, notably free speech.[27] There's also a tension with religious liberty, because, as in the bad old days of religious suppression, the state again finds itself in the business of deciding which ideas are so odious as to be intolerable. (When the two collide, there's something to be said for at least considering whether to accommodate religious objections to antidiscrimination laws.[28])

As a general matter, the maintenance of a free society depends on the ideas in citizens' heads. Those with political power need to understand what sustains a free society and act in a way that maintains it.

The problem antidiscrimination law addresses is the mirror image of the problem that the drug laws address. Libertarianism treats the individual in isolation, and demands only that his rights be respected. "In a free society," writes David Boaz, "we have our natural rights and our general obligation to respect the rights of other individuals. Our other obligations are those we choose to assume by contract."[29] It turns out, though, that actual freedom requires both internal and external conditions. Rights of nonaggression are insufficient to guarantee either.[30]

If antidiscrimination regulation is appropriate, then so are other restrictions on liberty that guarantee fair equality of opportunity. Consider restrictions on consensual sexuality.

Sex is an area where the libertarian objection to the nanny state becomes especially bitter. One of the most powerful slogans of libertarianism is that it aims to keep the state out of your bedroom. Here's the Libertarian Party platform again: "Consenting adults should be free to choose their own sexual practices and personal relationships."[31] Once more, the libertarians were right a lot of the time. With respect to homosexuality, fornication, and pornography, the law was stupid.[32]

On the other hand, here are three examples of restrictions on sexual freedom that make people freer.

For the first of these, return to antidiscrimination law. The prohibition of sex discrimination in employment has isolated exceptions.

Some of these derive from gender-based concerns of personal privacy: Hospitals can discriminate in hiring nurses in maternity wards, and retirement homes can discriminate when they hire personal caregivers for their patients. More interesting is the case of businesses that sell sexual titillation.

Nightclubs can discriminate on the basis of gender when they hire strippers. Businesses are not, however, permitted to discriminate for the sake of "plus sex" marketing, which packages sexual titillation together with other products or services. For example, airlines may not discriminate on the basis of sex in order to combine air travel with alluring flight attendants.[33] "When deciding sexual-titillation cases, courts effectively do two things: (1) they rigidly divide the work world between sex and nonsex businesses, and (2) they police the boundaries between these categories to ensure that the nonsex world does not shrink, even though it may grow."[34] This rule makes sense, because the sexualization of the workplace "alters the way [women] are treated by others, so that their intellectual and professional attributes are simply less likely to be recognized and encouraged."[35] Such focus on the body also has a detrimental effect on the performance of the women themselves.[36] Before the law intervened, women had to deal with sexualized workplaces pretty much everywhere. Constricting the market has made them freer.

Here is a second case. Sadomasochistic sex is another type of behavior between consenting adults that has been the object of officious interference. Yet a regulation-free world is impossible.

The libertarian claim was vigorously pressed in a 1993 English case involving an all-male club of sadomasochists. The club had operated secretly for more than ten years when it was discovered and prosecuted. The prosecution was based on a collection of videotapes that had come into the possession of police. The tapes had been made for the benefit of club members who could not be present when the activities took place. They showed the defendants torturing willing victims. The defendants were convicted of assault and sentenced to prison. The Law Lords upheld the convictions, holding that consent was not a defense to assault.[37] The European Court of Human Rights rejected the claim that the convictions constituted a violation of the "right to respect for . . . private and family life" guaranteed by Article 8 of the European Convention on Human Rights.[38]

The case for regarding the club's activities as beyond the law's legitimate concern has been made pithily by William Eskridge.:

> The SM club had been operating for a decade when Scotland Yard busted it, yet there was not a single person who claimed that he had been abused or mistreated by the participants. There was no evidence that any member of the SM club was sociopathic or had evidenced any violent tendencies outside the controlled context of the club; so far as can be determined, the members were model citizens, outlaws only after the House of Lords made them so. If you took a random sample of liaisons among twenty heterosexuals over the same period, you would not get such a good record.[39]

As Eskridge's last point suggests, there is also something that the majority culture can learn from the SM club. SM subcultures have developed elaborate rituals of consent and control, which reliably guarantee that the masochist is always the one in control of the interaction.[40] Meanwhile, in the mainstream culture of heterosexual sex, as many as one female in three is raped or sexually assaulted. Perhaps it would be a good thing if the SM subculture became *less* closeted, and the majority began to internalize that group's norms of consent.

The United States is more tolerant of sadomasochistic sex than England. It has been a very long time since there has been a prosecution. On the other hand, such practices are typically well concealed. The regime that now exists for SM subcultures in the United States resembles that which was sometimes (and sometimes still is) imposed on gays: what Eskridge calls "the mutually protective closet,"[41] in which those with atypical tastes are allowed to pursue their sexual interests on condition that they hide them from the majority.[42] For gays, the closet has been a terrible thing, not only because of the costs of concealment but because the whole institution rests on a false moral premise. It is hypothetical man, dying of thirst in the desert because the owner of the only oasis won't let him drink, is thus understood to be free.

Why should anyone want freedom, thus understood? The unspoken assumption is that, if you take away state power, people will be better able to make their way in the world. It would be nice if we all had the power to do that, but it isn't true. Everyone is sometimes vulnerable, and some people are always vulnerable, to circumstances that are not created by coercion, but that make it impossible to live as one wants. Franklin Roosevelt was right: "Necessitous men are not free men."

The idea of an entirely self-sufficient being has obsessed philosophers for a long time. But they understood that only God could be thus self-sufficient. (A persistent puzzle was why, given that God is perfect and needs nothing, there was any point in creating the universe.) The notion that any person could achieve such autarky is a delusion. Our dependency is built into our biology: we are born helpless and needy, dependent on strong webs of social obligation for our very survival. The ideal of the pure, hard, uncontaminated, impenetrable, invulnerable self has a persistent appeal, but it is typically accompanied by disgusted hostility toward people who remind us of our animal vulnerability and mortality. Those people tend to be subordinated groups—African Americans, Jews, women, homosexuals, untouchables, lower-class people.[46] To the extent that libertarianism entails indifference or hostility to the weak, it partakes of the same pathology.

A long-standing complaint against liberalism, from the left and the right, is that it exaggerates our separateness and fails to understand how deeply we are embedded in our social context. It conceives of the individual as entirely self-sufficient and independent, even though humans obviously are not like this. "The so-called *rights of man*," Karl Marx wrote, are nothing but the rights "of egoistic man, of man separated from other men and from the community . . . regarded as an isolated monad, withdrawn into himself."[47] Edmund Burke thought that the civil state "ought not to be considered as nothing better than a partnership agreement in a trade of pepper and coffee, calico or tobacco, or some other such low concern, to be taken up for a little temporary interest, and to be dissolved by the fancy of the parties. It is to be looked

not the case that homosexual conduct is per se inferior to
conduct.

But what if consent *always* authorized sadistic violence
in most jurisdictions, one cannot consent to spousal abu
understands that consent to such abuse is typically bogus,
of reasonable fear of retaliation. For that reason, it places l
freedom of consenting adults "to choose their own sexual p
personal relationships." Spouse abusers are routinely arreste
ecuted despite the (frequently insincere) protests of the vict
impossible to devise a rule that would respect genuinely con
domasochists while preventing spouse abuse. Once more, in
in the sexual sphere is unavoidable.

The third case is adult incest. Under the principle stated in
platform, it would obviously be permissible. But considerin
a mere classroom exercise. There is in fact a lot of sexual abu
ents and siblings—and this in a context where there is enormo
and legal pressure against it. What would be the likely effect
dynamics if the taboo were relaxed, and people were told t
thirteen-year-old will legally be fair game in a few years?

The deeper point is that the availability of some transaction
not only the parties but the broader pattern of social and
relationships—between employers and employees, between s
between parents and children.[44] These are not strictly speaki
nomic externalities, because they do not involve invasions of p
rights. They are *cultural* externalities. Once more, the fundamen
ing of post-Hayekian libertarianism is its inadequate attention
cultural preconditions of freedom.

Libertarianism's fundamental problem—revealed, in different wa
the problems of addiction and discrimination—is its underdevel
account of what is necessary for human liberty. Freedom is unders
to mean, in a definition that Charles Koch has embraced, "the abs
of coercion of a human being by any other human being."[45] Rothb

on with other reverence," being "a partnership in all science, a partnership in all art; a partnership in every virtue and in all perfection."[48] Unless people understand that they are embedded in tradition, "the commonwealth itself would, in a few generations, crumble away, be disconnected into the dust and powder of individuality, and at length dispersed to all the winds of heaven."[49] (Hayek quoted this passage from Burke with approval.[50])

The complaint is sound with respect to the libertarianisms of Rothbard, Nozick, and Rand. They are caricatures of liberalism—liberalism as perceived by its enemies.

Liberalism does not deny dependency. It rather aims to embed, within networks of mutual dependence that it takes for granted, a sphere of autonomy. In early proto-liberals like Locke, the sphere was primarily a religious one. It has expanded to encompass ordinary life as something that is, in its own way, sacred.[51]

Americans have distrusted government for a long time.[52] But America has also always been concerned about creating the conditions for improving one's condition, even when this requires state action. The well-known cult of the self-made man moralizes success: "Wealth, material goods, a decent standard of living, are coveted well-nigh universally. What does distinguish the American's pursuit of success is the particular significance he attaches to its achievement."[53] Success is taken as a sign of virtue; failure is a sign of sin. But this cult of success is a two-edged sword. It can be regarded as evidence that we live in a society where each gets what he deserves, where industry, frugality, and prudence are rewarded. Or it can be taken as evidence that our society is inadequate because it obviously does not furnish adequate opportunity to everyone.

The liberal ideal continues to drive American politics. All political parties rely on it. The dispute is about how to realize freedom—how to empower people to live the lives they want. Once more, this is a family quarrel within liberalism. The basic methodological problem for post-Hayek libertarians is that they focus on one obstacle to the realization of human freedom, the state, without attention to the others.

In order for people to genuinely be free, they need a reasonable set of opportunities from which to choose. A society is free to the extent that it makes available such opportunities. Government alone, of course, cannot provide them—though it can facilitate them, by subsidizing education, infrastructure, and basic research. And it can remove obstacles, as antidiscrimination law does.

A free society is a complex web of agency and structure. People make their history, but they don't make it just as they please. Liberalism aims to produce the kind of people who will take advantage of the opportunities it presents. Free people can develop only in a certain kind of context. Constraints on some people's freedom are justified when they are necessary to guarantee everyone's freedom.

The great promise of free markets is that, by making us richer, they can equip us to overcome not just the coercion of others but the recalcitrance of the world in which we must live. Poverty is unfreedom. But beyond distribution, liberty sometimes requires the exercise of government power in ways that put boundaries on people's choices. A cumulation of individual decisions can create a state of affairs in which large numbers of people are not free. A Hayekian justification for free markets was stated by Bill Clinton in his standard 1992 presidential campaign speech: "The ideal that if you work hard and play by the rules you'll be rewarded, you'll do a little better next year than you did last year, your kids will do better than you."[54] But this has a critical edge. Economic mobility in the United States is less than in Denmark, Norway, Finland, Canada, Sweden, Germany, or France.[55]

The core of liberalism is neither rights, nor limitations on state power, nor the protection of property. All of these are instrumental to the larger goal of creating conditions in which people have the power to decide for themselves what they want to do with their lives.

In its actual operation in American politics, libertarianism has ironically become an obstacle to that goal.

6

MOOCHERS

> It appears that we have unwittingly created a machinery which makes it possible to claim the sanction of an alleged majority for measures which are in fact not desired by a majority, and which may even be disapproved by a majority of the people; and that this machinery produces an aggregate of measures that not only is not wanted by anybody, but that could not as a whole be approved by any rational mind because it is inherently contradictory.
>
> —Friedrich Hayek[1]

This has been a study of political philosophy. We've concluded that some libertarian arguments are sounder than others. Who cares? What difference does it make? Has libertarianism had any effect?

Its effect has been profound. Libertarianism, in one form or another, has become a powerful force in American politics. It has competitors: Donald Trump's electoral victory inflamed tribalism and protectionism in both major political parties, and Marxism isn't dead on the left. But at this writing, policymaking in Washington is often divided between the party of Hayek and the party of Rothbard.

We will see this by examining the political influence of America's most powerful libertarian, Charles Koch. His Rothbardian intervention nearly crushed one Hayekian policy, the Obamacare law. More important, he has played an immense role in hamstringing the effort to slow climate change. Libertarianism, of which he has been the most effective advocate, endangers the human race.

This chapter concludes by considering the problem of the effect of money on politics—one of the sharpest points of disagreement between contemporary libertarians and their adversaries on the left. Koch's story yields pessimism about the effect on democracy of the inequality that free markets engender and that Hayek defends. Once one sees the importance of the political philosophy that powerful people happen to hold, other possibilities present themselves.

The rise within the Republican Party of Rothbardian thinking is a complex story, which begins long before Koch. In the mid-twentieth century, the party was quite Hayekian. Robert Taft supported government-funded old-age pensions and medical care. Thomas Dewey embraced broad social programs. Dwight Eisenhower, who built the interstate highway system, acknowledged that some people wanted to abolish Social Security and labor laws, but thought "their number is negligible and they are stupid." What distinguished Republicans was their emphasis on individual freedom and incentive. They offered honest and efficient government, to be contrasted with the coalition of corrupt big-city machines and southern racists that was the Democratic Party.[2]

The destruction of moderate Republicanism is a convoluted story. Historical accident played an important role: in the struggle for the 1964 presidential nomination, the forces of Barry Goldwater (who admired and sometimes quoted Hayek) were simply better organized than their opponents.[3] After he had the nomination, Goldwater (himself no racist) voted against the Civil Rights Act on libertarian grounds: "The freedom to associate means the same thing as the freedom not to associate."[4] In so doing, he transformed the Republican coalition. Eisenhower had gotten about 40 percent of the Black vote; Nixon in 1960, about a third; Goldwater, 6 percent. Goldwater was the first Republican ever to win in Georgia, and the first since Reconstruction to carry Alabama, Mississippi, and South Carolina. Richard Nixon's eagerness to woo the voters who had supported George Wallace in 1968 consolidated the racial polarization of American politics.

Libertarianism in all the forms we have examined is firmly opposed to racism. We have seen no trace of it in any of the arguments we have surveyed. Nonetheless, it is part of libertarianism's appeal to many Americans. Rothbard and Ron Paul both flirted with it, and American racists continue to be drawn to libertarianism. It is easier to oppose government power if you don't like what that power will be used for. The Rothbardian idea of abandoning the state for clusters of self-governing enclaves, some of which can be all white, captured the imagination of the racist right. Rand was no racist, but her language of moochers has more resonance when you think you know who those people are. The continuing vitality of this theme is evident when the Republican Party plunges into the despicable business of voter suppression. (Koch, who actively supports it, has not attempted to explain this obvious abandonment of libertarian egalitarianism.)

In 1964, business was not yet convinced that a rollback of the New Deal was in its interests. Goldwater tried to woo it, but it clustered around Lyndon Johnson, who won the election in a landslide.[5]

Until Reagan, libertarian ideas remained marginal in American governance. Nixon imposed wage and price controls. The political center was so far from Hayek in 1975 that Senators Hubert Humphrey, the Democratic former vice president and presidential candidate, and Jacob Javits, the liberal New York Republican, proposed a national economic planning agency.

Reagan succeeded in shifting American politics—and American understandings of liberty—in a Hayekian direction. He used the word *freedom* in his speeches more than any president before or since.[6] With the ascent of Clinton, Hayekian views took over the Democratic Party as well. "As president, Bill Clinton accomplished much of what Reagan could not: the dismantling of welfare, the deregulation of Wall Street, the expansion of free trade."[7]

But meanwhile, the Republican Party became increasingly Rothbardian: reflexively opposed to all taxation and regulation, the enemy of the administrative state—and friend to its enemies. It has become the home of unethical capitalists who want to be able to mooch and loot undisturbed. Trump, who had a long career as just that kind of capitalist, was the culmination of this trend. The administration made a sustained effort to defund any scientific research that might embarrass industry, leading to a systematic gutting of expertise throughout the federal bureaucracy.[8] Evidently liberty is in danger if scientists are allowed to discover what pollution does to childhood development.[9] The effect is particularly clear in the Environmental Protection Agency, where initiatives to dismantle regulations were drafted by lawyers and lobbyists employed by the regulated industries, without even consulting staff scientists.[10]

Rothbard's capture of the Republican Party is necessarily and permanently incomplete. Most Americans don't want to abolish the modern administrative state. The party relies heavily on older voters. They depend on Social Security and Medicare, a huge part of the federal budget. They're even willing to raise taxes on high earners in order to maintain them. But they fear there isn't enough money to go around. (The Obama-era Tea Party consisted mainly of older white people who did not want to pay for anyone else's benefits.[11]) So Republican proposals to cut retirement programs have always exempted those over fifty-five. Few regulatory and redistributive programs have been eliminated. They are run without enthusiasm in Republican administrations, but they remain in place, awaiting the return of the Democrats who believe in their missions. The pressure for savage cuts to all other programs thus becomes intense, but it isn't exactly libertarian.[12]

This perspective made it impossible for its proponents to understand Barack Obama. "Some of the smartest and most sophisticated people I know—canny investors, erudite authors—sincerely and passionately believe that President Barack Obama has gone far beyond conventional American liberalism and is willfully and relentlessly driving the United States down the road to socialism," former White House speechwriter David Frum reported. "No counterevidence will dissuade them from this belief: not record-high corporate profits, not almost 500,000 job losses in the public sector, not the lowest tax rates since the Truman administration."[13]

"He's a dedicated egalitarian," said Charles Koch. "I'm not saying he's a Marxist, but he's internalized some Marxist models—that is, that business tends to be successful by exploiting its customers and workers." His brother David agreed:

> He's the most radical president we've ever had as a nation, and has done more damage to the free enterprise system and long-term prosperity than any president we've ever had. . . . His father was a hard core economic socialist in Kenya. Obama didn't really interact with his father face-to-face very much, but was apparently from what I read a great admirer of his father's points of view. So he had sort of antibusiness, anti–free enterprise influences affecting him almost all his life.[14]

Charles sent a newsletter to his employees after the 2008 election declaring that America faced "the greatest loss of liberty and prosperity since the 1930s."[15] He declared in 2011 that he fears "a statist or collectivist society in which people are impoverished because one person is pitted against another as everyone attempts to gain by redistribution rather than producing goods and services that make people's lives better."[16]

There was a lot of this kind of thing. Obama's opponents were so persistent in tagging him with the label "socialist" that it got under his skin. After the question of socialism came up in an interview, he called the reporter back to expand on his explanation of why he wasn't a socialist.[17] He later declared: "I'm talking about lowering the corporate tax rate, my health care reform is based on the private marketplace, the stock market is doing pretty good the last time I checked and it is true that I am concerned about growing inequality in the system, but nobody questions the efficacy of a market economy in terms of producing wealth and innovation and keeping us competitive."[18]

Obama, and Biden (who has been less frequently tagged with the "socialist" label) after him, are part of a specific anti-socialist movement on the left, social democracy, which embraces a capitalist economy but demands a state strong enough to moderate its failures and excesses.[19] There are no Leninists left in American politics, and almost no democratic socialists, who hope to use electoral means to abolish capitalism. The political left in the United States, and most of Europe as well, has become broadly Hayekian. Even Bernie Sanders, who appropriated the socialist label, never proposed to nationalize the means of production. American leftists hardly ever own up to the power of Hayek's arguments,[20] but they implicitly accept them.

In fact, there's not that much daylight between Hayek and Obama. Obama continued the dominance of Hayekianism within the Democratic Party that began with Bill Clinton. The notion of Obama as a socialist presumes a Manichean view of politics in which the only alternatives are laissez-faire capitalism and North Korea.[21] We must fight totalitarians like Joseph Stalin and Dwight Eisenhower!

Obama was a market-friendly, good-government wonk, in the tradition of Dewey and Eisenhower. Those ideals were in retreat in the Republican Party. The biggest transportation bill of the George W. Bush administration was "a case study in bad governance, showering money on states without regard for national needs, financing new sprawl roads in sparsely populated areas while neglecting repairs to crowded urban transit systems." It was earmarked with 6,376 pet projects.[22] The Obama stimulus was obsessively clean of pork; some worthy projects were deleted because Obama worried that they would be misperceived. One of the enduring contributions of libertarianism is to infuse American politics with a constant concern for government waste, though, curiously, that concern has political bite only when Democrats are in power.

The shift within the Republican Party became clear in the massive struggle over the Affordable Care Act, also known as Obamacare. Hayek was unequivocally abandoned in favor of Rothbard. The shift was even spearheaded by Rothbard's friend, Professor Randy Barnett.

The case for government-funded health care has Lockean roots. "God hath not left one Man so to the Mercy of another, that he may starve him if he please."[23] Everyone has a right to the means of survival, and that entails not only a right to appropriate but also "a Title to so much out of another's Plenty, as will keep him from extream want, where he has no means to subsist otherwise."[24] Locke was thinking about food, of course, but death is death, however caused. The inability to afford lifesaving medical care is the functional equivalent of starvation. So a society that can afford to provide everyone with basic medical care is in the same moral position, with the same moral proviso limiting property rights, as a society with enough food for everyone. For Locke, withholding what others need to live is tantamount to murder.

Obamacare is fundamentally Hayekian. Recall that Hayek thought the state should "assist the individual in providing for those common hazards of life against which, because of their uncertainty, few individuals can make adequate provision," such as "sickness and accident."[25] He anticipated, in some detail, the design of the scheme Obama enacted, including even the hated mandate to purchase insurance: "There is little doubt that the growth of health insurance is a desirable development. And perhaps there is also a case for making it compulsory since many who could thus provide for themselves might otherwise become a public charge. But there are strong arguments against a single scheme of state insurance; and there seems to be an overwhelming case against a free health service for all."[26]

He rejected a government monopoly, which he thought would involve the usual inefficiencies. Instead, he envisioned multiple competing private insurance companies.

Obamacare makes insurance compulsory; it forbids insurers from discriminating against the sick; it subsidizes health care for those who cannot afford it. It thus delivers basic security with a market-based mechanism. It encourages competition. There are objections, within a Hayekian framework, to various aspects of Obama's scheme. Social welfare provision of any kind can create perverse incentives, such as welfare traps or uncontrollable costs. Obama had to give up some cost control measures in order to mollify health industries that had the power to kill the legislation; he barely had the votes for what he did pass.[27] So Republicans could reasonably have quarreled with those aspects of the law. They could even have modified them, had they been willing to support any coverage of the uninsured. That didn't happen.

Opposition was not Hayekian. It was Randian. To the extent that it was not based on raw political gamesmanship and outright lies, the fundamental objection was that it financed medical care by imposing taxes on people who hadn't done anything wrong. The Republican complaint against Obamacare mirrors Rothbard and Rand's complaints against Hayek.

During oral arguments in the case in which the Supreme Court addressed the constitutionality of the law (which we discussed briefly in the introduction), Justice Samuel Alito demanded that the United States concede that "what this mandate is really doing is not requiring the people who are subject to it to pay for the services that they are going to consume? It is requiring them to subsidize services that will be received by somebody else." Justice Ruth Bader Ginsburg responded: "If you're going to have insurance, that's how insurance works."[28] It is a big if. The most profound effect of the Obamacare battle has been a shift in the Republican Party's attitude toward sick people who can't afford to pay for medical care. If you get sick and you can't afford to pay for a doctor, that's your tough luck.

The situation before Obamacare had disadvantages from the standpoint of liberty. Employer-provided insurance is "community rated": rates are based on the average expected cost of the whole workforce, so that the healthy subsidize the sick. Individual insurance, on the other hand, was "experience rated": the insurer examined each applicant and charged based on that person's expected costs. A worker with a history of illness, or whose family members had such a history, was under enormous financial pressure to find a large employer to work for and to stay on that employer's payroll. That was "job lock," the pressure to keep one's job even if one could otherwise be better employed elsewhere—a phenomenon that, when the ACA was enacted, affected approximately a quarter of American workers.[29] Job lock was a particular disincentive to starting a small business, for which only experience-rated insurance is available. A less quantifiable burden is "marriage lock": people were reluctant to divorce even abusive spouses if that meant losing their health care.

Before Obama, similar schemes for health care reform were championed by Richard Nixon and Robert Dole. Obama's own plan was based in part on a proposal devised by the Heritage Foundation.[30] Hayek had long worried about the tendency "to resort to direct state controls or to the creation of monopolistic institutions where judicious use of financial inducements might induce spontaneous efforts."[31] The Heritage proposal followed the latter model: everyone would be required to purchase insurance, government would subsidize the poor, but private businesses would compete to provide the service.

The drive to privatize government-funded benefits was around long before Obamacare. Many contemporary Republicans want all social insurance—Social Security and Medicare, for example—to follow the Obamacare model of relying on private providers.[32] (The contradiction was noticed by the court of appeals judge—later associate justice—Brett Kavanaugh when he heard one of the Obamacare challenges.[33]) The Reagan administration, here as elsewhere influenced by Hayek, moved to privatize a broad range of government services, confident that this would improve government's efficiency. Clinton accelerated Hayekian tendencies that had already begun with Reagan. Today the federal government employs three times as many contract workers as government employees.[34]

Hayek was eager to explore such privatization, but he didn't purport to know what would work. Rothbard, characteristically confident about the effects of radical innovations, was certain that anything the state does can be done better by the private sector.

Privatization has dangers, however, which both Hayek and Rothbard ought to have foreseen. It calls into existence a new and persistent gang of moochers. If the state depends on private suppliers, then those suppliers will lobby for state favors and so distort state decision making. In military contracting, the problem is an ancient one. Libertarians worry about the power of public employee unions, but unions' resources are small compared with those of for-profit corporations. As those corporations grow in power, they increasingly get to make public decisions, and those decisions are now influenced by the companies' need for profit. The profit motive often guarantees high-quality product in the private sector. It has different effects with respect to public services.

Consider privately run prisons. Since 1989, the largest for-profit prison companies in the United States—the business is oligopolistic, with two companies controlling 75 percent of the market—have donated more than $10 million to candidates, and have spent nearly $25 million on lobbying. Between 2000 and 2010, the private federal prison population more than doubled. These companies house almost half the country's immigrant detainees.[35] They lobbied for "three strikes," "mandatory minimum," "truth-in-sentencing," and "immigration enforcement" laws, all of which produced longer sentences for larger numbers of prisoners.[36]

The cost savings associated with private prisons are tightly correlated with worse prison conditions. Wages are lower, pre-service training is reduced, and staff is reduced, to the point that prison safety is jeopardized. In one Idaho prison, the company falsified records to hide the shifts that were uncovered, and reached a tacit agreement whereby prison gangs controlled the facility.[37] (Perhaps this should be regarded as an experiment in decentralizing coercive power to private protective associations, as Rothbard proposed.) After a Justice Department report found that private prisons were unusually dangerous for both inmates and guards, the Obama administration decided to stop using them. The industry responded with large donations to the Trump campaign, and after his election, Trump reversed the decision.

Private prisons are not appropriate wielders of public power, and their incentives are such that they cannot possibly be politically legitimate.[38] One notable divergence concerns recidivism: private economic actors want their customers to come back. Rent-seeking special interests are always a danger, but libertarians ought to be especially wary of calling into existence interests that can prosper only by making the state more repressive.

Let's return to Obamacare. Privatization may make sense when there are multiple entities competing, on both quality and price, for government dollars. (Or it may not, depending on contingencies; if there is already a well-functioning and dedicated government bureaucracy, that culture might not be easily duplicated if its functions are transferred to the private sector.) Medicare has cost control problems. Politics aside, there was a reasonable case for trying a privatized solution to the problem of medical care.

The opposition to Obama's proposal, in the beginning, was purely political: Republican leaders were convinced that, if it could be defeated, Democrats would be punished in the next election. That happened in 1994 when Clinton's health bill failed, and they thought they could make it happen again.

When Obama proposed to tackle the health care problem, some Republicans were willing to work with him, and in the summer of 2009, the Senate Health, Education, Labor, and Pensions Committee adopted 161 Republican amendments to a health reform bill, in whole or in part. Obama desperately wanted the bill to be bipartisan. Republicans could have extracted a lot of concessions, if they were seriously interested in the details of a Hayekian approach to health care. But they divided on whether to work with Obama. Senator Jim DeMint hoped to repeat 1994: "If we're able to stop Obama on this, it will be his Waterloo. It will break him."[39]

The dispute among Republicans was resolved in August 2009, when town hall meetings held during the congressional recess were repeatedly disrupted by angry protesters. Their anger dominated the news. The Koch brothers played a major role: their political organization Americans for Prosperity held Hands Off My Health Care events in more than 250 cities and sponsored anti-Obamacare groups.[40] The people who turned out for the meetings were motivated in large part by a sustained campaign of disinformation, most prominently Sarah Palin's declaration that seniors and the disabled "will have to stand in front of Obama's 'death panel' so his bureaucrats can decide based on a subjective judgment of their 'level of productivity in society,' whether they are worthy of health care."[41] The protests showed moderate Republicans that it was too risky to associate themselves with Obama.

After that, the central Republican alternative proposal was the libertarian one of allowing insurance to be sold across state lines, which would have meant that the least-regulated state would dominate the market and thus effectively end all insurance regulation. They also embraced the somewhat less libertarian program of limits on medical malpractice lawsuits, which would reduce American health care spending by about one-half of 1 percent.[42] (Many libertarians, notably Rothbard and Mises, embrace liability as an alternative to regulation.) Neither would have much effect on the number of uninsured, because neither addressed the core problem that millions of Americans cannot afford to pay for health care. That requires redistribution of wealth, which evidently was no longer an option: the AFP intervention had taken it off the table. The Democrats reasonably concluded that it was impossible to work with Republicans on health care reform.[43]

Once the political decision had been made to oppose Obamacare, they needed a substantive position that was to the right of Hayek. They found one.

As a last resort after the law was passed, Republicans challenged it in court. The only arguments of principle available (and that is what you need in court) rested on a categorical rejection of redistribution—what I have elsewhere called Tough Luck Libertarianism. If you are too poor to buy medical treatment or health insurance, tough luck: you can't get something in a market unless you pay for it. If you have been sick in the past, that's tough, too: your insurance will be ruinously expensive and the policy won't cover the illnesses you are most likely to get. Government efforts to help you would be an outrageous violation of liberty.

The central claim of the constitutional challenge was that the state can't make you do things; that it may regulate only those who engage in some self-initiated action. It creatively read into the Constitution the notion that the law's trivial burden on individuals was intolerable, even when the alternative was a regime in which millions were needlessly denied medical care.[44] The action/inaction distinction came advertised as a great bulwark of liberty. Some bulwark. No one can live in the world without engaging in self-initiated actions all the time. If that's all it takes to trigger regulation, then government can push its citizens around in nearly any way it likes. What was so nakedly political about the proposed new limitation was that it had so little effect on existing law, and so would not be much of a constraint on Congress in the future. It was the weapon of a bee: it stings and it dies.[45]

The argument is useful for two purposes. One is political opportunism: any argument is good if it would help beat Obama. The other is that it is a step toward making the world a more Rothbardian place.

Barnett, the Georgetown law professor who devised the theoretical rationale for the challenge, had been a friend of Murray Rothbard's. Like Rothbard (but with far more legal and philosophical sophistication), he is tightly focused on the problem of restraining state power, he thinks that the state should have neither the power of taxation nor a monopoly of legitimate force, and his ideal is a network of private protective associations, which would police one another for misconduct. He is more frightened of government power than he is of untreated disease.[46] By the time the case got to the Supreme Court, that had become the official position of the Republican Party.

Reviewing this political history, I wrote in 2013:

> This is why so many people (including, perhaps, some Supreme Court justices) who were not Tough Luck Libertarians at all, who would find that philosophy repellent, nonetheless found themselves saying Tough Luck Libertarian things, and, in the opinion they finally wrote, making claims based on a Tough Luck *Constitution*—a constitution in which there is no realistic path to universal health care. That Constitution won't be attractive unless Tough Luck Libertarianism is right that it is acceptable to deny people the medical care they need. The challengers to the ACA talked a lot about slippery slopes—at the bottom of this one was a law requiring you to buy broccoli—but there's a slope in the other direction as well. Once you decide that it's acceptable to hold your nose and make this kind of argument, it will be easier next time.[47]

It was. After the Republicans took control of Congress and the presidency in 2017, their initial strategy, devised by House majority leader Paul Ryan, was "repeal and delay": a repeal whose implementation would be delayed for two years, allowing time to negotiate a replacement.[48] The Republican leadership claimed that this would motivate Democrats to work with them on constructing a small-government replacement. The plan carried the risk of no deal at all in the two-year window. It is not clear whether, for Ryan, that was a problem. As noted in chapter 2, he is a fan of Ayn Rand. He told an interviewer in September 2014, when he was still House Ways and Means chair: "I'd go back to the pre-Obamacare baseline. . . . I think that's the way to go, because we shouldn't assume we're going to have an explosive entitlement and then just replace it with our own."[49] He never expressly embraced repeal with no replacement at all, but that may have been what he was hoping for. A lot of Republican voters would have lost their insurance, but perhaps that could be blamed on the Democrats.

The strategy was abandoned when it became clear that a repeal without a replacement would lead to the quick collapse of insurance markets, leaving millions without coverage. So the Republicans were forced to devise a replacement. In the event, they came close to enacting five different repeal bills. There had been responsible Republican proposals to maintain broad coverage using more market-friendly mechanisms.[50] Trump had promised not to take away anyone's health care, and to replace Obamacare with something more generous and cheaper. His voters, many of whom depended on the law, believed him.[51] But the House Republican leadership was compelled by its libertarian wing, whose votes were indispensable, to embrace far harsher proposals. All of them would have taken insurance away from between twenty-two million and thirty-two million people, and most would have used the money saved for massive tax breaks for the rich.[52] The shift was largely brought about by Koch opposition to any reform that preserved subsidies for those who could not pay for health insurance.[53] Senator Rand Paul and House Freedom Caucus chair Mark Meadows explained why they were blocking any such reform: "Leadership wants to keep Obamacare-like subsidies to buy insurance but rename them refundable tax credits (families will be given up to $14,000 of other people's money)."[54] The opposition backfired because the House bill was too draconian for the Senate to stomach, Obamacare remained in place, and the issue helped the Democrats retake the House in 2018.

When the Supreme Court upheld the ACA, it construed the Constitution, on the basis of weak reasoning, to permit states to reject the statute's expanded Medicaid funding, which would have provided health care to the poorest citizens.[55] It makes no sense for any state to accept that invitation. When the ACA was negotiated, hospital associations agreed to accept cuts to their reimbursement rates, expecting that this would be more than made up for by money from patients newly insured through Medicaid. States refusing the money not only hurt their own health care systems and working poor, but they turn away a huge infusion of cash into their economies, which would create many, many jobs—good jobs, for doctors and well-paid medical technicians. That money has a powerful multiplier effect, creating jobs outside the health sector as well.[56] Yet as of this writing, twelve states have declined the money. Insurance has thus been denied to 2.3 million people.[57] Americans for Prosperity, which opposes any expansion of social welfare spending, brought more pressure to bear on state officeholders than doctors, hospitals, and the Chamber of Commerce could counter.[58] Had every state adopted the Medicaid expansion, about fifteen thousand deaths would have been prevented during the program's first four years.[59] Locke thought that people have a right to what they need to keep themselves alive. Hayek proposed subsidized health insurance. Rothbard thought that property rights are so sacrosanct that one may not redistribute even when lives depend on it. Here Rothbard has won.

People often act solely because an ideology has captured their imaginations. But an ideology can be a means as well as an end, and when this happens, the means can become an end. A political combatant reaches for the rhetoric that happens to be handiest to bash his opponent, and then finds afterward that it has become a lasting part of his platform. That happened with the Republicans and health care. Crude political strategy led them to support legislation whose major effect would be to devastate the lives of large numbers of Americans. If a foreign power were to do to Americans what the Republican health care bills attempted, it would be an act of war.

There remained important differences between Obama and Hayek. The most fundamental concerned the question of how to respond to a recession. Obama entered office amid a massive financial catastrophe. Hayek thought that the appropriate governmental response to such conditions was to do nothing and ride them out. He blamed recessions on government intervention that makes credit too easy to obtain (this became the standard Republican explanation for the 2008 bust), producing malinvestment. The only way to correct the distortion is to liquidate those investments with a correction, which should be allowed to readjust the economy as quickly as possible. Rothbard held the same view. (One may, however, wonder whether the neatness of this account of the business cycle can be reconciled with Hayek's account of unknowably complex spontaneous orders.[60])

Hayek's great rival, Keynes, argued that the opposite response was appropriate: in a recession, government should massively spend in order to stop the unraveling of otherwise sound businesses and restore the lost demand. Obama's response was firmly Keynesian: his Recovery Act spent $831 billion to stimulate the economy—50 percent bigger in constant dollars than the entire New Deal.[61] The stimulus was a spectacular success, saving or creating about three million jobs and increasing output by more than 2 percent.[62] Hayek is right that recessions sometimes weed out malinvestment, but the collapse of 2008 was destroying thousands of well-functioning enterprises. A notable example is the rescue of Chrysler and General Motors, which saved about a million jobs. More generally, the ability of central banks to intervene softened business cycles throughout the twentieth century, with less severe oscillations of boom and bust. Here Obama saw beyond Hayek.

This time the Republicans really were the Hayekian party. They fought intensely to stop the stimulus, and their alternative—only four Senate Republicans opposed it—consisted of nothing but tax cuts.[63] Had they prevailed, the American economy would likely have gone into a catastrophic and prolonged depression. Much of this was reckless political gamesmanship: they were so focused on stymieing Obama that the welfare of the country no longer mattered. But they could not have rationalized doing that without the comfort of libertarian mythology. (Since Obama didn't need their votes, they may also have judged that this irresponsible posturing would be harmless, at least in the short run.)

Blanket hostility to everything the state does explains one of the scariest developments in American politics, the atrophy of the public sector.

Hayek understood that "where . . . it is impracticable to make the enjoyment of certain services dependent on the payment of a price, competition will not produce the services."[64] Some activities have positive externalities: if government fails to perform them, they won't be done. All libertarians (except the anarchists) agree that this is true of police and military protection, and that these therefore must be supplied by the state.[65]

The conditions for sustained economic growth include protection of property rights, enforcement of contracts, and open trade across borders. But growth also requires elements that libertarians have been tirelessly attacking: a well-functioning banking system with a central bank able to manage the macroeconomy, quality communications and transportation infrastructure, publicly funded research and education, regulation of markets to prevent externalities, enforcement of nondiscrimination rules that prevent the waste of human capital, and efficient public administration, including a well-functioning tax system.[66]

One important public good is research and development of new technologies. Such research aids many firms, and so there is not enough incentive for any firm to invest in it. We considered this basic Hayekian point in chapter 1. In the mid-1960s, R&D spending by the federal government was nearly 2 percent of GDP. It dropped to around 0.6 percent in fiscal year 2019. The United States now ranks tenth worldwide in government R&D as a share of the economy, and most of what we do is defense related.[67]

Or consider basic infrastructure. The construction of the interstate highway system produced almost a third of the increase in America's productivity in the late 1950s, and about a quarter in the 1960s.[68] That was then. The American Society of Civil Engineers reported in 2021 that bringing US infrastructure up to acceptable levels would require $2.6 trillion in additional spending. Leaving that issue unaddressed would cost $10 trillion in lost GNP by 2039. About one in four bridges are structurally deficient.[69] Infrastructure spending in China and India is almost 10 percent of GDP. It is about 5 percent in Europe, and 3 percent in Mexico. The United States has not exceeded 3 percent since the mid-1970s.[70] Once again, Americans for Prosperity has played a role; it has fought at the state level to defeat appropriations for highway repairs and infrastructure investments.[71] It also fought hard to defeat President Joseph Biden's infrastructure legislation.[72]

From 2003 to 2015, the National Institutes of Health lost 22 percent of its capacity to fund research because of budget cuts and sequestration.[73] Between 2008 and 2012, more than forty-five thousand jobs were eliminated from state and local health departments.[74]

Hostility to the public sector has been elevated to a matter of principle, by people whose views matter. Thus presidential candidate Mitt Romney: "Did you know that government—federal, state, and local—under President Obama, has grown to consume almost forty percent of our economy? We're only inches away from ceasing to be a free economy."[75] Would we really be freer without roads, bridges, Social Security, Medicare, Medicaid, police, firefighters, environmental protection? Of course, much of this is politically untouchable, so the drive for small government inevitably focuses on spending that has no powerful protectors—public goods that benefit everyone in general and no one in particular.

Atrophying investment in the public sector has damaged and continues to damage the overall performance of the American economy. Unlike failures of regulation, this cannot be attributed to the success of powerful interests, because there are no such interests. Just as the benefits of public goods are broad and diffuse, so are their costs. Wealthy people benefit from tax cuts, but the undersupply of public goods is bad for business (and the same people whose taxes are cut tend to hold a lot of stock). Rothbardian ideology is at work. Taxes must be reduced. The state must shrink. So if anything is part of the public sector, it must go.

American prosperity after World War II was the product of a robust public sector and an active regulatory state. The same pattern holds everywhere. In the modern world, the richest countries are the ones that have expanded their governments the most.[76] Small-government ideology threatens American decline.

It is hard to show that libertarian philosophy has been the cause of any particular political development. We can say that there has been a growing demand, by an increasingly potent political faction, to cut back on government regulation and public sector funding. In his first inaugural address, Ronald Reagan declared, "government is not the solution to our problem; government is the problem." Bill Clinton adopted a similar theme: "The era of big government is over." Policymaking is always affected by the framework within which we think about it.

Recall, from chapter 1, that there are two kinds of errors in science. A type I error is the (false) detection of an effect that has not in fact occurred. A type II error is the failure to detect an effect that has in fact occurred. We said that, in the context of regulation and redistribution, unnecessary government intervention is type I error, and the failure to intervene is type II error. Libertarianism, I argued, focuses on type I error and is oblivious to type II. In practice, then, it produces a lot of type II error.

The easiest case—the kind of inaction that counts as type II error for any kind of libertarianism—is passivity in the face of aggression against or reckless endangerment of persons or property. The sheriff has a duty to stop the lynching. He shouldn't send the drunk driver on his way. The state (or, if there is no state, the private protective associations) may not stand by while some people injure others. Yet libertarian rhetoric has been deployed, sometimes successfully, to prevent the state from performing this minimal function.

As this book goes to press, the Supreme Court is considering a new limitation on the administrative state, forbidding Congress from delegating to major agencies the kind of regulatory discretion they have had for decades. The judges who propound this view claim to be following the original meaning of the Constitution, but the originalist credentials of this limitation are dubious.[77] If this theory is adopted, Justice Elena Kagan observed, "then most of Government is unconstitutional—dependent as Congress is on the need to give discretion to executive officials to implement its programs."[78] The philosophical movement this book has been examining can help to make sense of this strange development in constitutional law.

Rothbard is the most explicit of the libertarians in his disregard for type II error. As we saw in chapter 3, he (in one of his moods) would require proof "beyond a reasonable doubt" that there is "strict causality from the actions of the defendant to the victimization of the plaintiff" before pollution can be stopped, even if that protects most forms of environmental destruction. Rothbard's priorities were clear: "It is far better to let an aggressive act slip through than to impose coercion and commit aggression ourselves."[79] Pollution could cause massive death and damage. Large parts of the earth could become uninhabitable. But cheer up: at least the state's power would be restrained. In criminal law, the "beyond a reasonable doubt" standard is not a license for crime, because no criminal can be confident that the police will not be able to discover the necessary evidence. But applied to pollution, Rothbard's rule amounts to a guarantee that one can ruin other people's persons and property with impunity.

Which brings us to an examination of one more libertarian thinker.

Charles Koch is, in his own way, as influential as any of the libertarians we have examined in this book. He, more than his late younger brother, David, is the moving force in the brothers' political activities. As a young man, he read deeply in libertarian texts. He was friendly with Hayek and Rothbard. He talked David into being the Libertarian vice presidential candidate in 1980, because he was too busy running the family company to do it. He is an industrialist, not a philosopher. But he has energetically supported libertarian causes and funded libertarian think tanks, many years before he became a household name. His growing network has mobilized not only his own vast wealth but hundreds of millions from other wealthy business owners, moving the Republican Party in a libertarian direction and helping it win elections.

Government, he declared in 1979, "is to serve as a night watchman, to protect individuals and property from outside threat, including fraud. That is the maximum."[80] This limitation, he thinks, promotes "true democracy," where people "can run their own lives and choose what they want to buy, choose how to spend their money." ("Now in our democracy you elect somebody every two to four years and they tell you how to run your life.")[81] His present influence has come after many years of being marginal, with no support from business, when he refused to compromise his principles.[82]

From an early age, Koch was an avid reader of Hayek, whom he once persuaded to visit his libertarian think tank, the Institute for Humane Studies.[83] Two other writers, however, appear to have had an even greater impact on him.

Koch has written that his worldview was shaped by "two life-changing books," Ludwig von Mises's *Human Action* and F. A. Harper's *Why Wages Rise*. He told an interviewer that he "traces his belief system" to the latter.[84] "Harper demonstrated that real wages are determined by the productivity of labor. . . . The more productive an employee is, the more an employer will need to pay to retain him."[85] Harper taught him that "wages rise not because of unions or government action, but because of marginal productivity gains—people get more money when they produce more value for other people."[86] The point was valid when Harper wrote: a rising standard of living depended on rising productivity. But the correlation between productivity and wages ended about forty years ago. Harper showed that wages can't rise faster than productivity, but he didn't prove that they couldn't rise more slowly. From 1973 to 2014, productivity grew 72 percent, while average hourly wages increased by 9 percent.[87]

Harper thought that small government followed readily from the presumption of mutual opacity. Any government assessment of needs "will have no necessary relationship to your hopes and expectations," because "the Commissar of the Peoples' Needs never met you—probably doesn't even know that you exist."[88] It follows that any reduction in the size of government will make people better off. "The greatest opportunity now for a quick increase in the worth of wages is to reduce the cost of governing ourselves so that more of the wage can be kept."[89]

Harper is right that, when government takes taxes, that money is unavailable to the consumer. But he pays no attention to what the taxes are paying for. Without an assessment of that, there's no way to know whether doing without government services and keeping the money makes the taxpayer better off.

Koch's other transformative influence is Mises, whose monumental treatise deduces an elaborate economic theory from a few parsimonious premises. Koch writes that Mises "showed in unparalleled depth and scope that a free society based on scrupulous respect for private property, the consistent rule of law, and the right to freely exchange goods and services is the system most conducive to human well-being, progress, civility, and peace."[90]

Like his student Hayek, Mises was an Austrian refugee from the Nazis. Like Hayek, he was shaped by the experience. Long before Hayek, he showed that socialist central planning could not deploy resources rationally. He is, however, far more categorical than Hayek in condemning government intervention in the economy, which he blames for "wars and civil wars, ruthless oppression of the masses by clusters of self-appointed dictators, economic depressions, mass unemployment, capital consumption, famines."[91]

Mises writes that "the specific method of economics is the method of imaginary constructions." These constructions are "conceptual image[s] of a sequence of events logically evolved from the elements of action employed in its formation."[92] The theorems of economics are a priori, "products of deductive reasoning that starts from the category of action."[93] He thought he could deduce from simple premises, such as the fact that people enter transactions to make themselves better off, that prosperity is promoted by an economic system with clear property rights, contract enforcement, stable currency, and other such basics.

Austrian School economics made a valuable contribution by insisting on those basics. Modern economics agrees about the value of free trade, but in the past century, it has also developed increasingly sophisticated accounts of market failures, notably financial crises, externalities, and systemic instability that periodically destroys economic value by devastating otherwise efficient businesses. Economics today is also intensely empirical, striving to map these failures and determine their causes and magnitudes. Mises, however, never departs from his model.

It's as if someone devised a theory of engineering that left out friction. In some contexts, engineers can get away with that, because sometimes the amount of friction is trivial. But the consequence is a pretty crude approach to engineering. What the engineering analogy leaves out is that it is rarely the case that when engineers fail to notice friction, someone gets rich. A theory like Mises's is a handy tool for those who mooch unearned gains when markets fail and so don't want law to correct the failures. The neatness of his a priori constructs is also in deep tension with Hayek's account of unknowably complex spontaneous orders.

He is skeptical of the state. "Government is in the last resort the employment of armed men, of policemen, gendarmes, soldiers, prison guards, and hangmen. The essential feature of government is the enforcement of its decrees by beating, killing, and imprisoning. Those who are asking for more government interference are asking ultimately for more compulsion and less freedom."[94] He stops short of Rothbard's anarchism. Property must be protected. "One must take exception to the often-repeated phrase that government is an evil, although a necessary and indispensable evil."[95] Beyond that minimum, he rejects even such familiar restrictions on contractual obligation as corporate limited liability and bankruptcy, without which modern capitalism probably could not function.

Mises acknowledges that some actions have positive externalities, and so will be undersupplied by the market, but he responds only with a screed against wasteful government subsidies. He cites Henry Hazlitt's *Economics in One Lesson*, but Hazlitt is less crude than this; he acknowledges that some public works are necessary, "streets and roads and bridges and tunnels . . . buildings to house legislatures, police and fire departments."[96] Hazlitt's objection is to "public works as a means of 'providing employment.'"[97] But that still doesn't say which public expenditures are in fact justified. Here Koch follows Mises: Americans for Prosperity has blocked public transit projects and spending on roads and bridges.

Koch's most important political interventions were his opposition to Obamacare, and in particular to its reliance on taxation to provide health care to those who cannot afford it, and his resistance to any regulation that would ameliorate climate change. He has not explained the connection between his positions on those issues and his libertarian philosophy. This is a puzzle, because the most attractive forms of libertarianism repudiate those positions: Locke and Hayek thought that everyone had a right to the material means of self-preservation, and activities that promote climate change aggress against others' persons and property. Mises had views relevant to both those issues.

On both issues, Mises parted company with Hayek, who thought that, because the distributions produced by the market in significant measure reflect luck, a social minimum financed by taxation is appropriate. That would include health insurance. Mises, however, feared any redistribution whatsoever. "In fact, the Welfare State is merely a method for transforming the market economy step by step into socialism."[98] He was mighty categorical: "Welfare policies inevitably always fail."[99] Health insurance was dangerous. "Insurance against diseases breeds disease." What promotes recovery is "the desire and the necessity of becoming well again and ready for work."[100] Here the deductive method parodies itself: the body's resistance to infection responds to price signals! Mises also evidently rejected Hayek's claim that markets do not reliably reward virtue. He told Ayn Rand: "You have the courage to tell the masses what no politician told them: you are inferior and all the improvements in your conditions which you simply take for granted you owe to the effort of men who are better than you."[101]

Mises's views on pollution were similarly extreme. He is even more insistent on mutual opacity than Hayek. He thinks that people have no knowable preferences other than those that are revealed in their actions. That is why one can't say that government expenditure is ever justified: there's no market to prove that it is. Thus he offers a theoretical backstop for Rothbard's claim that one can't price pollution.[102]

He understands the problem of externalities. Absent appropriate cost internalization, a businessman "will embark upon certain projects only because the laws release him from responsibility for some of the costs incurred."[103] When this happens, "the economic calculation established by them is manifestly defective and their results defective."[104] But like Rothbard and unlike Hayek, he sees no possible answer other than the adjustment of property rights "by a reform of the laws concerning liability for damages inflicted and by rescinding the institutional barriers preventing the full operation of private ownership."[105] The possibility that such an adjustment may be impossible—to take a pertinent example, no one can own the earth's atmosphere and thus be incentivized to keep its greenhouse gases low—is not considered. Neither Harper nor Mises even considers the possibility of pollution that produces cumulative harms, and so can't be remedied by individual tort suits.

It is, of course, impossible to know how important Harper's and Mises's ideas are now in Koch's view of the world. But we have his own testimony that they are very important. They map onto his political behavior fairly precisely.

Koch is one of the richest people in the world, with a net worth of about $50 billion.[106] He inherited a midsize oil refining concern, which is now the second-largest privately held company in the United States. He attributes his success to his capacity to look at the world from a Hayekian perspective. The market is full of unknown information that, if detected and properly used, could create enormous new value, some of which can be captured by the business that exploits it. Throughout his business empire Koch encourages employees to seek such opportunities. And when he invests, he is willing to incubate ideas that will take years to pay off, because his privately held company need not cope with investors' desire for short-term returns. In 1981, he wisely rejected a $20 million offer to take his company public.[107]

His business philosophy aims to apply Hayek's ideas. "Market-based management" is decentralized decision making, giving mechanics, clerks, and factory workers the authority to restructure their own jobs to increase productivity. Salary caps were removed; an unusually capable employee could earn more than his supervisor. "I went out and interviewed people and they were tearful," one Koch consultant reported. "We're talking people without high school degrees, getting paid by the hour, no air-conditioning, at a manufacturing plant, but for these people their lives had really changed. Like one guy, he points out his work area because now he is in charge of it. He decides how the work will come through it. He has authority."[108] Much of his business is private equity, purchasing businesses and making them more profitable. The effects have sometimes been impressive. After Koch bought Georgia-Pacific and applied his management techniques to the company, *Forbes* reported that one of its plants "is producing the same amount of paper towel and toilet paper as before with half the workforce and sharply higher profits."[109]

On the other hand, it's doubtful how much of his wealth comes from this philosophy. He inherited what was already one of the largest private companies in America and reinvested 90 percent of its profits. The most important reason for his success is a spectacularly lucrative state-enforced monopoly—the kind of parasitism that he categorically condemns. The Clean Air Act of 1970 imposed limits on pollution by oil refiners, but it included grandfathering exemptions for existing plants, which were also allowed to expand their operations. One of these was Koch's, near Pine Bend, Minnesota—a refinery that already benefited from a special exemption from federal limits on oil imports. The Pine Bend refinery thus was protected from competition, and became one of very few distributors of gasoline in the Midwestern United States. Koch's books trumpet his business's remarkably above-market returns.[110] Such returns were, however, the inevitable result of his monopoly: he became one of the world's richest men because American consumers paid artificially inflated prices for energy. Which depends on continuing massive use of fossil fuels.[111]

Wallace S. Moyle concludes that the "market-based management" philosophy, which all Koch employees are required to master, is "a jumble of bromides having no relationship to Mises's philosophy other than Koch's own dogged insistence that they go together. Employees trained in MBM invoke the principles of human freedom the way ancient Egyptian bureaucrats invoked the pharaoh's manifestations of Ra: not because it helps them do their jobs but because it pleases the boss."[112]

If this management style captures some of the virtues of an unregulated free market, it also re-creates its pathologies. Georgia-Pacific saw worsened working conditions and a spike in workplace injuries and fatalities.[113] The Koch approach entails, a Texas deputy attorney general wrote in a 2001 affidavit, that

> each section of the Koch pipeline must show a profit, and this profit must increase every quarter. Environmental and safety compliance does not pay off quarter by fiscal quarter, and thus employees are not rewarded or encouraged to strive for safety or compliance. Indeed, safety improvements are regularly delayed or ignored even when recommended by employees. Employees at Koch are told that every decision has to be judged by its economic effect and how the decision will affect the company's profitability.[114]

Any solution to this problem must come from top management—the analogue of central regulation. But Koch is averse to such top-down regulation. So he created a laissez-faire world, where each of his employees has an incentive to produce value and ignore externalities.

And then there's the matter of risk. On August 24, 1996, in a small town fifty miles southeast of Dallas, Texas, Danielle Smalley was packing to leave for college the next day. The seventeen-year-old smelled gas. Her father checked the propane tank beside the trailer they lived in, but it wasn't leaking. Her family was too poor to own a telephone, so she and her friend Jason Stone offered to drive to a neighbor's to make the call to the gas company. Crossing a dry creek bed, the truck stalled. She turned the ignition.

The fireball reached hundreds of feet in the air. The concussion was felt miles away. The teenagers were on fire as they tried to run from the truck. Their hair and clothes were incinerated. The only way to tell the corpses apart was to examine their genitals.

The pipeline, several hundred feet from Smalley's subdivision, had been carrying liquid butane: lighter fluid. It had been constructed in the 1980s, and had a history of corrosion problems from the beginning. Koch Industries had taken it offline in 1993, when a newer pipeline went into operation, but increasing demand made it worth $8 million annually to put the old pipeline back into service. When the company did that, it ran a test that found corrosion in 583 locations in a single forty-six-mile length. It patched the most damaged spots, left the others untouched, and started the butane flowing in 1996. Smalley and Stone were burned alive eight months later.

During the closing statement at the trial, the attorney for Danielle's father projected a clock on a screen and paused for sixty seconds to give the jurors an idea of how long it had taken Danielle to die. "There is no more horrible death than a burn death," he told them. "There is no more horrible way to lose somebody than to see them burn to death in front of your eyes." The jury awarded $296 million, then the largest wrongful death award in American history.[115]

The Kochs have since sold most of their pipelines.

Charles Koch is not an evil person. As I noted in the introduction, he is in fact intensely idealistic. He became deeply involved in politics because he embraced libertarian hopes. Although he has become the most important supporter of the Republican Party, he parts company with it on issues of personal liberty, such as immigration and drug regulation. He denounced Trump's protectionism. He has been willing to endure massive public vilification to fight for what he believes in.

He lives without ostentation. He taught his children that they are entitled to no special privileges on account of their wealth. In 1993, his sixteen-year-old son, Chase, blew through a red light and killed a twelve-year-old boy who was crossing the street. It was rumored that the Kochs would use their influence to avoid charges. Instead, Charles escorted Chase to the boy's funeral, "where every eye on the church was on them," one attendee remembered. Chase later pleaded guilty to a misdemeanor charge of vehicular manslaughter. Charles was determined to keep his billionaire status out of it.[116]

It is the thesis of this book that his political idealism is misplaced—that he is making these sacrifices for an unworthy utopia. Suppose that we lived in the libertarian paradise that he is striving to bring about. Its Hayekian virtues are clear: strong civil liberties, open borders, free trade, an end to rent-seeking regulations.

But in that world, what would protect the Danielle Smalleys? It is, of course, impossible to live in a world without risk. Accidents will happen. We are back to trade-offs between costs and benefits. Someone has to decide which dangers to the public are too great to endure.

That someone should not be Koch.

Here the virtues of entrepreneurship become vices. Competitive pressures, together with the personality traits that make successful capitalists, militate toward sometimes foolhardy risk-taking. It is immensely valuable to have a class of people who are thus reckless with their own money. They produce the innovations that have enriched us all. It is different when the objects of risk are other people's lives. Danielle Smalley was not a coinvestor with Koch Industries. No sane regulator could have permitted butane to flow through decaying pipelines in residential areas.[117]

Koch accurately describes the explosion as "the first and only time since our company's founding in 1940 that one of our pipelines caused the death of innocent bystanders."[118] But reckless risks remain part of the company's strategy with respect to pollution, above all the pollution that creates climate change.

When Koch describes his own philosophy, he emphasizes Hayekian themes.[119] In practice, however, and sometimes even in theory, he's closer to Rothbard: "We've seen libertarians go into government. We've seen the Milton Friedmans and the Alan Greenspans in government, and they haven't decreased it; they've helped say, 'How can this work more efficiently?' which in the end expands government. It is particularly tragic in their case, because they perhaps were very effective when they were out of government. But in government, they get co-opted; they become spokesmen for it and emasculate the opposition."[120]

Anything that government does evidently is illegitimate. Koch writes: "Morally, lowering taxes is simply *defending* property rights. . . . Nor is it valid to say that reducing your taxes simply shifts your 'fair share' of the tax burden to someone else. There is *no* 'fair' share. Our goal is not to *reallocate* the burden of government; our goal is to *roll back* government. We should consistently work to reduce *all* taxes, our own and those of others."[121]

This is tantamount to Rothbard's anarchism: taxation is theft, everything the state does is illegitimate. Another early influence on Koch's views was Robert LeFevre, whose Freedom School he attended and (as early as 1966) funded, and whose attachment to property rights was even more extreme that Rothbard's. LeFevre thought it impermissible to cut ropes a kidnapper had bound you with if they weren't your ropes.[122]

We saw that Rothbard and Rand had difficulty coping with the problem of pollution. So, evidently, does Koch. (He eventually fired Rothbard from the Cato Institute for insubordination, but his viewpoint remains heavily Rothbardian.) The Environmental Protection Agency ranked Koch Industries one of only three companies that was a top ten polluter of air, water, and climate.[123] (Some of this is an inevitable consequence of being one of the largest petroleum companies.) The company has piled immense mounds of petroleum coke, a by-product of oil refining, in poor inner-city neighborhoods in Detroit and Chicago. The dust blew in clouds off the piles, covering homes and entering residents' lungs. Koch Industries maintained that the piles were harmless, but the coke is so laden with toxic chemicals that the Environmental Protection Agency allows no new licenses to burn it in the United States. It is exported to countries with weaker environmental regulations.[124]

Koch thought that regulation should be given the "barest possible obedience" and wrote, "Do not cooperate voluntarily, instead, resist whenever and to whatever extent you legally can. And do so in the name of *justice*."[125] After paying out millions in fines and legal judgments for multiple violations (and a pattern of lying about them), his company made a concerted effort to comply with the law.[126] Reflecting on the experience in 2007, Charles Koch wrote, "we were caught unprepared by the rapid increase in regulation. . . . While business was becoming increasingly regulated, we kept thinking and acting as if we lived in a pure market economy."[127] This way of putting it, Jane Mayer observes, implies that "the problem wasn't so much Koch Industries' conduct as the legal regime in which it operated."[128] Koch writes that increases in regulation "have universally damaged the ability of businesses to create real value and contribute to societal well-being."[129] *Universally?* Barack Obama's assessment of the Koch brothers is fair: "For them, all taxes were confiscatory, paving the road to socialism; all regulations were a betrayal of free-market principles and the American way of life."[130]

Koch now follows a policy he calls "10,000 percent compliance," meaning that 100 percent of laws are to be obeyed 100 percent of the time.[131] The policy was faithfully followed to prevent a recurrence of Koch's environmental violations in the 1990s, which produced criminal charges and millions in fines. There have continued to be dozens of violations of workplace safety rules, which are cheaper to transgress. One worker's death was ruled to be related to "serious" violations, but the resulting fines were only $35,050, and other deaths produced even smaller penalties.[132]

He brought the same organizational skills to his political activities. Americans for Prosperity, the largest of the Koch lobbying organizations, has a staff of twelve hundred, more than three times the staff of the Republican National Committee, with directors in thirty-four states.[133] It routinely hires Republican legislative and campaign operatives, who tend eventually to move back to Republican posts, where they are likely to further Koch agendas. Thus the Koch network is increasingly and pervasively intertwined with the Republican Party.

Koch money has been used to finance primary challenges to Republican officeholders who fail to support positions that the party's own voters reject: reduction or privatization of Social Security and Medicare, massive tax cuts for the rich, elimination of public sector collective bargaining rights, climate change denial. The consequence is a growing Republican unanimity in favor of those positions.[134] Without Koch's persistent support, libertarian ideas might not be influential enough today to attract my attention or yours.

Americans for Prosperity, his political organization, consistently demands tax cuts, the elimination of business regulations, Medicaid cuts, reducing public education funding, and opposing all environmental laws, state and federal.[135] This kind of undiscriminating antistatism is not Hayekian. It is Rothbardian.

The opportunities for mooching and looting are obvious. Citizens for a Sound Economy, an antiregulation advocacy group founded by the Koch brothers in 1985, is a cautionary tale. The group lobbied to cut the federal antitrust enforcement budget after Microsoft donated

$380,000. A telecommunications deregulation proposal followed a $1 million contribution from the phone company US West. A reclamation plan that would reduce cane-growing acreage in the Florida Everglades was opposed after three sugar companies gave $700,000. Major support from the tobacco industry was followed by opposition to tax increases on cigarettes and other tobacco regulations.[136] Koch worries about special interests capturing regulators and extracting favors from them, but students of regulation also worry about what has been called "corrosive capture": disabling government from correcting market failures, thus licensing predatory behavior.[137] Is Dracula a libertarian?

The most important externality that markets are not now accounting for is climate change. There are about $6 trillion in fossil fuel reserves. If all of those are used, the earth's temperature will rise by 16 degrees Fahrenheit.[138] The tolerable upper bound is 3.6 degrees. The largest increase that has happened since life appeared on earth was a 6-degree rise during the end-Permian extinction, 251 million years ago, which wiped out 95 percent of the species on the planet. The 16-degree rise won't happen, because everyone would die first and the burning of fossil fuels would then cease. The danger, according to a Pentagon assessment, "is real, urgent, and severe." A US National Security Strategy report warns: "The change wrought by a warming planet will lead to new conflicts over refugees and resources; new suffering from drought and famine; catastrophic natural disasters; and the degradation of land across the globe."[139]

This is the biggest externality in the history of economics. Coal is the worst fossil fuel: when one accounts for the cost in pollution, every unit that is burned has *negative* economic value.[140] Moreover, from a libertarian standpoint, the effects of climate change involve clear violations of property rights. People in less developed countries, which have not benefited from the industrialization that is producing climate change, are likely to bear immense costs—in some cases, the loss of all their land to rising sea levels.[141]

Koch understands externalities: "When property rights are unclear or ill-defined . . . owners don't benefit from all the value they create and don't bear the full cost from whatever value they destroy. Their use of the property will not be optimally focused on creating value in society. In the past, when owners were not liable for injury to person or property caused by pollution, noise or accidents, they made less effort to prevent them."[142]

Since it isn't possible to have property rights in earth's atmosphere, the next best Hayekian solution is some kind of tax on carbon consumption, so that those who burn it will have to bear the costs they are creating. Unlike direct regulation, a tax leaves decisions to individuals based on their true costs. It creates incentives for just the kind of innovation that, Hayek emphasized, free markets are best at delivering.

Koch has done more than anyone else to block this remedy.

He was promoting skepticism about climate change as early as 1991, when President George H. W. Bush said that he would support a treaty limiting carbon emissions.[143] At that time, Republicans generally accepted the scientific consensus about the danger of climate change, but Koch immediately began funding junk science attacking that consensus.[144] When Bill Clinton proposed an energy tax, which would have taxed fossil fuels but exempted renewable energy, the Koch organization mobilized to defeat it. Koch's principal political lieutenant, Richard Fink, explained: "Our belief is that the tax, over time, may have destroyed our business."[145] Koch similarly beat back Obama's cap-and-trade bill, which would have imposed a price on carbon emissions.[146] Since then, Americans for Prosperity has pushed lawmakers to sign a "No Climate Tax" pledge promising to oppose "any legislation relating to climate change that includes a net increase in government revenue." Those who resisted, such as Indiana Republican senator Richard Lugar, were overwhelmed by Koch money and lost their seats in primary challenges. Representative Bob Inglis, a very conservative South Carolina Republican, had been a close ally of the Kochs until he began learning about the science of climate change and supported a carbon tax. Suddenly Koch Industries stopped returning his phone calls, and helped organize activists who turned his town hall meetings into circuses of angry shouting. He was ultimately defeated in his primary by a previously unknown lawyer named Trey Gowdy who had received generous Koch funding.[147]

It has become clear that any Republican officeholder who proposes to do anything, however market-friendly, about climate change risks being destroyed by Americans for Prosperity. Nearly half of all Republican representatives signed the pledge in the 111th Congress (2009–10). Three-fifths did in the 113th Congress (2013–14). This was not a reflection of constituent preferences: in the districts represented by legislators who signed the pledge, 73 percent of voters support action to regulate carbon dioxide, and 58 percent believe it threatens future generations.[148] It may not even reflect the legislators' own considered views, since they dare not say what they believe. The American Republican Party was, until the rise of far-right European parties, the only political party in the world that denied that the human race faces this threat.[149] On climate policy, Rothbard has triumphed over Hayek.

The coal and petroleum industries, with Koch leading them, have expended enormous efforts to cast doubt on the science and persuade the world that climate change either is not happening or is not caused by human activity.[150] Americans for Prosperity's budget massively increased in response to the threat of restrictions on carbon emissions: $5.7 million in 2007, $10.4 million in 2009, $17.5 million in 2010.[151] AFP, which is tightly controlled by Koch, has worked hard to disseminate preposterous claims that the scientific community is conspiring in order to empower the state.[152] The techniques of lying and distortion are largely copied from the earlier tactics of the tobacco industry when for decades it obfuscated the link between smoking and lung cancer.[153]

Libertarian think tanks, notably the Cato Institute, have been potent sources of the misinformation.[154] Unlike Americans for Prosperity, the think tanks are not Koch's marionettes. Their scholars are free to write what they like. But they are predisposed to be skeptical of claims that there is any problem that demands a large government response.

Koch has offered little explanation for his activism on climate change.

What he has said is manifestly false: that the science is uncertain, that government intervention can accomplish nothing.[155] "These policies that the U.S. government has, others have proposed or promulgated have been just symbolic. They have made essentially no difference. . . . You look at all the progress in having less greenhouse gases and it's due to innovation, not regulation."[156] He said this in 2017, after he had spent millions to defeat any effective government response, and after nearly eight years in which Obama had nonetheless imposed restrictions on automobile and power plant emissions, regulated appliances to force them to become more energy efficient, and invested billions in renewable energy. (In fairness, Koch Nitrogen has been a leader in carbon-capture technology.) Moreover, the carbon tax, which Koch worked so hard to prevent, would have promoted exactly the kind of cutting-edge innovation that he says he wants. If carbon-based energy were priced at its true social cost, then for the past several decades, there would have been greater incentives to devise new forms of green energy. Koch has stood in the path of innovation.

Is Koch deliberately lying? No one is forcing him to grant interviews at all. He may well be saying what he believes. What he believes is what his Rothbardian premises lead him to believe. He never seems to have cared about money for its own sake. On the other hand, as one attempts to reconstruct his thinking, he obviously cares intensely about his business, and his extensive holdings in the petroleum industry are obviously relevant.

A libertarian frame of reference led others to similar conclusions. George Will accused scientists of "trying to stampede the world into a spasm of prophylactic statism."[157] Charles Krauthammer: "Now the experts will regulate your life not in the name of the proletariat or Fabian socialism but—even better—in the name of Earth itself."[158] Ed Crane, the head of the Cato Institute: "Global warming theories just give the government more control of the economy."[159]

The climate change denial movement reached its peak with the election of Donald Trump. Trump, the protectionist who aims to promote favored industries, is obviously no libertarian.[160] His climate denialism probably reflects political opportunism: the notion of a conspiracy of lying scientists, which Koch did so much to promote for years before the 2016 election, fits nicely into the paranoid narrative Trump relies upon. Trump's deregulatory agenda, which rolled back climate change efforts across nearly every federal department, was an echo of Koch's years of work politicizing the issue.[161]

Koch has written that his aspiration is "to create a harmony of interest in society. For business to survive and prosper, it must create real long-term value in society through principled behavior."[162] Whatever long-term value Koch has created is swamped by the greatest catastrophe the human race has faced in many millennia.

This is not libertarianism. It betrays libertarianism's deepest commitments.

That conclusion supports Jane Mayer's assessment:

> One thing I've learned from covering a lot of really powerful people in politics, some of whom have done some pretty nefarious things . . . is that it's very rare that people are sitting there twisting their mustache and saying, "I'm gonna get away with this!" If you ask Charles Koch if he thinks he's doing something good for America, he probably would tell you sincerely that he thinks he is—it's just that his ideology also happens to be exactly what's great for his fortune. He's rationalized this and created an ideology that's perfectly self-serving.[163]

In the early stages of this book, I thought Mayer was too harsh on Koch. I still think her picture of him in her writings understates his idealism. But I'm now persuaded that her overall judgment is sound. Koch replicates in his own life the trajectory that this book traces. He began as a sincere libertarian idealist. He has somehow talked himself into a position that allows him to maximize his wealth by inflicting enormous suffering and loss on other people. Corruption is not always conscious.

The case of Koch may here be paradigmatic. Libertarianism has powerful attractions for many rich people who haven't read Hayek, who aren't interested in theory in the way that Koch is, who simply like the notion that political justice demands that millions of dollars be transferred from the public fisc into their own pockets, and that they be allowed to pollute and defraud with impunity. This book is predicated on the assumption that philosophy matters. The assumption is often sound. Many libertarians sincerely believe what they say, and are open to argument. This book is for them. But it is also true that in politics, particularly politics involving the distribution of wealth, many people's underlying motivations are no more sophisticated than those of a dog who sees a discarded end of a frankfurter on the sidewalk. Theory be damned. I want that money.

Return to the disagreement between Rawls and Hayek, which we discussed in chapter 2. The deepest tension between them concerns the concentration of wealth that modern capitalism engenders. Hayek thought that inequality is a necessary product and continuing precondition of economic growth. Rawls worried that it distorts the exercise of political power: the rich will be able to exercise an undemocratic degree of authority over everyone else. Capitalism "permits very large inequalities in the ownership of real property (productive assets and natural resources) so that the control of the economy and much of political life rests in a few hands."[164]

This exaggerates the correspondence between wealth and political outcomes, which is much more contingent than Rawls thinks.[165] Nonetheless, Rawls was right to worry. In contemporary America, the rich are far better able than the poor to make their policy preferences prevail. Their opinions have much more impact on policy than low-income groups, whose views in practice have no effect at all.[166]

The problem is not just an American one. Oligarchical tendencies are a constant of political life. There has never been an advanced society without large inequalities, and those with wealth have always had disproportionate control over the apparatus of the state.[167] It is not, however, inevitable that state power will be constrained in a Randian way. As noted in chapter 1, there is considerable wealth concentration in the Scandinavian countries and Germany, but they manage to have generous social programs.

America's problem is a peculiar combination of paranoid Randianism at the top and political disorganization and powerlessness at the bottom. Neither—here Hayek can answer Rawls—is a necessary incident of capitalism.

Hayekian thinking deserves some of the blame for America's asymmetry of power. Hayek took for granted that the masses would have their views reflected in politics—perhaps too well reflected, as populist pressures pushed the state toward redistributive taxation. He was especially skeptical of labor unions, which cartelized labor at the expense of the less organized. Reagan's election in 1980 brought a new federal hostility toward unions. Since then, for that and other reasons, the labor movement has collapsed. In the 1950s, 40 percent of private sector workers were unionized. The number in 2012 was less than 7 percent.

There was a lot not to like about the unions. They always were disproportionately white, sometimes corrupt and overtly racist.[168] They benefited a minority of workers at the expense of others. But they did place upward pressure on wages, union and nonunion (since nonunion employers worried about the possibility of unionization), and they were the only source of organized power that the working class had. Their disintegration has promoted monopolies, accelerated economic inequality, and exacerbated the disproportionate political power of the rich.[169] That skewing of politics will persist until new institutions form to represent the interests of people who are not rich. The obstacles to the development of such institutions are formidable, but democracy is in danger without them.[170]

At this point, working class voters feel diffuse rage, ready to be harnessed by demagogues like Trump. This was Obama's biggest failure. The growth of wealth on his watch was spectacular: the net worth of American households and nonprofit institutions grew from $67 trillion in 2007 (the peak before the recession) to $94 trillion in 2017.[171] (You would think that the richest Americans would all have loved him. You would be wrong.)

Yet the employment situation was a catastrophe. "Between early 2000 and late 2016, America's overall work rate for Americans age 20 and older underwent a drastic decline. It plunged by almost 5 percentage points (from 64.6 to 59.7)."[172] Millions of working-age people have left the labor pool altogether.[173] Many live on disability benefits. They spend their days watching television, surfing the internet, often abusing drugs. They are frightened and angry.

Obama barely acknowledged their existence. Here is his final State of the Union address: "The United States of America, right now, has the strongest, most durable economy in the world. We're in the middle of the longest streak of private sector job creation in history. More than 14 million new jobs, the strongest two years of job growth since the '90s, an unemployment rate cut in half."[174] What he said was technically true, but only because the unemployment statistic does not count those who have despaired of finding work and are no longer looking. The employment numbers are also insensitive to the kinds of jobs that are created: insecure, part-time work without benefits counts as "employment."[175] Hayek thought these people would just have to take their chances. If Obama disagreed, he didn't trumpet the fact, and neither did Hillary Clinton.

No wonder so many voters who had supported him turned to Trump, an economic illiterate who at least was talking about creating jobs.

More to the point of this book is the ideology that is increasingly prevalent among the American elite. The top 1 percent of Americans have distinctive political views. They are "much more favorable toward cutting social welfare programs, especially Social Security and health care," and "much less willing than others to provide broad educational opportunities, by 'spend[ing] whatever is necessary to ensure that all children have really good public schools they can go to' or 'mak[ing] sure that everyone who wants to go to college can do so.' They are less willing to pay more taxes in order to provide health coverage for everyone, and they are much less supportive of tax-financed national health insurance." They are also "significantly less favorable to increasing government regulation of Wall Street firms, the health care industry, small business, and especially big corporations."[176] Campaign contributions from the richest families go to Republicans by a roughly 60-to-40 ratio, and that does not include the dark money that is hidden from public scrutiny.[177] The more a politician is dependent on wealthy donors, the farther to the right the politician is likely to be.[178]

Moreover, among the rich, the libertarians are by far the most active and organized. The Kochs have been holding summits—once annual, now twice a year—that billionaires flock to attend. Attendance now often exceeds five hundred, often in husband-and-wife pairs. Guests must pledge a minimum of $100,000 per year. Congressional leaders Mitch McConnell and Paul Ryan, governors Scott Walker and Chris Christie, and presidential hopefuls attend. Some sessions amount to auditions for invited candidates.[179] A single fundraising session raised nearly $900 million.[180] One hotel staffer reported hearing pledges in increments of $5 million.[181] Liberal and moderate billionaires have nothing like the Koch network, and tend to be less interested in political mobilization.

Rawls is right that, in conditions of inequality, the rich can do dreadful things with their power. But that is contingent on what they happen to believe. Calling the rich "conservative," or even "libertarian," obscures the most important aspect of their view. That view is not Hayekian. They are in the grip of a crude version of Rothbard—and many have sunk below Rothbard, all the way to Rand. Their power is dangerous because, in the name of liberty, they want to destroy their fellow citizens' economic security and deprive them of protection from pollution, fraud, and manipulation. The burden of this book has been to show that this philosophy relies on a defective and indefensible conception of liberty.

The growing inequality of wealth in America, and the disproportionate power of money in politics, are of course ubiquitous themes in modern American discourse. Yet the discussion often relies on a strange assumption: that what Americans for Prosperity does is normal political behavior for rich people, a natural consequence of inequality. It is not. Affluence does not entail a compulsion to plunge the lower classes into desperate insecurity.

Revolutionary libertarian ideas are not the sort that usually accompany great wealth. One peculiarity of the Koch network is that wealthy elites in most societies are conservative in the classic sense of the word: averse to abrupt change, reverent toward tradition. They don't want upheaval, because if the world is turned upside down, they might not be able to keep what they have. America's radical rich, on the other hand, are ready to tear it all down for the sake of Rothbard's paradise. The farmer in Aesop's fable killed the goose that laid the golden eggs because he foolishly thought he could get more gold that way. To capture the situation of America's radical rich, one would have to change the story, so that the farmer, gone utterly mad, believed that the goose was conspiring to take all his property.[182] Edmund Burke presciently warned the French revolutionaries that, if they relentlessly attacked all habits of custom and obedience, then the army would see no good reason to obey them, and "some popular general" would end up ruling the country.[183] Within a few years, Napoleon was in charge. America's radical rich should skeptically scrutinize Rothbard's confidence that, after we sweep big government away, their property rights will be secure.

To make the paradox even stranger, America's ruling class is historically unique because it really does have a story to tell on its own behalf. In most societies, the rich have been useless parasites—landlords extorting tribute from peasant farmers, kings demanding tribute from those landlords, and so forth. At best, they offered military protection from other bandits. After the Great Enrichment, on the other hand, America's billionaires can honestly say that the system that enriches them is good for everybody. Everyone has a stake in the status quo. Rawls's philosophy is no threat to us, because around here, inequalities really do benefit everyone.

But the social safety net rankles. Why the constant yearning to blow it up?

The fault line in libertarian thought that we have been exploring in this book mirrors one in conservative thought more generally. Some conservatives have thought that social order, with the hierarchy that accompanies it, benefits everyone.[184] Others, however, have regarded the lower classes as a despicable rabble whose needs count for nothing, who deserve nothing, and who should be crushed if they challenge their betters.[185]

The bit of Hayek that is most neglected, that the American left ignores and that the right finds hardest to digest, is his claim that dumb luck has a lot to do with success in a capitalist economy. Those who are on the bottom are not there because they are worse or less deserving people. Their needs count for as much as anyone's.

Luck plays an important role in every human life. This creates some embarrassment for the winners. They need a coping strategy. We are back to the fundamental problem confronted by Rawls, whose little brothers died of diseases that at least one of them caught from him. It must have haunted him all his adult life. Rawls responded by proposing a social contract that aimed to minimize the effect of arbitrary misfortune, giving the losers, to the extent possible, a stake in the system.

But we can imagine a different, more comfortable response. Young Jack Rawls might have decided that he was better, that his brothers didn't deserve to survive, that they would have been unproductive moochers, that the world is already fundamentally fair.

Would it have been better for him to be in that state? Nozick famously asked us to imagine the opportunity to plug into an "experience machine," a device that would stimulate our brains to imagine good experiences, while we lay motionless in a tank. The moral of that story, he thought, is that we care about more than experience. We want to really be doing things, not imagining ourselves to be doing them. "Someone floating in a tank is an indeterminate blob. . . . Plugging into the machine is a kind of suicide."[186]

A central part of the liberal ideal is to make one's life choices with full awareness of the range of human possibility, to go through life awake rather than sleepwalking. That was why Milton thought God was right to allow Adam to be tempted, so that there could be a genuine choice between good and evil.

A Randian Rawls would have been a more contented person than real Rawls, who all his life contemplated the problem of justice with itchy dissatisfaction. But he would not really have known how to think about his privileged position, or how to justify it. He would be imprisoned in a smug fantasy. Living the dream, indeed.

But of course it is not only the very rich who are drawn to the charms of extreme libertarianism. It is well entrenched in popular culture. In the COVID epidemic, this has had catastrophic consequences.

CONCLUSION

As I was writing this book, the COVID-19 epidemic broke out, killing (as of March 2022) approximately a million Americans and more than six million people worldwide. Two septugenarians, who had been Rothbard's friends and remain among his most prominent disciples, debated government efforts to control the disease.

Lew Rockwell, Rothbard's literary executor and Representative Ron Paul's former chief of staff, in a piece titled "What Would Murray Say About the Coronavirus?," offers a view that is characteristically extreme. He denies that spreading a deadly disease is a form of aggression that could justify restrictions such as quarantines. He quotes Rothbard:

> It is important to insist, however, that the threat of aggression be palpable, immediate, and direct, in short, that it be embodied in the initiation of an overt act. Any remote or indirect criterion—any "risk" or "threat"—is simply an excuse for invasive action by the supposed "defender' against the alleged "threat." . . . Once one can use force against someone because of his "risky" activities, the sky is the limit, and there is virtually no limit to aggression against the rights of others. Once permit someone's "fear" of the "risky" activities of others to lead to coercive action, then any tyranny becomes justified.[1]

Rockwell argues that the mere risk of contagion is not sufficiently "palpable, immediate, and direct" to satisfy Rothbard's conditions. "People are not threatening others with immediate death by contagion. Rather, if you have the disease, you might pass it on to others. Or you might not. What happens if someone gets the disease is also uncertain."[2]

This argument elicited a protest from another old Rothbardian, Walter Block. "The reductio ad absurdum of this point of view is that quarantines are *never* justified, unless death from infection follows 'immediately' that is, only seconds after infection. But this appears to be a conclusion not compatible with any reasonable interpretation of the NAP [nonaggression principle] of libertarianism."[3] That principle "proscribes not only physical invasions but also the threat thereof,"[4] and "if spreading illnesses is not a rights violation, then nothing is."[5]

Block is saner, but Rockwell is more Rothbardian. Rothbard, you'll recall, would require that, before coercive action can be taken against pollution, there must be proof "beyond a reasonable doubt" that there is "strict causality from the actions of the defendant to the victimization of the plaintiff."[6] It follows that an infected person would have the right to freely mingle with others unless the law could meet that impossible burden of proof.

Even if one accepted Block's claim, that spreading disease is a kind of aggression, the state would be weirdly selective in the protection it afforded. Here is the deepest flaw in a political philosophy that holds that the state can do no more than protect rights.[7] The virus itself violates no rights. Quarantines might be justified (if one accepts Block's interpretation of aggression), but other measures that are *less* restrictive of individual liberty—the subsidized research that produced the vaccine, or the use of public money to give free immunizations—would themselves count as impermissible rights violations. Taxation is robbery.

The world is full of misfortunes that humans don't cause but have the power to collectively prevent. They cannot act against those misfortunes unless the state can do more than protect rights. In the libertarian vision of a minimal state, disasters such as climate change and

COVID must be patiently endured. The entire world would become—partly because of libertarianism, it *has* become—like Gene Cranick's home: we must stand back and watch it burn.

The first and most important problem COVID poses for libertarianism is that it calls attention to the fact that, in nature, pandemics sometimes happen. Plagues periodically ravage animal and plant species. Humans are distinctive in our capacity, sometimes, to consciously detect and respond to disease.

That could have happened after the outbreak of COVID in China.[8] Since the George W. Bush administration, the United States had a sophisticated pandemic detection and response apparatus. Shortly before Trump took office, the federal Pandemic Prediction and Forecasting Science and Technology Working Group issued a report describing its increasingly sophisticated use of remote-sensing and AI tools, which, it said, "provide opportunities to mitigate large-scale outbreaks by predicting more accurately when and where outbreaks are likely to occur, and how they will progress." A warning about the outbreak of the disease appeared in the president's briefing book no later than January 1, 2020. There had been a long history of cooperation between American and Chinese public health officials. In normal times, the United States would have quickly offered China its assistance in identifying and controlling the pandemic, as it had done with earlier diseases such as SARS and Ebola. High-level diplomatic pressure and Chinese self-interest might have produced collaboration in containing the outbreak. The worldwide pandemic might never have happened at all.

One of the programs had identified more than 160 different coronaviruses that potentially might develop into pandemics, including the closest known relative to COVID19. The Trump administration, eager to cut government spending, decided to scrap it in September 2019, a few months before the first reports of the new virus in Wuhan, China. Dozens of scientists and analysts were fired.

It is easy to focus on the specific failings of Trump, who never bothered to read his briefings. He had ended most cooperation with China (for example, yanking out all of America's Centers for Disease Control observers), creating an atmosphere of suspicion that made it hard to coordinate in an emergency. The few administration officials who specialized in relations with that country were focused on trade and had no interest in disease.

But the larger lesson is that the complex structures of taxpayer-funded forecasting and international cooperation that Trump smashed are the only imaginable means for containing outbreaks like this one. The problem was not just him. The imperative to shrink the size of government is not peculiar to Trump.

When confronted with problems that only state action can solve, libertarians rarely acknowledge that their philosophy entails death and destruction. Instead, they tend to shut their eyes. We saw that in climate change denial, and again with COVID, most prominently in Richard Epstein's infamous prediction that no more than five hundred Americans would die of the disease.[9]

A second lesson of the pandemic, however, is that sometimes the narrative of stupid, clumsy bureaucrats stifling private initiative is deadly accurate. Once the disease had arrived in the United States, reliable testing was urgently needed. The Centers for Disease Control and Prevention insisted that its test was the only one that could be used, and forbade independent laboratories from developing their own. It turned out that the CDC's test was fatally defective. For more than a month, as the disease was spreading, the CDC wouldn't let other labs develop alternatives or use the very effective test that was being deployed outside the United States by the World Health Organization.[10] This is the kind of story that Milton Friedman liked to tell, and shows yet again that Friedman was right some of the time.

A third lesson is that partnership between big government and big business, of the kind that libertarians loathe, can do wonders. Massive federal spending induced a higher level of risky investment than the private sector would otherwise have been able to muster, while enlisting the stupendous capabilities of Big Pharma. The work undertaken by those businesses built upon decades of state-funded basic science, especially in the expensive field of molecular biology. The speed with which the vaccines were developed is one of the most astounding accomplishments in history. It was quickly manufactured in enormous volumes. The entire American population could have been immunized by summer 2021.

But that didn't happen. The main reason the disease continued to kill tens of thousands was resistance to vaccines and masks in the name of individual liberty.

We saw this show before, in the battle over Obamacare. The Florida attorney general claimed there is a substantive constitutional right "to make personal healthcare decisions without governmental interference."[11] In the first decision invalidating the statute, the Republican-appointed judge declared: "At its core, this dispute is not simply about regulating the business of insurance—or crafting a system of universal health insurance coverage—it's about an individual's right to choose to participate." [12] Another judge, echoing a trope that by then had already become popular, worried that "Congress could require that people buy and consume broccoli at regular intervals."[13] The Broccoli Horrible, as Justice Ruth Bader Ginsburg later called it, brilliantly resonated with conservative fears, tinged with gender anxiety, about the welfare state. Jared Goldstein observes that it "calls to mind an overbearing mother who thinks she knows what's best for us and can tell us what to do," and thus evokes a "nanny state" in which "Mommy is in power."[14] The fear of being thus infantilized and emasculated elicits an instinctive revulsion. The statute's opponents offered a narrative of self-reliance and invulnerability.[15]

The same rhetoric resurfaced during the COVID epidemic, as Republican politicians opposed mask and vaccination requirements. The identification of liberty with disease and death was remarkable, but it was not new. In defiance of the principle that businesses and their customers should be free to transact as they see fit, Florida governor Ron DeSantis attempted to forbid cruise ships—an unusually dangerous environment because of their confined spaces—from requiring passengers to be vaccinated.[16] Governor Kristi Noem of South Dakota, where the disease was spreading with record-breaking speed, wrote: "If folks want to wear a mask, they should be free to do so. Similarly, those who don't want to wear a mask shouldn't be shamed into wearing one. And government should not mandate it. We need to respect each other's decisions."[17] At a Trump rally, she said that the absence of restrictions made South Dakotans "happy because they are free."[18] As of September 1, 2021, one in every five hundred people in South Dakota had died of the disease—among the highest death rates in any state.[19] They rail against socialism, but they resemble Stalin and Mao in their blithe willingness to accept quite a lot of death as the price of their utopia.

Charles Koch, and the organizations he funded, again played a major role in resisting public health efforts. They opposed federal COVID relief, opposed lockdowns and masks, urged that all businesses remain open and that customers and workers continue to mingle unmasked, and promoted a strategy of permitting the disease to roar through the population unchecked in hopes of eventually achieving herd immunity. Some governors followed that strategy, leading to far more deaths than their neighboring states.[20] Koch denounced the "impulse . . . to control people," arguing that the appropriate response was "individual initiative." [21]

Senator Josh Hawley introduced an amendment to the Senate budget resolution restricting federal funding to K–12 schools that mandate COVID vaccines for students, mandate students wear masks, or do not resume in-person instruction.[22] Senator Ted Cruz denounced as "authoritarian" a requirement that federal employees be vaccinated: "The American people must maintain their individual liberties and the right to make their own medical decisions."[23] New Hampshire enacted a "medical freedom" law declaring the "natural, essential and inherent right to bodily integrity, free from any threat or compulsion by government to accept an immunization."[24] Governor Tate Reeves of Mississippi, responding to President Biden's vaccine mandates for private businesses, wrote on Twitter: "This is still America, and we still believe in freedom from tyrants."[25] Libertarian rhetoric led to massive vaccine resistance among Republican voters, which in turn led to (at least) tens of thousands of preventable deaths.[26] The Supreme Court, with a new Republican-appointed majority, invented new constraints on federal power to prevent the Occupational Safety and Health Administration from addressing the greatest danger to workers in history, invalidating a regulation that (the Court did not dispute) would have saved thousands of lives.[27]

This is a new and unfamiliar conception of freedom. Some blamed libertarianism for vaccine and mask resistance,[28] but the standard libertarian story is that people have the right to do what they want as long as they don't hurt anyone else.[29] Now we were told that they have a right of choice even if they *do* hurt or even kill other people. If this is right, then we have been very unfair to drunk drivers, who also are exercising their liberty.[30]

This book engages with philosophical arguments for libertarianism: consequentialist claims like those of Hayek, Epstein, and Mises, and rights-based arguments like those of Rothbard, Nozick, and Rand. But political philosophers sometimes need to get over themselves.[31] Most people hold their political views for reasons that have nothing to do with philosophy. One lesson of the battles over Obamacare and COVID is that libertarianism has a deeper emotional source than either of these: a peculiar vision of the heroic solitary individual, who sustains himself without any external support. *I don't depend on anybody. I can take care of myself.*[32]

It is a delusion. Humans are communal animals. We are born helpless. We are not able to forage for ourselves at birth, like lizards. Without settled practices of mutual aid we would die within a few hours. It is because early hunter-gatherer groups cared for their infants 90,000 years ago that there were still humans 89,900 years ago. And, of course, if we survive into old age, we again become vulnerable and dependent. Admirers of capitalism are fond of quoting the biologist E. O. Wilson's dismissal of socialism: "Karl Marx was right, socialism works, it is just that he had the wrong species." Ants can have systems in which individuals care only about the colony as a whole, but humans do best when they look after themselves. But Wilson's point can easily be overstated. Wilson thought "we get maximum Darwinian fitness by looking after our own survival,"[33] but in fact humans have always lived in cooperative groups.

Humans need both self-reliance and cooperation. Doctrinaire libertarians, too, have the wrong species. Martha Nussbaum observes that some exercises of political power reflect "impossible aspirations to purity, immortality, and nonanimality, that are just not in line with human life as we know it."[34] (Libertarianism's growing popularity is probably a reaction to disappointment about institutions, which tempts people to fantasize that they can get along by themselves.)[35] The burgeoning markets and diversity of lifestyles that libertarians laud can happen only in a state strong enough to operate autonomously from the powerful interests within it.[36] Freedom is an achievement. It is a *collective* achievement. Libertarianism tends to consider people in isolation from the systems in which they are embedded, but the risks to which they are vulnerable are often systemic risks. The notion of a life without vulnerability, dependence, and need is an infantile fantasy.

The issue of health care takes us back to the fire that destroyed Gene Cranick's home—a fire that became the object of national discussion in the context of the battle over Obamacare. The libertarians who defended the firefighters who stood back and watched the house burn were right that if government can protect everyone against fire, then logically it would have the power to address a huge range of misfortunes, and that this entails a much bigger government than they would like. Those misfortunes—the undeserved poverty that free markets inevitably produce, crumbling infrastructure, pollution, dizzying economic cycles of boom and bust, financial disaster when jobs disappear, addiction, commercial fraud, dangerous workplaces and consumer products, pervasive discrimination, climate catastrophe, untreated disease and premature death—are all like Cranick's fire. They are disasters that don't derive from provable rights violations, which extreme libertarianism therefore demands that we passively watch and endure. It hopes to persuade us to call this misery freedom.

ACKNOWLEDGMENTS

In some ways, I've been writing this book all my life. I first was drawn to academic work when, as a student, I read the literature on gay rights and found that it was largely based on the idea that the state should never interfere with transactions between consenting adults. I was less comfortable than most of the scholars in that area with a principle that entailed that heroin should be available at the corner store, and so, in my earliest work, tried to reformulate the claim in terms of equality rather than liberty.

In my doctoral dissertation, I found myself pushing back against libertarian objections to antidiscrimination law. In so doing, I first encountered the generosity and stubbornness of Richard Epstein, whom I couldn't convince then and won't convince now.

I've found myself pushing back against libertarian assumptions many times. This book is in part a response to the provocation of John Tomasi's *Free Market Fairness*, an important synthesis of Rawls and Hayek. My approach is not his, but reading him helped to set me on this path.

I was drawn deeper into the specifically libertarian literature by the Obamacare case. In the course of writing about that litigation, which culminated in *The Tough Luck Constitution and the Assault on Health Care Reform*, I read *Atlas Shrugged*. (No, unlike everyone else, I didn't read it in high school.) I found it tough going, barely mentioned it in the book, and was sorry that I had worked so hard with so little result. To some extent, this project began as a manifestation of the fallacy of sunk costs, undertaken in the spirit of the man who has lost $100 at the blackjack table and is determined to get it back.

Among the friends and colleagues who have either endured my musings on this topic or read drafts are Albert Alschuler, Mark Alznauer, Jack Balkin, Peter Boettke, David Boaz, Jason Brennan, Jennifer Burns, Steve Calabresi, Henry Cohen, Peter DiCola, Richard Epstein, James Farr, Sam Fleischacker, Samuel Freeman, Christopher Freiman, Paul Gowder, Todd Henderson, Geoffrey Kabaservice, Josh Kleinfeld, Kitty Koppelman, Margaret Koppelman, Nancy Koppelman, Erica Landsberg, Christopher Leonard, Steve Lubet, Eric Mack, Jamie Mayerfeld, John McGinnis, James Nelson, Martha Nussbaum, Jim Pfander, Valerie Quinn, Marty Redish, Nadav Shoked, Vivasvan Soni, Matt Spitzer, Max Stearns, John Tomasi, Jim Tourtelott, Barry Weingast, Dan Wikler, Kevin Vallier, Matt Zwolinski, and Todd Zywicki. I'm sure I've left many off this list who deserves an equal degree of thanks; apologies for the omissions. Thanks also to audiences at the Nuffield Workshop in Political Theory, Oxford University, the University of Texas School of Law, Northeastern University, Notre Dame Law School, the Liberty Fund, and the Northwestern Law faculty workshop.

The manuscript was the object of mini-courses at Northwestern Law in the winters of 2017–18 and 2020–21, where it was subjected to withering critiques by some very smart students.

Special thanks to the Liberty and Law Center at Antonin Scalia Law School, George Mason University, and the Searle Center on Law, Regulation, and Economic Growth, Northwestern University, for hosting conferences in March 2018 to discuss the manuscript, and to David Bernstein, Ilya Somin, Daniel Polsby, Chris Newman, Tom Palmer, Nigel Ashford, Randy Barnett, Walter Olson, Trevor Burrus, Jonathan Adler, Samuel Bagenstos, Brian Doherty, William A. Galston, Brink Lindsey, Deirdre McCloskey, Steven Teles, and Will Wilkinson for attending.

The fabulous research assistance of Tom Gaylord has been

indispensable. Emily Roznowski and Deepa Ramakrishnan German also did research for me. Jeff Britting of the Ayn Rand Institute provided archival materials. Jane Brock helped to prepare the manuscript.

A portion of chapter 3 previously appeared as Andrew Koppelman, "Involving Orcs," review of *Mean Girl: Ayn Rand and the Culture of Greed*, by Lisa Duggan, *New Rambler*, Dec. 11, 2019. Reprinted by permission.

Special thanks to my publicist, Sarah Russo, and my agents, Andrew Stuart and Paul Starobin, for helping me find my way to St. Martin's, and to my editor, Michael Flamini, for his confidence in this project and generous help with the manuscript.

ANALYTICAL TABLE OF CONTENTS

Introduction *1*

Libertarian political philosophy makes astonishing cruelty a political ideal *1*

but its best known form is a corrupted variant *4*

Modern libertarianism began with Friedrich Hayek's plea for freedom and prosperity *8*

Now it takes multiple forms *9*

some of them not very nice *10*

Hayek offers a sophisticated analysis and partial defense of the inequality that free markets generate *14*

unlike the delusional romanticism of Murray Rothbard, Robert Nozick, and Ayn Rand *16*

Libertarianism has been captured by opportunists who want to inflict harm with impunity, and now actively promote environmental catastrophe *18*

Even in its most attractive form, libertarianism is an inadequate political philosophy, and points beyond itself *21*

1. Prosperity: Hayek's case against socialism *25*

In the 1930s, central economic planning was embraced by most intellectuals and most of the public *25*

Modern libertarianism was born with Hayek's protest against that idea *27*

Hayek introduced the idea of markets as a way to cope with too much information—more than any planner could know......30

And thought that, if the human race was going to become less poor, undeserved inequality had to be accepted......35

But because inequality was undeserved, redistribution was not unjust, although sometimes imprudent......38

Hayek worried about abuses of government power, but some programs that scared him, such as Social Security, have promoted individual liberty......43

He didn't categorically oppose regulation. He thought it was sometimes imperative......46

Overregulation is destructive, but so is underregulation......53

Hayek understood that free markets don't suppose that everyone is self-seeking, but depend on shared traditions and ideals in order to operate. Police and courts at least must be trustworthy. Similarly with other regulators......57

There are deep tensions between Hayek's embrace of tradition and his commitment to progress, and between ordinary people's need for stability and the demands of a dynamic economy. The task of navigating these tensions can't be reduced to mechanical rules......58

Hayek's views have been restated, in a crude antistatist form, by Milton Friedman......64

And, more subtly, by Richard Epstein......66

Hayek's framework provides an appropriate field of battle between the libertarian right, suspicious of government intervention, and the social democratic left, concerned about the immediate needs of the least well off. Both will sometimes be correct......70

Hayek, however, has no coherent conception of rights, and rights are the moral center of libertarianism. For such a conception, we must turn to other authors.......71

2. Rights: The nonlibertarian liberalism of Locke and Rawls......74

Libertarian rights claims usually rest on a commonsensical story about property......74

Which purportedly derives from John Locke, the philosopher of the American founding......77

But Locke's arguments don't support absolute property rights......79

People are entitled to what they have worked to produce......82

The institution of property is good for everyone. 83

But these principles don't mean that the poor have a moral duty to starve 84

Locke doesn't justify everything that happens in free markets 87

A fair social contract benefits the worst-off members of society 94

The libertarian claim, that a safety net violates property rights, misunderstands what property is 97

A social contract must give everyone reasons to support it 100

3. Tyranny: The fantasy worlds of Rothbard, Nozick, and Rand 107

In the late 1960s, libertarianism morphed into romantic anarchism 107

Led by Murray Rothbard, the most influential philosopher you never heard of 111

Rothbard proposed an indefensible fetishization of absolute property rights 113

And his case against regulation is even weaker 119

Robert Nozick, the most academically respectable libertarian, borrows a lot from Rothbard, including his mistakes 124

The most widely read libertarian is Ayn Rand, whose fiction, however, doesn't quite support her enthusiasm for unregulated capitalism 130

Rand's philosophical arguments are even worse than Rothbard's 134

Rand's ideal is a lot less attractive than Hayek's 143

Rights claims shouldn't rely on melodramatic fantasy 149

4. Nanny: The case for (some) paternalism 151

Libertarians don't like it when the state interferes with people's choices ... 151

But sometimes such interference makes us freer, for instance by making addictive drugs hard to get 154

In order to be free, we need to be capable of governing ourselves, and that doesn't happen automatically 158

Sometimes paternalistic interference makes it more likely that we will get what we want 161

Libertarians are sometimes so eager to defer to choices that they can't see when people are deceived and defrauded 168

Free markets depend on trust, and when law tolerates fraud, it undermines that trust 171

5. Liberty: The case for antidiscrimination law 173

Libertarians think antidiscrimination law violates business owners' rights 173

but discrimination sometimes systematically blocks access to freedom and prosperity 174

Prohibitions of discrimination can promote people's ability to shape their own lives 180

Here libertarianism is an obstacle, not a path, to liberty 183

6. Moochers: How libertarianism was corrupted and betrayed 187

Libertarians have become an increasingly powerful faction within the Republican Party 188

Their philosophy shaped the fight against Obamacare 192

and is a continuing threat to preconditions of successful capitalism such as basic research and infrastructure investment 201

A reflexive bias against government action is dangerous 205

Charles Koch has been an enthusiastic libertarian for more than half a century 206

He cites the same philosophy as the basis of his political activism 217

which has accelerated disastrous climate change, benefited his business by harming others, and so betrayed libertarianism's deepest commitments ... 218

The influence of money on politics is a problem for democracy, but libertarianism's popularity among billionaires makes it worse 223

Conclusion: Libertarianism and the COVID epidemic 230

COVID revealed anew the strengths and pathologies of libertarianism 230

And showed that its appeal, for many, is a childish fantasy of self-sufficiency 236

NOTES

INTRODUCTION

1. Friedrich Hayek, *The Constitution of Liberty*, 113 (1960).
2. Glenn Beck, *Glenn Beck Program*, Oct. 5, 2010, radio broadcast, transcript, https://www.glennbeck.com/content/articles/article/198/46276/.
3. Roy Edroso, "Libertarian Fire Department Lets House Burn Because Owner Didn't Pay $75; Rightbloggers Applaud Free Market, Suffering," *Village Voice*, Oct. 11, 2010.
4. The fire chief did state in a press conference: "This tragedy was not the fault of the South Fulton Fire Department or the city of South Fulton, but rather the failure, the fault was the failure of the Cranick family not to pay that subscription." Christy Hendricks, "Fire Chief Responds to Questions After Home Left to Burn," KVVS12, Oct. 6, 2010.
5. Mara Liasson, *Morning Edition*, NPR, May 25, 2001.
6. Americans for Tax Reform, The Taxpayer Protection Pledge Signers: 112th Congressional List, Americans for Tax Reform, 2012.
7. Bruce Watson, "Tennessee Fire Ignites National Debate on Public Services," AOL.com, Oct. 7, 2010.
8. Chad Lampe, Tenn. "Town Fights Fire with Money," *Weekend Edition*, NPR, March 18, 2012. As of this writing, the fire department confirmed that the arrangement is still in force.
9. NBC News, "'No Pay, No Spray' Case: Firefighters 'Threatened,'" Oct. 7, 2010.
10. Kevin Williamson, "Pay-for-Spray Fire Department: Doing the Right Thing," The Corner, *National Review*, Oct. 4, 2010.
11. NBC News, "No Pay, No Spray."
12. Michael Laris, "Tenn. Family's Loss After Not Paying Fire Fee Resonates in Montgomery," *Wash. Post*, Oct. 13, 2010.

13. Joseph Simonson, "Bernie Sanders: Soviet Socialism 'Not My Thing' but 'Denmark and Sweden Do Very Well,'" *Wash. Examiner*, Apr. 6, 2019. Earlier in his career, he was far more radical. In a 1976 interview, he said, "I favor the public ownership of utilities, banks and major industries." Andrew Kaczynski and Nathan McDermott, "Bernie Sanders in the 1970s urged nationalization of most major industries," CNN, Mar. 14, 2019.
14. Jennifer Schuessler, "Hayek: The Back Story," review of *The Road to Serfdom*, by Friedrich Hayek, *N.Y. Times*, July 9, 2010, Sunday Book Review.
15. Erik Hayden, "'Pay-to-Spray' Fire Fighters Let House Burn Down," *Atlantic*, Oct. 5, 2010. Broadcaster Keith Olbermann declared that the house fire revealed "the America envisioned by the Tea Party." Olbermann, *Countdown with Keith Olbermann*, MSNBC, Oct. 4, 2010.
16. Fred L. Block, *Capitalism: The Future of an Illusion* (2018).
17. David Boaz, *The Libertarian Mind: A Manifesto for Freedom*, 6 (2015).
18. Jason Brennan, *Libertarianism: What Everyone Needs to Know*, xi (2012)
19. Jan Narveson, *The Libertarian Idea*, 175 (1988).
20. Tibor Machan, "Preface," in *The Libertarian Reader*, vii (Tibor Machan, ed. 1982).
21. Brian Doherty, *Radicals for Capitalism: A Freewheeling History of the Modern American Libertarian Movement*, 3 (2007).

    It may be helpful to distinguish libertarianism from two similar philosophies: classical liberalism and neoliberalism. These are often lumped together. John Tomasi is not idiosyncratic when he uses *libertarianism* to denote "a family of liberal views that gives exceptionally high priority to the economic liberties of capitalism." *Free Market Fairness*, xxv (2012).

    Doherty's definition is stricter, and it is the one that I follow in this book. Classical liberalism, which arguably falls within Tomasi's definition, was a nineteenth-century doctrine opposed to feudalism and nationalism, which aimed at unimpeded free trade and careers open to talents. It had no deep commitments concerning regulation to prevent external harms. Most of the regulations it opposed had a different purpose, the protection of monopolies and of the privileges of the nobility. Neoliberalism, which developed in response to the collapse of the Austro-Hungarian Empire after World War I, aims to constrain state interference with markets in order to promote economic growth. Noneconomic questions, such as paternalistic legislation or antidiscrimination law, do not concern either of these. Neither embraces the absolute antistatism of libertarianism. Hayek was a variety of classical liberal, and was a founder of neoliberalism, but he is of interest here as an early precursor of libertarianism, as defined by Doherty. Libertarianism begins with one strand of Hayek's thought and takes it to extremes that Hayek himself rejected.
22. Charles Murray, *What It Means to Be a Libertarian: A Personal Interpretation*, xi (1997).

23. See Brennan, *Libertarianism: What Everyone Needs to Know*, 24–25, 172–73.
24. I cannot address them all. For further discussion, see Doherty, *Radicals for Capitalism*. Wilfred Cantwell Smith's observation, that no one can know enough about Buddhism or Hinduism to say that either is true or false and know what he is saying, is pertinent. *Questions of Religious Truth*, 74 (1967).
25. The federal district court decisions are discussed in Andrew Koppelman, "Bad News for Mail Robbers: The Obvious Constitutionality of Health Care Reform," 121 *Yale L.J. Online* 1 (2011).
26. Transcript of Oral Argument, Dept. of Health and Human Services v. Florida (No. 11–398), Supreme Court of the United States, Mar. 27, 2012, 20.
27. Id. at 29.
28. Trump, however, gave it new friends on the left. Andrew Koppelman, "Liberal Conservatism," review of *How to Be a Conservative*, by Roger Scruton, *New Rambler*, Aug. 26, 2020.
29. Andrew Koppelman, "Socialists for Capitalism," *Niskanen Center* (blog), Feb. 2, 2021.
30. Bowers v. Hardwick, 478 U.S. 186, 194 (1986).
31. Andrew Koppelman, "The Miscegenation Analogy: Sodomy Law as Sex Discrimination," 98 *Yale L. J.* 145 (1988). Many years later, the Supreme Court embraced the argument, in litigation in which I participated. See Brief of Amici Curiae William N. Eskridge Jr. and Andrew Koppelman, Bostock v. Clayton County, Georgia, No. 17–1628, 2019 WL 2915046.
32. Hayek was more skeptical of programs that go beyond a minimum income to maintain middle-class status for some, like Social Security. As I will argue, this position was inconsistent with his more basic commitments.
33. Jason Brennan, "Rawls' Paradox," 18 *Const. Polit. Econ.* 287, 294-95 (2007), citing D. Dollar and A. Kraay, "Growth is good for the poor," 7 *J. Econ. Growth* 195 (2002).
34. World Bank Group, *Poverty and Shared Prosperity 2016: Taking On Inequality* (2016.)
35. Homi Kharas and Kristofer Hamel, "A Global Tipping Point: Half the World Is Now Middle Class or Wealthier," Brookings Institution, Sept. 27, 2018.
36. Rand Paul, *The Tea Party Goes to Washington*, 35 (2011).
37. *Atlas Shrugged*, 961 (1957; Signet 1996).
38. Robert Nozick, *Anarchy, State, and Utopia*, 79 (1974).
39. Sarah A. Donovan et al., "The U.S. Income Distribution: Trends and Issues," *Cong. Res. Serv. Rept.* R44705, Jan. 13, 2021, 14; Edward N. Wolff, "Household Wealth Trends in the United States, 1962 to 2019: Median Wealth Rebounds . . . But Not Enough," *NBER Working Paper* 28383, Jan. 2021, 43.
40. Wolff , *Household Wealth Trends*, 14.
41. Lane Kenworthy, "Why the Surge in Income Inequality?," 46 *Contemp. Sociology* 1, 2 (2017).

42. Richard B. Freeman, *America Works: The Exceptional U.S. Labor Market* 41–57 (2007); Congressional Budget Office, "Trends in the Distribution of Household Income Between 1979 and 2007" (Oct., 2011).
43. Joseph E. Stiglitz, *The Price of Inequality*, 3 (rev. ed. 2013).
44. Jacob S. Hacker, *The Great Risk Shift: The New Economic Insecurity and the Decline of the American Dream* (rev. ed. 2019).
45. Lane Kenworthy, *Social Democratic Capitalism*, 134–36 (2020).
46. William D. Nordhaus, "Schumpeterian Profits in the American Economy: Theory and Measurement," *NBER Working Paper* No. w10433, Apr. 2004.
47. See Jake Rosenfeld, *What Unions No Longer Do* (2014).
48. To some extent, they already have. See Stiglitz, *The Price of Inequality*, 35-64; Brink Lindsey and Steven Teles, *The Captured Economy: How the Powerful Enrich Themselves, Slow Down Growth, and Increase Inequality* (2017); Robert B. Reich, *Saving Capitalism* (2016); Luigi Zingales, *A Capitalism for the People* (2012).
49. Lindsey and Teles, *The Captured Economy*, 64–89; Neil Netanel, Copyright's Paradox, 54–80 (2010).
50. The libertarian roots of partisan opposition to the Affordable Care Act are explored in Andrew Koppelman, *The Tough Luck Constitution and the Assault on Health Care Reform* (2013).
51. John Locke, *Two Treatises of Government*, 2.34, 291 (Peter Laslett ed. 1988).
52. It may be helpful to clarify the concept of "growth," a term that has become controversial because it is sometimes understood to mean consuming an increasing, unsustainable volume of natural resources. The aim of economic analysis, however, is to satisfy human wants, a goal that is sometimes but not always connected to ecological damage. The concept of growth more appropriately refers to technological progress, which has been the actual source of prosperity. If that progress continues, there is no reason why we cannot devise means to raise humanity's standard of living more effectively than we do now, with less or even no environmental damage. See Fred L. Block, *Capitalism: The Future of an Illusion* 183–88 (2018).
53. See, e.g., Tomasi, *Free Market Fairness*; Matt Zwolinski, "A Hayekian Case for Free Markets and a Basic Income," in *The Future of Work, Technology, and Basic Income* (Michael Cholbi and Michael Weber eds. 2019); Andrew Lister, "The 'Mirage' of Social Justice: Hayek Against (and for) Rawls," 25 *Critical Rev*. 409 (2013); Brink Lindsey, "Liberaltarians," *New Republic*, Dec. 4, 2006; Will Wilkinson, "Is Rawlsekianism the Future?," *Cato at Liberty* blog, Dec. 4, 2006; Don Arthur, "Hayek and Rawls: An Unlikely Fusion," Evatt Foundation (2008), http://evatt.org.au/papers/hayek-rawls.html.

CHAPTER 1: PROSPERITY

1. F. A. Hayek, "The Road to Serfdom, an Address Before the Economic Club of Detroit," Apr. 23, 1945, quoted in Bruce Caldwell, introduction, in *The Road to Serfdom: Text and Documents*, 20 (2007).
2. Susan Previant Lee and Peter Passell, *A New Economic View of American History*, 362–63 (1979).
3. Angus Burgin, *The Great Persuasion: Reinventing Free Markets Since the Great Depression* 13 (2012); see also Bruce Caldwell, *Hayek's Challenge: An Intellectual Biography of F. A. Hayek*, 232-37 (2004).
4. On the early history of the Austrian School, see Janek Wasserman, *The Marginal Revolutionaries: How Austrian Economists Fought the War of Ideas* (2019); Quinn Slobodian, *Globalists: The End of Empire and the Birth of Neoliberalism* (2018).
5. Burgin, *The Great Persuasion*, 24.
6. Quoted in Alan Ebenstein, *Friedrich Hayek: A Biography*, 91 (2003).
7. Quoted in Bruce Caldwell, *Introduction*, in *The Road to Serfdom: Text and Documents*, 12 (2007).
8. Kim Phillips-Fein, *Invisible Hands: The Businessmen's Crusade Against the New Deal*, 10–13 (2009).
9. According to the leading history of post-World War II American conservatism, its publication "enabled those who felt routed to draw the lines and confidently take sides once more." George H. Nash, *The Conservative Intellectual Movement in America Since 1945* 6 (rev. ed. 1996).
10. Eric Foner, Free Soil, *Free Labor, Free Men: The Ideology of the Republican Party Before the Civil War* (1970). Early Republicans did resemble contemporary libertarians in their tendency to regard poverty as the fault of the poor, even in times of economic depression, such as the aftermath of the Panic of 1857. Id., 23–29.
11. Friedrich Hayek, *The Constitution of Liberty*, 11 (1960).
12. Franklin D. Roosevelt, State of the Union address, Jan. 6, 1941.
13. Hayek, *The Constitution of Liberty*, 12.
14. Roosevelt, State of the Union address, 1941.
15. John Tomasi catalogues libertarians who emphasize the benefits of free markets for the poor in *Free Market Fairness*, 123–161 (2012).
16. Randy Barnett, *Our Republican Constitution: Securing the Liberty and Sovereignty of We the People*, 21 (2016). The same crude narrative runs through George F. Will, *The Conservative Sensibility* (2019).
17. Franklin D. Roosevelt, State of the Union address, Jan. 11, 1944.
18. Caldwell, *Hayek's Challenge*, 3.
19. Alan Ebenstein, *Friedrich Hayek: A Biography*, 293; Brian Doherty, *Radicals for Capitalism: A Freewheeling History of the Modern American Libertarian Movement* 11 (2007).

20. Hayek, *The Constitution of Liberty*, 7.
21. Phillips-Fein, *Invisible Hands*, 39.
22. Burgin, *The Great Persuasion*, 87–91. One key paragraph in *The Road to Serfdom*, approving of "an extensive system of social services" and limits on "the smoke of factories," did however survive the abridgment, so careful readers should have understood that Hayek was not advocating a minimal state. See *The Reader's Digest* condensed version of *The Road to Serfdom* 38 (Institute of Economic Affairs 1991).
23. Matt Zwolinski and John Tomasi, *The Individualists: Radicals, Reactionaries, and the Struggle for the Soul of Libertarianism* (forthcoming 2022).
24. Friedrich Hayek, *The Road to Serfdom*, 49 (1944; rev. ed. 1976).
25. Friedrich Hayek, "The Use of Knowledge in Society," 35 *Am. Econ. Rev.* 519 (1945); Friedrich Hayek, "Competition as a Discovery Procedure," in *The Essence of Hayek* 254 (Chiaki Nishiyama and Kurt R. Leube eds., 1984).
26. Wasserman, *The Marginal Revolutionaries*, 151.
27. Friedrich Hayek, *Law, Legislation, and Liberty, v. 2: The Mirage of Social Justice*, 2 (1976).
28. Deirdre McCloskey, *Bourgeois Equality: How Ideas, Not Capital or Institutions, Enriched the World*, xii (2016).
29. Hayek, *The Constitution of Liberty*, 36.
30. Friedrich Hayek, "The Moral Element in Free Enterprise," in *Studies in Philosophy, Politics, and Economics*, 233 (1967).
31. Hayek, *Law, Legislation, and Liberty, vol. 2*, 3.
32. See Simon Griffiths, *Engaging Enemies: Hayek and the Left* (2014).
33. Timothy Stoltzfus Jost, *Health Care at Risk: A Critique of the Consumer-Driven Movement*, 114 (2007). Some libertarian writers evade this point by silently conflating human wants with wants that markets can satisfy; see Alan Haworth, *Anti-Libertarianism: Markets, Philosophy, and Myth*, 30–31, 60–61, 110 (1994).
34. John Rawls, *A Theory of Justice* 276/244 rev. (1971; revised ed. 1999).
35. Merriam-Webster.com Dictionary, s.v. "socialism," accessed Feb. 12, 2022, https://www.merriam-webster.com/dictionary/socialism.
36. Frank Newport, "Democrats More Positive About Socialism Than Capitalism," Gallup, Aug. 13, 2018.
37. Frank Newport, "The Meaning of 'Socialism' to Americans Today," Gallup, Oct. 4, 2018.
38. Sam Frizell, "Here's How Bernie Sanders Explained Democratic Socialism," *Time*, Nov. 19, 2015.
39. The confusion about the term was promoted by Republicans' habit of calling President Obama a socialist. See Andrew Koppelman, "A Short Guide to Obama and Socialism," *Balkinization* blog, Mar. 9, 2009.
40. See, e.g., David French, "Dear Democrats, Ownership Isn't Theft," *National Review*, Dec. 20, 2017.

41. Hayek, *Law, Legislation, and Liberty*, vol. 2, 71.
42. Id., 74.
43. Luigi Zingales, *A Capitalism for the People*, 3, 17 (2012).
44. Hayek's efficiency argument, that capital should be allocated to those who have shown their skill in investing it, presumes that success is not all a matter of luck. David Miller, *Principles of Social Justice*, 188 (1999).
45. Hayek, "The Moral Element," 234–35. John Rawls and T.M. Scanlon embrace the same idea. T.M. Scanlon, *Why Does Inequality Matter?* 36–37 (2018).
46. On the complex and interdependent relationship between free markets and ideas of virtue, see Deirdre McCloskey, *The Bourgeois Virtues: Ethics for an Age of Commerce* (2006).
47. Hayek, *Law, Legislation, and Liberty, vol. 2*, 131. Today this claim is anachronistic, as the gains from growth increasingly concentrate at the top.
48. Hayek, *The Constitution of Liberty*, 42–43.
49. Id., 394.
50. William D. Nordhaus, "Schumpeterian Profits in the American Economy: Theory and Measurement," *NBER Working Paper* No. 10433, Apr. 2004.
51. McCloskey, *Bourgeois Equality*; Deirdre McCloskey, *Bourgeois Dignity: Why Economics Can't Explain the Modern World* (2010).
52. Hayek, *The Constitution of Liberty*, 320.
53. This is anachronistic, as modern colossi like Apple and Samsung race to outdo each other in the speed of innovation.
54. Hayek, *The Constitution of Liberty*, 320.
55. Id.
56. Friedrich Hayek, *Law, Legislation, and Liberty, v. 3: The Political Order of a Free People* 79 (1979).
57. David Schmidtz, *Elements of Justice*, 140–49 (2006).
58. Hayek, *The Constitution of Liberty*, 129.
59. Id., 42.
60. Id., 44.
61. Nancy Koppelman, *One for the Road: Mobility in American Life, 1787–1905*, unpublished PhD diss., Emory University, 1999; Margaret Guroff, *The Mechanical Horse: How the Bicycle Reshaped American Life* (2016).
62. Hayek, *The Constitution of Liberty*, 44.
63. Id., 88.
64. Id., 448. Here we see a curious convergence between Hayek's views and those of Karl Marx. Marx, too, emphasized that no one, not even the owners of the biggest businesses, is in control of a capitalist economy: man "treats other men as means, degrades himself to the role of a mere means, and becomes the plaything of alien powers." "On the Jewish Question," in *The Marx-Engels Reader* (Robert C. Tucker ed., 2d ed. 1978), 34. The market has its own logic, which disciplines employer as well as employee: "In bourgeois society capital is independent and has individuality, while the living person

is dependent and has no individuality." Marx, *The Communist Manifesto*, in *The Marx-Engels Reader*, 485. It was this alienation that was the deepest wrong of capitalism: "The process of production has the mastery over man, instead of being controlled by him." Karl Marx, *Capital, v. 1*, 81 (tr. Samuel Moore and Edward Aveling, 1967). Hayek agreed that this resistance to conscious control was a central fact about capitalism, but regarded it as the necessary precondition of freedom.

65. Hayek, *The Constitution of Liberty*, 91.
66. Id., 90.
67. Ebenstein, *Friedrich Hayek: A Biography*, 45.
68. It is thus a misunderstanding to say that Hayek's defense of inequality posits a "heroic legislator of value" or "the notion that the freedom of some is worth more than the freedom of others." Corey Robin, *The Reactionary Mind: Conservatism from Edmund Burke to Donald Trump*, 158–59 (2d ed. 2018).
69. Lane Kenworthy, "Income Distribution," in *The Good Society*, July 2020, https://lanekenworthy.net/income-inequality/.
70. Will Wilkinson, "Don't Abolish Billionaires," *N.Y. Times*, Feb. 21, 2019.
71. US Bureau of the Census, Statistical Abstract of the United States: 1967, 88th ed., 321 (GNP of $355.3 billion in 1950, $487.8 billion in 1960.)
72. Lane Kenworthy, *Social Democratic Capitalism*, 38–65 (2020).
73. Thomas Piketty et al., "Optimal Taxation of Top Labor Incomes: A Tale of Three Elasticities," 6 *Am. Econ. J.: Econ. Pol'y* 230 (2014); Thomas L. Hungerford, "Taxes and the Economy: An Economic Analysis of the Top Tax Rates Since 1945 (Updated)," Cong. Research Service, Dec. 12, 2012; *Does Atlas Shrug? The Economic Consequences of Taxing the Rich* (Joel B. Slemrod ed. 2000).
74. Hayek, *The Road to Serfdom*, 120–21.
75. Id., 37.
76. Bernard Harcourt, "How Paul Ryan enslaves Friedrich Hayek's The Road to Serfdom," *The Guardian*, Sept. 12, 2012.. Hayek spent considerable effort attacking the idea of "social justice," but what he meant by the term was intervention in the operation of the economy to ensure just outcomes, not a social minimum. For clarification, see Tomasi, *Free Market Fairness*, 142–61.
77. Hayek, *Law, Legislation, and Liberty, vol. 3*, 55.
78. Hayek, *The Constitution of Liberty*, 257.
79. Nicholas Wapshott, *Keynes Hayek: The Clash That Defined Modern Economics* 200 (2011).
80. Friedrich Hayek, *Law, Legislation, and Liberty, v. 1: Rules and Order* 142 (1973).
81. Hayek, *Law, Legislation, and Liberty, vol. 3*, 56.
82. Kenworthy, *Social Democratic Capitalism*, 2–3.

83. Hayek, *Law, Legislation, and Liberty, vol. 1*, 142.
84. Hayek, *The Constitution of Liberty*, 259.
85. Id., 297.
86. Id., 294.
87. Id., 297.
88. Hayek, Preface, in *The Road to Serfdom*, 1976 ed., xx.
89. Elizabeth Anderson, *Common Property: How Social Insurance Became Confused With Socialism*, Boston Review, July 25, 2016.
90. Hayek, *Law, Legislation, and Liberty, vol. 1*, 142.
91. Hayek, *The Constitution of Liberty*, 229.
92. Charles Reich, "The New Property," 73 *Yale L.J.* 733, 771 (1964). The article persuaded the Supreme Court to broaden its understanding of constitutionally protected property rights. Goldberg v. Kelly, 397 U.S. 254 (1970).
93. Reich, "The New Property," 773, quoting Walter Lippmann, *The Method of Freedom* 101 (1934).
94. Anderson, "Common Property." On the corrosive effects of intergenerational dependency before Social Security, see Hendrik Hartog, *Someday All This Will Be Yours: A History of Inheritance and Old Age* (2012).
95. Boaz, *The Libertarian Mind: A Manifesto for Freedom* 186 (2015). Milton and Rose Friedman make the same claim. Free to Choose: A Personal Statement 106 (1980).
96. Adam Smith, *An Inquiry into the Nature and Causes of the Wealth of Nations*, III.iii.12, 405 (1776; R. H. Campbell and A. S. Skinner eds. 1976).
97. Hayek, *The Road to Serfdom*, 38.
98. On the health consequences of fine particulate exposure, see Doug Brugge, *Particles in the Air: The Deadliest Pollutant Is One You Breathe Every Day* (2018).
99. Juliet Eilperin and Brady Dennis, "Trump administration rejects tougher standards on soot, a deadly air pollutant," *Wash. Post*, Dec. 7, 2020.
100. Sean Reilly, "EPA scraps science panel: 'Your service . . . has concluded,'" *E&E News*, Oct. 12, 2018.
101. Lisa Heinzerling, "Cost-Nothing Analysis: Environmental Economics in the Age of Trump," 30 *Colo. Nat. Resources, Energy & Envtl. L. Rev.*, 287 (2019).
102. "Cost and Benefit Considerations in Clean Air Act Regulations," Congressional Research Service report R44840, May 5, 2017.
103. A useful overview, sensitive to libertarian concerns, is Thomas A. Lambert, *How to Regulate: A Guide for Policymakers* (2017).
104. Jacob S. Hacker and Paul Pierson, *American Amnesia: How the War on Government Led Us to Forget What Made America Prosper*, 65–66 (2016). Public funding of research has another attraction: because the discoveries are not patented, competing businesses can instantly take advantage of them.
105. Id., 3. In *The Libertarian Mind* (278), David Boaz breezily claims: "When resources are taxed away from those who earn them to be spent by government

officials, they do not work as efficiently to satisfy consumer needs as do resources directed by private owners."

106. The gap that divides him from contemporary minimal-staters should have been clear from the beginning:

> Where, for example, it is impracticable to make the enjoyment of certain services dependent on the payment of a price, competition will not produce the services; and the price system becomes similarly ineffective when the damage caused to others by certain uses of property cannot be effectively charged to the owner of that property. . . . Thus neither the provision of signposts on the roads nor, in most circumstances, that of the roads themselves can be paid for by every individual user. Nor can certain harmful effects of deforestation, of some methods of farming, or of the smoke and noise of factories be confined to the owner of the property in question or to those who are willing to submit to the damage for an agreed compensation.

Hayek, *The Road to Serfdom*, 38–39; see also Law, Legislation, and Liberty, v. 3, 41–46.

107. Deirdre McCloskey, "The Two Movements in Economic Thought, 1700–2000: Empty Economic Boxes Revisited," 26 *Hist. Econ. Ideas* 63 (2018).

108. Harold Demsetz, "Information and Efficiency: Another Viewpoint," 12 *J. L. & Econ.* 1 (1969).

109. This is a central theme of the scholarship of James Buchanan, whose influence on modern libertarianism is, however, exaggerated (and whose views are misrepresented) in Nancy MacLean, *Democracy in Chains* (2017). MacLean's narrative is full of fabrications, most egregiously the accusation, on the basis of no evidence, that Buchanan's work was animated by a desire to overturn *Brown v. Board of Education*. The success of this unreliable book, which was nominated and then short-listed for a National Book Award, has done much to garble the left's understanding of libertarianism. On the distortions of MacLean's account, see Andrew Koppelman, "Corrupting the National Book Award?," *Balkinization* blog, Oct. 26, 2017, https://balkin.blogspot.com/2017/10/corrupting-national-book-award.html.

110. Milton Friedman and Rose Friedman tell the sad story in *Free to Choose*, 194–200.

111. *Law, Legislation, and Liberty, v. 3* is an extended treatment of the problem.

112. An invaluable corrective here is Steven Croley's careful delineation of the political dynamics of federal administration (and devastating critique of the public choice theory) in *Regulation and Public Interests* (2008).

113. Even if, per impossibile, the police were a network of private security firms, as some libertarians wish, they would need somehow to be immune from bribery and corruption.

114. *Law, Legislation, and Liberty*, v. 3, 170–71.
115. Id., 108.
116. Cass R. Sunstein, *Simpler: The Future of Government* 5 (2013).
117. It is arguable that, even within a Hayekian framework, cost–benefit analysis is biased against regulation, because many benefits resist quantification, particularly the prevention of injuries to people. On the other hand, so do costs.
118. Id. at 34. He later observed that the Trump administration confirmed that the aggregate benefits of Obama-era regulations vastly exceeded their costs. "The Sense Behind the Noise on Trump's Regulation Policy," *Bloomberg*, Mar. 1, 2018.
119. Sunstein cites Hayek's claim about the limitations of planning to explain why it is important to solicit public comment before finalizing rules. Simpler, 81. This "check on mistakes" is, of course, far less precise than prices.
120. US Government Spending History from 1900, http://www.usgovernmentspending.com/past_spending (2021).
121. George A. Akerlof and Robert J. Shiller, *Phishing for Phools: The Economics of Manipulation and Deception*, 154 (2015).
122. The same bias would be formalized by John Tomasi's proposal in *Free Market Fairness* (241) that interferences with economic liberty should "have to pass a high degree of judicial scrutiny." Many administrative law scholars worry about ossification, the accumulation of legal constraints that make prompt and efficient rulemaking impossible. Any proposal for a heightened judicial role should be assessed in light of its likely impact on both types of error.
123. Brink Lindsey and Steven Teles, *The Captured Economy: How the Powerful Enrich Themselves, Slow Down Growth, and Increase Inequality*, 19 (2017).
124. Id., 20.
125. Id., 22.
126. Id., 35–89; see also Reich, *Saving Capitalism*, 3–86.
127. Reich, *Saving Capitalism*, 31–34.
128. Id., 34–36.
129. Suresh Naidu, Eric A. Posner, and Glen Weyl, "Antitrust Remedies for Labor Market Power," 132 Harv. L. Rev. 536 (2018).
130. See Ellen Frankel Paul, *Hayek on Monopoly and Antitrust in the Crucible of United States v. Microsoft*, 1 *N.Y.U. J. L. & Liberty*, 167 (2005).
131. Thomas O. McGarity, "Still Free to Harm: A Response to Professor Farber," 92 *Tex. L. Rev.* 1629, 1632 (2014).
132. Thomas O. McGarity, *Freedom to Harm: The Lasting Legacy of the Laissez Faire Revival* (2013), shows that libertarian rhetoric is often deployed to defeat regulation.
133. Steven Teles, "Kludgeocracy in America," 17 *Nat. Affairs* 97 (Fall 2013).
134. For a catalog of the dysfunctions, see Michael B. Tanner, *The Inclusive Economy: How to Bring Wealth to America's Poor* (2018).

135. Lindsey and Teles, *The Captured Economy*, 136.
136. Id., 160–61.
137. Id., 161.
138. Some libertarians have noticed this. See, e.g., Tyler Cowan, "What libertarianism has become and will become—State Capacity Libertarianism," *Marginal Revolution* blog, Jan. 1, 2020.
139. Friedrich Hayek, *The Fatal Conceit: The Errors of Socialism*, 12 (1988).
140. *The Constitution of Liberty*, 36.
141. Friedrich Hayek, "Individualism: True and False," in *The Essence of Hayek*, 147.
142. Hayek, *Law, Legislation, and Liberty*, v. 1, 36.
143. Hayek, *The Constitution of Liberty*, 26.
144. Hayek, "Individualism: True and False," 140.
145. John Gray, *Hayek on Liberty*, 148 (3d ed. 1998).
146. *Capitalism, Socialism, and Democracy* 83 (3d ed. 1942), footnote omitted.
147. Sean Illing, "Why we need to plan for a future without jobs," *Vox*, Oct. 17, 2016.
148. According to one estimate, approximately 90 percent of the lost manufacturing jobs were eliminated by automation. Michael J. Hicks and Srikant Devaraj, "The Myth and Reality of Manufacturing in America," Ball State University, June 2015.
149. Freeman, *America Works*, 129.
150. Joseph Stiglitz, *Globalization and Its Discontents* Revisited (2018); Brink Lindsey, *Human Capitalism* (2013).
151. Ross Douthat and Reihan Salam, *Grand New Party: How Republicans Can Win the Working Class and Save the American Dream* 147 (2008). Douthat and Salam's book was written before the 2008 meltdown of the mortgage market.
152. Jeff Larrimore et al., "Report on the Economic Well-Being of U.S. Households in 2019, featuring Supplemental Data from April 2020," *Bd. Governors Fed. Res. Sys.* 21 (May 2020).
153. Zingales, *A Capitalism for the People*, 115.
154. Hayek, *Law, Legislation, and Liberty*, v. 1, 142.
155. Hayek, *Law, Legislation, and Liberty*, v. 2, 122.
156. Hayek, *The Road to Serfdom*, 210.
157. Karl Polanyi, *The Great Transformation*, 130–34 (1944).
158. Dani Rodrik, "Populism and the Economics of Globalization," 1 *J. Int'l Bus. Pol'y*, 12 (2018).
159. David C. Kang, *Crony Capitalism: Corruption and Development in South Korea and the Philippines* 3 (2002).
160. Paul Cohen, "Lessons from the Nationalization Nation: State-Owned Enterprises in France," *Dissent*, Winter 2010; Jacques Neher, "For U.K., a French Lesson on Closing Coal Mines," *N.Y. Times*, Oct. 24, 1992.
161. See Slobodian, *Globalists*.

162. Ernst-Joachim Mestmäcker, quoted in id., 209.
163. *Law, Legislation, and Liberty*, v. 3.
164. He had no discernible role in formulating Pinochet's policies. See Bruce Caldwell and Leonidas Montes, "Friedrich Hayek and His Visits to Chile," 28 *Rev. Austrian Econ.*, 261 (2015). On the other hand, his approval of Pinochet's regime reveals authoritarian tendencies in his political philosophy. Thomas Biebricher, *The Political Theory of Neoliberalism*, 73–74 (2018).
165. Douglass C. North, John Joseph Wallis, and Barry R. Weingast, *Violence and Social Orders: A Conceptual Framework for Interpreting Recorded Human History* (rev. ed. 2013). Thanks to Will Wilkinson for pointing out the relevance of this work to the critique of Hayek.
166. This conception of democracy, in which voters choose among elites, is developed in Schumpeter, *Capitalism, Socialism, and Democracy*. Modern political science scholarship supporting Schumpeter's view is reviewed in Christopher H. Achen and Larry M. Bartels, *Democracy for Realists: Why Elections Do Not Produce Responsive Government* (rev. ed. 2017).
167. Celine McNicholas et al., "Unlawful: U.S. employers are charged with violating federal law in 41.5 percent of all union election campaigns," Econ. Pol'y Institute, Dec. 11, 2019.
168. Thomas A. Kochan et al., "Worker Voice in America: Is There a Gap between What Workers Expect and What They Experience?," 72 *ILR Rev.* 3 (2019).
169. See Jake Rosenfeld, *What Unions No Longer Do*, 24–29 (2014).
170. *The Constitution of Liberty*, 267–84.
171. Reinhold Niebuhr, *The Children of Light and the Children of Darkness* 17 (1944).
172. David Harvey, *A Brief History of Neoliberalism*, 96–97 (2005); Amy Chua, *World on Fire: How Exporting Free Market Democracy Breeds Ethnic Hatred and Global Instability*, 43–45, 136–38 (2002); Stiglitz, *Globalization and Its Discontents Revisited*, 211–12.
173. Kenworthy, *Social Democratic Capitalism*.
174. Doherty, *Radicals for Capitalism*, 308–9.
175. *Free to Choose*, 222.
176. Milton Friedman, *Capitalism and Freedom*, 108–15 (1962).
177. Id., 115.
178. Paul Krugman, "Who Was Milton Friedman?," *New York Review of Books*, Feb. 15, 2007. It is however worth noting that, like Hayek, Friedman proposed an approach to medical needs that essentially anticipated Obamacare, requiring people to buy insurance in the private sector and subsidizing those who could not afford it. Milton Friedman, "Gammon's Law Points to Health-Care Solution," *Wall Street Journal*, Nov. 12, 1991.
179. Burgin, *The Great Persuasion*, 184–85. Burgin is referring to the leading nineteenth-century social Darwinists, Herbert Spencer and William Graham Sumner.

180. *Free to Choose*, 31–32.
181. Burgin, *The Great Persuasion*, 183.
182. Id., 185. Deirdre McCloskey is sometimes susceptible to the same immoderation, conflating familiar welfare state measures with socialism. Compare her criticisms of Bismarck's welfarism in *Bourgeois Equality* (604–7) with the grudging concession of a legitimate role for the welfare state in *Bourgeois Dignity* (445) and the quotations on p. 606 of *Bourgeois Equality*, which make clear that Bismarck meant to protect the status quo by giving marginal people a stake in the system and so forestalling revolution. McCloskey's account of the rise of capitalism is a marvelous overview of the role of ideas in transforming economic life, but she sometimes seems to contemplate the problem of poverty from twenty thousand feet, so that if it's improving in the aggregate, details like Social Security don't matter. But in fact lots of people depend on it, and would be in pretty bad shape without it.
183. James W. Ely, "Impact of Richard A. Epstein," 15 *Wm. & Mary Bill Rts. J.* 421, 427 (2006),
184. Jeffrey Rosen, "The Unregulated Offensive," *N.Y. Times*, Apr. 17, 2005.
185. See Richard A. Epstein, *Simple Rules for a Complex World*, 53–148 (1995).
186. See Richard A. Epstein, *Principles for a Free Society: Reconciling Individual Liberty with the Common Good* (1998).
187. He acknowledges that his views "have evolved in ways that turn out to be more sympathetic to government administration than I had once supposed." *Design for Liberty*, 6 (2011). He occasionally shows how the anarcho-libertarians, whom I consider in chapter 3, misunderstand how markets work. *Principles for a Free Society*, 43–44, 67, 112, 124; "My Rand Paul Problem," Hoover Institution Defining Ideas, Feb. 3, 2014; "The Libertarian Quartet," *Reason*, Jan. 1999 (reviewing Randy Barnett, *The Structure of Liberty*).
188. Richard A. Epstein, "The Kidney Crisis," Hoover Institution Defining Ideas, Oct. 27, 2014; Richard A. Epstein, "The Human and Economic Dimensions of Altruism: The Case of Organ Transplantation," 37 *J. Leg. Stud.* 459 (2008).
189. Richard A. Epstein, *The Classical Liberal Constitution* (2014).
190. For his own account of the differences between himself and Friedman, see Richard A. Epstein, "Setting Krugman Straight," Hoover Institution Defining Ideas, Aug. 19, 2014.
191. *The Classical Liberal Constitution*, 353. The same concession to the necessity of regulation is made by Charles Murray, *What It Means to Be a Libertarian: A Personal Interpretation*, 115 (1997).
192. See, e.g., Richard A. Epstein, "The Role of Defeat Devices in Environmental Protection: Beyond the VW Scandal," *Forbes*, Sept. 27, 2017.
193. He also breaks with many libertarian administrative law scholars, by advocating judicial deference to agency expertise on substantive questions of policy. Richard A. Epstein, *The Dubious Morality of Modern Administrative Law* (2020).

194. See Richard A. Epstein, *Takings: Private Property and the Power of Eminent Domain* (1985).
195. *The Classical Liberal Constitution*, 356.
196. Id.
197. Jonathan Chait, "Richard Epstein Can't Stop Being Wrong About the Coronavirus," *New York* Intelligencer, Apr. 21, 2020.
198. Richard A. Epstein, '*Hayek's Constitution of Liberty—a guarded retrospective*,' 30 *Rev. Austrian Econ.* 415, 429 (2016). See also Richard A. Epstein, "Hayekian Socialism," 58 *Md. L. Rev.*, 271 (1999).
199. *Design for Liberty*, 146; *Principles for a Free Society*, 130–31, 151–53.
200. Richard A. Epstein, "Decentralized Responses to Good Fortune and Bad Luck," 9 *Theoretical Inq. in Law*, 309 (2008).
201. *Design for Liberty*, 148.
202. See Richard A. Epstein, *Mortal Peril: Our Inalienable Right to Health Care?* (1997).
203. Elinor Ostrom, *Governing the Commons: The Evolution of Institutions of Collective Action* (1990). This is the central claim of Charles Murray's libertarianism. See Charles Murray, *What it Means to Be a Libertarian: A Personal Interpretation* (1997).
204. Kenworthy, *Social Democratic Capitalism*, 76–79.
205. *The Classical Liberal Constitution*, 167.
206. Id., 571.
207. Id., 168.
208. Edward Conard, *Unintended Consequences: Why Everything You've Been Told About the Economy is Wrong* 23 (2012).
209. Federal Reserve Bank of St. Louis, Real Gross Domestic Product (GDPA); Real gross domestic product per capita (A939RX0Q048SBEA), updated Jan. 29, 2022.
210. The modern Hayekian Edward Conard is so obsessed with growth that he denounces charitable contributions and liberal arts majors because they divert resources from production. See Unintended Consequences, passim; Edward Conard, *The Upside of Inequality: How Good Intentions Undermine the Middle Class* (2016).
211. *Hayek on Liberty*, 152.
212. See *Wendy Brown, Undoing the Demos: Neoliberalism's Stealth Revolution* (2015).
213. Daniel Rodgers, *Age of Fracture*, 10, 76 (2011).
214. *Law, Legislation, and Liberty*, v. 3, 168; similarly *The Road to Serfdom*, 90–92.
215. *Law, Legislation, and Liberty*, v. 3, 174.
216. *The Constitution of Liberty*, 53.
217. Hayek, *Law, Legislation, and Liberty*, v. 2, 41.
218. Id., 108.

219. *Murray N. Rothbard vs. the Philosophers: Unpublished Writings on Hayek, Mises, Strauss, and Polanyi*, 65 (Roberta A. Modugno ed. 2009).
220. Id., 67.
221. *The Constitution of Liberty*, 398.
222. *The Road to Serfdom*, 13.
223. My analysis of his multiple philosophical commitments is drawn from Chandran Kukathas, *Hayek and Modern Liberalism*, 166–204 (1989).
224. See id., 130–65.

CHAPTER 2: RIGHTS

1. F. A. Hayek, "The Dilemma of Specialization," in *The State of the Social Sciences*, 463 (Leonard D. White ed. 1956).
2. My example is loosely adapted from Luke 2:1-20. In the Bible story, Joseph has a home, but because of a census, he is not allowed to remain there, but must travel. Having a home does one no good when one is not permitted to sleep in it.
3. Rand Paul and Mark Meadows, "Let's fully repeal ObamaCare, then have an open debate on how to replace it," Fox News, Mar. 6, 2017.
4. I set aside the question of whether Locke is himself a liberal, or whether his reliance on divine authority makes him at best a proto-liberal. See Timothy Stanton, "Authority and Freedom in the Interpretation of Locke's Political Theory," 39 *Pol. Theory* 6 (2011).

   There is also controversy about the extent to which he was personally involved in slavery. Compare Holly Brewer, "Slavery, Sovereignty, and "Inheritable Blood": Reconsidering John Locke and the Origins of American Slavery," 122 *Am. Hist. Rev.* 1038 (2017), with James Farr, "Locke, Natural Law, and New World Slavery," 36 *Pol. Theory* 495 (2008).

   Liberals for centuries have expressly relied upon themes from Locke's work, and those themes are what I consider here.
5. "Letter to John Trumbull, Feb. 15, 1789," in *Writings* 939 (Merrill D. Peterson ed. 1984). Locke's importance was likewise acknowledged by Karl Marx, who wrote that Locke "was the classical expression of bourgeois society's ideas of right as against feudal society, and moreover his philosophy served as the basis of the whole of subsequent English political economy." Theories of Surplus-Value, v. 1, 367 (1969).
6. But see *Danielle Allen, Our Declaration: A Reading of the Declaration of Independence in Defense of Equality* (2014).
7. These are not necessarily the arguments that were most important to Locke himself. Locke's claim about the prosperity of day laborers in England, for example, aims "to bring out the tremendous productive power of labor, not to show that a system of property rights does justice to the poor." Samuel Fleischacker, *A Short History of Distributive Justice*, 37 (2004).

8. Eric Mack, *John Locke*, 131–38 (2013).
9. John Locke, *Two Treatises of Government* 2.4, 269 (Peter Laslett ed. 1988).
10. Id., 2.4, 269.
11. Id., 2.6, 271.
12. Id., 2.27, 287–88.
13. Id., 2.124, 350–51.
14. John Locke, *A Letter Concerning Toleration*, 47 (James H. Tully, ed. 1983) (1689).
15. Locke, *Two Treatises*, 2.95, 331.
16. Murray Rothbard, *Economic Thought before Adam Smith: An Austrian Perspective on the History of Economic Thought, v. 1*, 316–17 (1995).
17. Murray Rothbard, *For a New Liberty: The Libertarian Manifesto* 39 (rev. ed. 1978).
18. Id., 52.
19. Id., 25.
20. Murray Rothbard, *The Ethics of Liberty*, 221 (NYU Press 1998).
21. Locke, *Two Treatises*, 2.25, 286.
22. Id., 2.28, 288.
23. Id., 2.27, 288.
24. Id.
25. Jeremy Waldron, *The Right to Private Property*, 185 (1988).
26. Locke papers, quoted in *James Tully, A Discourse on Property: John Locke and his Adversaries*, 121 (1980).
27. A. John Simmons, *The Lockean Theory of Rights*, 273 (1992).
28. On the importance of reciprocity in Locke, see Mack, *John Locke*, 35–40.
29. Locke, *Two Treatises*, 2.34, 291.
30. Id., 2.50, 302.
31. Eric Mack, *Libertarianism*, 17 (2018).
32. Locke, *Two Treatises*, 2.48, 301.
33. Id., 2.34, 291.
34. Id., 1.42, 170.
35. George Sher, *Desert*, 39–40 (1987).
36. John Tomasi, *Free Market Fairness* 182 (2012). This does not, however, mean that such activity is a fundamental right that should be presumptively free from regulation, as Tomasi argues. See my review, "Notre Dame Philosophical Reviews," May 5, 2012, http://ndpr.nd.edu/news/30638-free-market-fairness/.
37. Locke, *Two Treatises*, 2.41, 297.
38. Robert Lee Hale, "Coercion and Distribution in a Supposedly Non-Coercive State," 38 *Pol. Sci. Q.* 470, 473 (1923).
39. David Schmidtz, *Elements of Justice* 156 (2006); Robert Nozick, *Anarchy, State, and Utopia*, 177 (1974).

40. Pollock v. Williams, 322 U.S. 4, 18 (1944)(Jackson, J.). For evidence that this is necessary but not sufficient, see Elizabeth Anderson, *Private Government: How Employers Rule Our Lives (and Why We Don't Talk about It)* (2017).
41. Locke, *Two Treatises*, 2.37, 294.
42. "Considerations of the Consequences of Lowering Interest," quoted in Ian Shapiro, *The Evolution of Rights in Liberal Theory*, 127 (1986). Locke wrote in a time when the economy was improving and wages were rising (see Shapiro, 83), but that doesn't matter to his argument.
43. Locke, *Two Treatises*, 1.42, 170. Contrast Rothbard, who, we saw earlier, thought that property can mean a right to starve others.
44. Id., 2.131, 353.
45. Id., 1.42, 170.
46. See Waldron, *The Right to Private Property*, 273, 282–83.
47. Locke, *Two Treatises*, 1.42, 170.
48. Locke says "he that sells his corn in a town pressed with famine at the utmost rate he can get for it does no injustice against the common rule of traffic, yet if he carry it away unless they will give him more than they are able, or extorts so much from their present necessity as not to leave them the means of subsistence afterwards, he offends against the common rule of charity as a man and if they perish is no doubt guilty of murder." John Locke, *Venditio*, in *Locke: Political Writings*, 445 (David Wooton ed. 2004).
49. Locke, *Two Treatises*, 1.42, 170.
50. Mack, *John Locke*, 72–74.
51. Robert Filmer, *Patriarcha and Other Writings*, 225, 236 (Johann P. Sommerville ed. 1991).
52. Locke, *Two Treatises*, 1.9, 148.
53. Tully, *A Discourse on Property*, 61, 85, 89.
54. Samuel Freeman, "Illiberal Libertarians: Why Libertarianism is Not a Liberal View," 30 *Phil. & Pub. Aff.* 105, 149 (2001). Freeman notes that his argument is not applicable to Hayek, who never endorsed Rothbard's conception of property rights.
55. As recently as 1900, per capita medical expenditure in the United States was $5, which is $100 in present dollars. In 2018 it was $11,172. David Dranove, *Code Red: An Economist Explains How to Revive the Healthcare System Without Destroying It*, 9 (2008); U.S. Department of Health and Human Services, Centers for Medicare and Medicaid Services, National Health Expenditure Data, Historical (2019). Of course, if one actually becomes gravely ill, the costs can be much higher.
56. He did, however, assume women's natural subordination in marriage, which could be conceived in contractual terms. He would have been untroubled if our hypothetical woman felt pressured to marry a rich man. See Carole Pateman, *The Sexual Contract* (1988). This of course contradicts his claim

that one may not "justly make use of another's necessity, to force him to become his Vassal."

57. It is controversial whether Locke really defended, or merely tolerated, such acquisitiveness. Compare Tully, *A Discourse on Property*, 103–4, 175–76, with Jeffrey Isaac, "Was John Locke a Bourgeois Theorist? A Critical Appraisal of MacPherson and Tully," 11 *Canadian J. Pol. & Soc. Theory* 107 (1987).
58. Leo Strauss, *Natural Right and History* 250–51 (1953).
59. Quoted in Brewer, *Slavery, Sovereignty, and "Inheritable Blood"*, 1068.
60. *A Letter Concerning Toleration*, 37.
61. Which is not to say that the development of capitalism required those rights violations—a notion thoroughly refuted in Deirdre McCloskey, *Bourgeois Dignity: Why Economics Can't Explain the Modern World* (2010).
62. The problem of asymmetric information is discussed more fully in chapter 4.
63. Hayek, as we have seen, had the same problem. Both of them undervalued democratic accountability as a way of guaranteeing the rights they prized.
64. Locke, *Two Treatises*, 2.28, 289.
65. Richard Ashcraft, "Liberal Political Theory and Working-Class Radicalism in Nineteenth-Century England," 21 *Pol. Theory* 249 (1993).
66. Locke, *Two Treatises*, 2.34, 291.
67. Alan Ryan, *On Politics: A History of Political Thought From Herodotus to the Present*, 479 (2012).
68. Simmons observes that "Locke simply never discusses any cooperative ventures but those whose terms are settled in advance by the consent of the parties." *The Lockean Theory of Rights*, 269 n.116.
69. John Bates Clark, *The Distribution of Wealth: A Theory of Wages, Interest, and Profits* (1899). Clark's claim has continuing appeal for some. See, e.g., N. Gregory Mankiw, "Spreading the Wealth Around: Reflections Inspired by Joe the Plumber," 36 *Eastern Ec. J.* 285 (2010).
70. John Rawls, *A Theory of Justice* 308/271 rev. (1971; revised ed. 1999).
71. *What Social Classes Owe to One Another* 141 (1883). Hayek quotes this passage, and comments: "This is true only if 'merit' is used in the sense in which we have used 'value,' without any moral connotations, but certainly not if it is meant to suggest proportionality to any endeavor to do the good or right thing, or to any subjective effort to conform to an ideal standard." The Constitution of Liberty, 440 n.10 (1960). On this point he essentially agrees with Rawls.
72. *A Theory of Justice*, 308/271 rev. The point is powerfully elaborated in Samuel Freeman, "Capitalism in the Classical and High Liberal Traditions," in *Liberalism and Distributive Justice*, 31–39 (2018). Nozick concedes the point and does not rely on Clark's argument. Distribution according to marginal product is yet another patterned principle, to be rejected for the same reason that Nozick rejects all patterned principles. Nozick, *Anarchy, State, and Utopia*, 194. (Thanks to Eric Mack for pointing out the relevance of this

passage.) Nozick does say in several places that one of the attractions of free markets is that they tend to give people some approximation of their marginal product. See id., 187–88, 301–2, 304–5.

73. An additional objection to the marginal-value idea, when it is used to justify returns on capital, is that "the contribution of capitalists is not a natural contribution (in the way that the contribution of workers and productive resources is) but is instead an institutional artifact." It is only because ownership of capital is attributed to them by the positive law that they are deemed to have made any contribution at all. Freeman, "Capitalism in the Classical and High Liberal Traditions," 37. Other difficulties with Clark's conception are reviewed in Guglielmo Forges Davanzati and Andrea Pacella, *A Capital Controversy in Early Twentieth Century: Veblen vs. Clark*, 51 *J. Econ. Issues* 118 (2017).
74. Clark, *The Distribution of Wealth*, 8.
75. Id.
76. *Anarchy, State, and Utopia*, 169.
77. Id., 290.
78. Alan Haworth, *Anti-Libertarianism: Markets, Philosophy, and Myth*, 92–93 (1994).
79. Milton Friedman, *Capitalism and Freedom*, 166 (1962).
80. Whether it reduces the incentive to work is a complex question. Some workers will decide that, because of taxation, an additional hour of work is not worth it. Others will conclude that they need to work more hours in order to secure the income they want. The relative proportions are difficult to quantify.
81. Center on Budget and Policy Priorities, Chart Book: The Earned Income Tax Credit and Child Tax Credit, May 24, 2016. A leading libertarian policy guide is torn. In a section on poverty policy, it acknowledges the program's success and proposes to expand it to single adults, to increase the frequency of its payments, and to eliminate the marriage penalty in its administration. *Cato Handbook for Policymakers* 443–44 (8th ed. 2017). In a section on the federal budget, on the other hand, it proposes to cut the program by 50 percent. Id., 320. A primary reason that the cut is demanded is because the program "imposes a large cost on other people who pay the taxes to fund the benefits." Id., 449.
82. The same objection, that there is no way to precisely allocate credit for production in a complex division of labor, destroys efforts on the left to transform Lockean self-ownership into a basis for redistribution. See Barbara Fried, "Left-Libertarianism: A Review Essay," 32 *Phil. & Pub. Aff.* 66 (2004).
83. Locke, *Two Treatises*, 1.53–54, 179–80.
84. Shapiro, *The Evolution of Rights*, 146–47. Locke's inconsistency is noted in Nozick, *Anarchy, State, and Utopia*, 288–89, but Nozick does not resolve it. Nozick worsens the problem by dispensing with Locke's proviso that one

can't agree to be a slave. Id., 331. Nozick's reformulation of Locke thus leads to Filmer's conclusion, except that the owner of newly produced people is more likely to be the mother than the father: she produced the child, and the father contributed one factor of production in a consensual transaction. Slavery and matriarchy are not what Nozick had in mind. See Susan Moller Okin, *Justice, Gender, and the Family*, 74–88 (1989).

85. John Rawls, *Lectures on the History of Political Philosophy* 152–55 (Samuel Freeman ed. 2007); John Rawls, *Political Liberalism*, 286–88 (1993). Rawls's reading of Locke on this point is contested. "Whether Locke assumed that the members of his political society were substantial property-owners or whether he held a more extended view of political membership is one of the most controversial questions in the secondary literature on Locke." Richard Ashcraft, *Locke's Two Treatises of Government*, 166 (1987). Locke's position is at least ambiguous, and Rawls's modification of social contract theory removes the ambiguity.
86. Ryan, *On Politics*, 480.
87. Thomas Pogge, *John Rawls: His Life and Theory of Justice*, 5–6 (2007). Pogge reports that both brothers died of diseases they got from John. Rawls's widow, Mardy, told Professor Samuel Freeman, who edited Rawls's papers, that Rawls felt confusedly guilty for Tommy's death, even though he knew that it was not his fault. Rawls may not have made this clear in his conversations with Pogge. Samuel Freeman, personal communication to author, Aug. 8, 2021.
88. Ben Rogers, "John Rawls," obituary, *Guardian*, Nov. 27, 2002.
89. Rawls, *Lectures on the History of Political Philosophy*, 152.
90. He never relies on anything like Locke's claim that we have obligations because we are God's creations, and also rejected Locke's idea of a prepolitical entitlement to property. Rawls thus relies on contractualism in a deeper way than Locke: our rights, including our property rights, are artifacts of the social contract, and so their specification depends on what a fair social contract would entail.
91. Adam Smith had a similar view of joint contribution: "It is but equity . . . that they who feed, cloath and lodge the whole body of the people, should have such a share of the produce of their own labour as to be themselves tolerably well fed, cloathed, and lodged." Adam Smith, *An Inquiry into the Nature and Causes of the Wealth of Nations*, I.viii.36, 96 (1776; R. H. Campbell and A. S. Skinner eds. 1976).
92. Rawls, *Political Liberalism*, 6. The notion that government is to be judged by its treatment of the least advantaged was anticipated by others, although without Rawls's precision. Thus Edmund Burke, in 1788: "When the God whom we adore appeared in human form, He did not appear in a form of greatness and majesty, but in sympathy with the lowest of the people, and

thereby made it a firm and ruling principle, that their welfare was the object of all government, since the Person who was the Master of Nature chose to appear Himself in a subordinate situation." Quoted in Conor Cruise O'Brien, *The Great Melody: A Thematic Biography of Edmund Burke* 375–76 (1992).

93. John Rawls, *Justice as Fairness: A Restatement*, 59–60, 63 (2001).
94. T. M. Scanlon, *Why Does Inequality Matter?* 139 (2018).
95. Id., 141.
96. *A Theory of Justice*, 75/65 rev.
97. Hayek, *Law, Legislation, and Liberty*, v. 2, 132.
98. Karl Marx, *Capital, v. 1*, 92 (International Publishers 1972), quoted in Rawls, *Lectures on the History of Political Philosophy*, 351. Marx understood that, in a growing economy, there might be "a constant growth in the labourer's means of subsistence." *Capital, v. 1*, 523. But this did not satisfy him, because higher wages would "be nothing but *better payment for the slave*, and would not conquer either for the worker or for labour their human status and dignity." "Economic and Philosophic Manuscripts of 1844," in *The Marx-Engels Reader* (Robert C. Tucker ed., 2d ed. 1978), 80. Human status and dignity are of course Rawls's central concerns. Rawls summarizes Marx's ideal in terms that could also describe his own view: "What concerns [the members of society] is how social and economic institutions are to be organized so that they can cooperate on fair terms and use their combined labor effectively with the forces of nature in ways to be decided by society as a whole." *Lectures on the History of Political Philosophy*, 351.
99. Rawls, *Justice as Fairness: A Restatement*, 174.
100. Katrina Forrester, *In the Shadow of Justice: Postwar Liberalism and the Remaking of Political Philosophy* 104–39 (2019); William A. Edmundson, *John Rawls: Reticent Socialist* 3–5 (2017). This was not his own view. He was more inclined toward either democratic socialism (in which "the means of production are owned by society," *Justice as Fairness: A Restatement*, 138) or "property-owning democracy," a market economy in which government continually intervenes to ensure widespread dispersal of the ownership of capital. In this respect, he was mistaken about the implications of his own argument. See Andrew Koppelman, "Rawls and the Market Economy," 51, *National Affairs* 130 (2022).
101. Nozick, *Anarchy, State, and Utopia*, 235.
102. "Whether or not people's natural assets are arbitrary from a moral point of view, they are entitled to them, and to what flows from them." Id., 226. But what flows from natural assets—my earlier example of basketball talent is borrowed from Nozick—is contingent on the rewards available in their economic environment, including its tax laws. They are not entitled to any particular economic environment. Market exchanges, Will Kymlicka observes,

"involve legal rights over things, over external goods, and these things are not just created out of nothing by our self-owned powers." *Contemporary Political Philosophy: An Introduction*, 107 (1990). What self-ownership entails is that I can't be forced to play basketball if I don't want to.

103. Nozick, *Anarchy, State, and Utopia*, 171. Freeman observes that libertarians often take property to be "an intuitively clear notion, involving the nearly unrestricted freedom to control and determine what is done with a thing." "Illiberal Libertarians," 129. Existing systems of positive law, however, vary in the entitlements associated with ownership. Id.
104. Locke held the same view. See Tully, *A Discourse on Property*, 164–65.
105. Id., 132.
106. Nozick, *Anarchy, State, and Utopia*, 234.
107. There is some uncertainty as to whether Rawls's principle, if incorporated into the structure of property rights in the way he describes, is patterned according to Nozick's definition. Nozick says a principle is patterned if "it specifies that a distribution is to vary along with some natural dimension, weighted sum of natural dimensions, or lexicographic ordering of natural dimensions." Id., 156. The difference principle says nothing about an overall ordering, but only about the situation of those on the bottom, and so it is not patterned according to this definition. (Rawls expressly rejects "pattern criteria, those that require the actual distribution to exhibit certain ascertainable features." "Some Reasons for the Maximin Criterion," in *Collected Papers* 229 (Samuel Freeman ed. 1999.)) Nozick's attack on patterns is however immediately followed and amplified by his claim that redistributive taxation is slavery, suggesting a broader understanding of what counts as a patterned argument. See also Eric Mack, "Robert Nozick's Political Philosophy," *Stanford Encyclopedia of Philosophy*, 4.2 (2018) (taking the slavery argument to be an argument against patterns).
108. Nozick, *Anarchy, State, and Utopia*, 163.
109. Id., 157 n.
110. Id.
111. John Tomasi claims that there is such a proviso in every major libertarian thinker. *Free Market Fairness*, 126–27, 132, 134, 136, 139–40.
112. Ronald Replogle, *Recovering the Social Contract*, 53–55 (1989).
113. David Hume, "Of the Original Contract," in *Essays Moral, Political, and Literary* 465 (Eugene F. Miller ed. 1987).
114. Waldron, *The Right to Private Property*, 273.
115. Id., 271–83.
116. Id., 273.
117. Hobbes and Rousseau offer interest-based arguments, though they rely on different interests, physical safety (Hobbes) and the need not to be dominated by others (Rousseau). Kant's argument is duty-based. Interpreters have read Locke both ways.

118. See Thomas Nagel and Liam Murphy, *The Myth of Ownership* (2002). For a defense of the argument against some libertarian objections, see Andrew Koppelman, "Does Respect Require Antiperfectionism? Gaus on Liberal Neutrality," 22 *Harv. Rev. of Phil.* 53, 58–59 (2015).
119. Ajay Mehrotra, *Making the Modern American Fiscal State: Law, Politics, and the Rise of Progressive Taxation*, 1877–1929 (2014).
120. Nozick, *Anarchy, State, and Utopia*, 180–81.
121. Philip Rucker, "Sen. DeMint of S.C. Is Voice of Opposition to Health-Care Reform," *Wash. Post*, July 28, 2009.
122. Andrew Lister, "Markets, Desert, and Reciprocity," 16 *Pol. Phil. & Econ.* 47 (2017).
123. "The idea of entitlement presupposes, as do ideas of (moral) desert, a deliberate effort of will, or acts intentionally done." Rawls, *Justice as Fairness: A Restatement*, 75.
124. Rawls, *A Theory of Justice* 88–89 rev. The language is slightly different on p. 103 of the original edition. See Schmidtz, *Elements of Justice*, 62. For similar statements, see *A Theory of Justice* 10/10 rev.; 310–11/273 rev.
125. Scanlon, *Why Does Inequality Matter?*, 119.
126. Id., 120.
127. Id.
128. Id., 124.
129. Lane Kenworthy, *Social Democratic Capitalism* 25–26 (2020); Robert E. Goodin, "Stabilizing Expectations: The Role of Earnings-Related Benefits in Social Welfare Policy," 100 *Ethics* 530 (1990).
130. Harry Frankfurt, "Equality as a Moral Ideal," in *The Importance of What We Care About* 134 (1988).
131. Quoted in Forrester, *In the Shadow of Justice*, 126.
132. Rawls, *A Theory of Justice*, 277/245 rev. Eric Mack argues (*Libertarianism*, 129) that this continual intervention is in tension with his claim that, in a just society, "there are no unannounced and unpredictable interferences with citizens' expectations and acquisitions." *Political Liberalism*, 283. Inheritance and gift taxes and bequest restrictions would be rules announced in advance of any acquisition of wealth. But they are obviously insufficient to prevent radical inequalities, since inherited wealth is less important than it once was in creating huge fortunes. Most of the world's richest people now are self-made. Chris Edwards and Ryan Bourne, *Exploring Wealth Inequality* 9 (Cato Institute, Nov. 5, 2019). Any effort to radically reduce wealth inequality would therefore invite Mack's objection.
133. Hayek, *Law, Legislation, and Liberty*, v. 2, 132.
134. "The fact is simply that we consent to retain, and agree to enforce, uniform rules for a procedure which has greatly improved the chances of all to have their wants satisfied, but at the price of all individuals and groups incurring the risk of unmerited failure." Id., 70.
135. Id., 131.

136. Others have reached the same conclusion. See Tomasi, *Free Market Fairness* 151–161; Kevin Vallier, "Rawlsianism," in *Arguments for Liberty* 161 (Aaron Ross Powell and Grant Babcock eds. 2016); Andrew Lister, "The 'Mirage' of Social Justice: Hayek Against (and For) Rawls," 25 *Crit. Rev.* 409 (2013); Loren E. Lomasky, "Libertarianism at twin Harvard," 22 *Soc. Phil. & Pol'y* 178 (2005); Richard A. Epstein, "Rawls Remembered: An appreciation from the Right," *National Review Online*, Nov. 27, 2002 (arguing that Rawls entails classical liberalism); Daniel Shapiro, "Why Rawlsian Liberals Should Support Free Market Capitalism," 3 *J. Pol. Phil.* 58 (1995); Brink Lindsey, "Liberaltarians," *New Republic*, Dec. 4, 2006; Will Wilkinson, "Is Rawlsekianism the Future?," *Cato at Liberty* blog, Dec. 4, 2006; Don Arthur, "Hayek & Rawls: An Unlikely Fusion," Evatt Foundation (2008), http://evatt.org.au/papers/hayek-rawls.html. For an argument that Hayek should be understood as a social contract theorist, see Robert Sugden, "Normative Judgments and Spontaneous Order: The Contractarian Element in Hayek's Thought," 4 *Const. Pol. Economy* 393 (1993).

137. Hayek, *Law, Legislation, and Liberty*, v. 2, 100, quoting John Rawls, "Constitutional Liberty and the Concept of Justice," in *Nomos IV: Justice* 102 (1963).

138. Id. He later claimed that this statement was not altogether sincere:

> I was trying to remind Rawls himself of something he has said in one of his earlier articles, which I'm afraid doesn't recur in his book: that the conception of correcting the distribution according to the principles of social justice was unachievable, and that therefore he wanted to confine himself to inventing general rules which have this effect. Now if he was not prepared to defend social distributive justice, I thought I could pretend to agree with him. But studying his book further, my feeling is he doesn't really stick to that he had announced first. And that there is so much egalitarianism, really, underlying his argument that he is driven to much more intervention than his original conception of justice has.

Oct. 28, 1978 interview with James Buchanan, available as "Hayek and Buchanan: Rawls, Egalitarianism and Social Justice," YouTube, https://www.youtube.com/watch?v=uRhs26o03ok, and Nobel Prize–winning economist oral history transcript (1983), p. 219, https://archive.org/details/nobelprizewinnin00haye/page/n473/mode/2up?q=rawls

139. Hayek, *Law, Legislation, and Liberty, v. 2*, 189.

140. For evidence that Hayek was right about the implications of Rawls's principles, see Jason Brennan, *Rawls' Paradox*, 18 *Const. Polit. Econ.* 287 (2007); Tomasi, *Free Market Fairness*, 226–37.

CHAPTER 3: TYRANNY

1. Ayn Rand, *Atlas Shrugged*, 188 (1957; Signet 1996). You will notice that all the other epigraphs are from Friedrich Hayek. This one is different because this chapter examines a very different kind of libertarianism.
2. Lee Edwards, *Goldwater: The Man Who Made a Revolution* 344–45 (1995).
3. Brian Doherty, *Radicals for Capitalism: A Freewheeling History of the Modern American Libertarian Movement* 346–53 (2007); Justin Raimondo, *An Enemy of the State: The Life of Murray N. Rothbard*, 176–77 (2000).
4. Libertarian Party 2020 Platform, https://www.lp.org/platform/.
5. Richard A. Epstein, *The Classical Liberal Constitution*, 17 (2014).
6. Ron Paul, "The Political Importance of Murray Rothbard," in *Man, Economy, and Liberty: Essays in Honor of Murray N. Rothbard*, 329 (Walter Block and Llewellyn H. Rockwell Jr., eds. 1988).
7. John Ganz, "The Forgotten Man: On Murray Rothbard, philosophical harbinger of Trump and the alt-right," *Baffler*, Dec. 15, 2017.
8. Raimondo, *An Enemy of the State*, 101.
9. Murray Rothbard, "Confessions of a Right-Wing Liberal," *Ramparts*, June 1968, 48.
10. Raimondo, *An Enemy of the State*, 196.
11. Id., 214; Daniel Schulman, *Sons of Wichita: How the Koch Brothers Became America's Most Powerful and Private Dynasty* 100–101 (2014).
12. David Gordon, "The Kochtopus vs. Murray N. Rothbard," *Economic Policy Journal*, Mar. 28, 2014.
13. Murray Rothbard, *For a New Liberty: The Libertarian Manifesto*, 27 (rev. ed. 1978).
14. *An Austrian Perspective on the History of Economic Thought: Economic Thought Before Adam Smith, vol. 1*, 317 (1995).
15. Or in Hayek. Rothbard regarded Hayek's work as "extremely dangerous" because it approved of a great deal of state activity. "Confidential Memo to the Volker Fund on F. A. Hayek's Constitution of Liberty," in *Murray N. Rothbard vs. the Philosophers: Unpublished Writings on Hayek, Mises, Strauss, and Polanyi* 61 (Roberta A. Modugno ed. 2009). On the other hand, he published a gracious appreciation after Hayek won the Nobel Prize in Economics. "Hayek and the Nobel Prize," *Human Events*, Nov. 16, 1974.
16. Murray Rothbard, *The Ethics of Liberty*, 46 (NYU Press 1998).
17. Id., 46–47.
18. David Hume, "An Enquiry Concerning Human Understanding," in L.A. Selby-Bigge, ed., *Enquiries Concerning Human Understanding and the Principles of Morals* 142 (3d ed. 1975).
19. *Ethics of Liberty*, 14 n. 15.
20. Id., 45.

21. Matt Zwolinski, "Reading The Ethics of Liberty, Part 4—Rothbard's Second Argument for Self-Ownership," *Bleeding Heart Libertarians*, Oct. 4, 2012.
22. Nadav Shoked, "The Duty to Maintain," 64 *Duke L. J.*, 437 (2014).
23. Randy Barnett makes the identical error when, after justifying property rights on Hayekian grounds, he takes up the problem of unmet need or market failure as raising the question whether "the requirements of justice should be ignored or overridden." *The Structure of Liberty*, 166 (1998). Hayekian reasoning does not entail the requirements of justice as Barnett understands them. On a similar error in Gerald Gaus, see Andrew Koppelman, "Does Respect Require Antiperfectionism? Gaus on Liberal Neutrality," 22 *Harv. Rev. of Phil* 53, 58–59 (2015).
24. Matt Kibbe, *Don't Hurt People and Don't Take Their Stuff: A Libertarian Manifesto* (2014); Matt Zwolinski, "The Libertarian Nonaggression Principle," 32 *Soc. Phil. & Pol'y*, 62 (2016).
25. Rothbard, *For a New Liberty*, 31.
26. Id., 39.
27. Id., 23.
28. Id., 24.
29. Id., 25.
30. Id., 25.
31. Jeffrey Winters, *Oligarchy* (2011).
32. Douglass C. North, John Joseph Wallis, and Barry R. Weingast, *Violence and Social Orders: A Conceptual Framework for Interpreting Recorded Human History* 53 (rev. ed. 2013). In such an order, the creative destruction engendered by capitalist innovation would be intolerable: "The creation of new economic organizations directly threatens existing economic organizations and their patterns of rents." Id., 116.
33. Id., 274.
34. Id., 72.
35. Id., 169–81.
36. Mancur Olson, *Power and Prosperity: Outgrowing Communist and Capitalist Dictatorships* (2000).
37. Robert Kagan, "Not Fade Away: The myth of American decline," *New Republic*, Jan. 10, 2012.
38. *Ethics of Liberty*, 100. Jan Narveson, *The Libertarian Idea*, 274 (1988), reluctantly and tentatively reaches the same conclusion.
39. *Ethics of Liberty*, 57.
40. Friedrich Hayek, *The Constitution of Liberty*, 136 (1960).
41. *Ethics of Liberty*, 221. Jan Narveson similarly rejects any regulation of natural monopolies, because "the use of one's resources for whatever purposes one will is the hallmark of liberal freedom." *The Libertarian Idea*, 203. Nozick thought that property rights should be overridden in such a situation. Robert Nozick, *Anarchy, State, and Utopia*, 180 (1974).

42. Murray Rothbard, "Power and Market," in *Man, Economy, and State* 1117–21 (2nd ed., Mises Institute 2009).
43. James W. Child, "Can Libertarianism Sustain a Fraud Standard?," 104 *Ethics* 722 (1994). In chapter 4, I elaborate the point, which also applies to Rand.
44. Murray Rothbard, Law, "Property Rights, and Air Pollution," 3 *Cato J.* 55, 58–59 (Spring 1982).
45. Murray N. Rothbard, "Toward a Reconstruction of Utility and Welfare Economics," in *The Logic of Action One: Method, Money, and the Austrian School* 211 (1997).
46. Rothbard had difficulty accounting for the actual history of pollution in industrial economies. Alan Haworth, *Anti-Libertarianism: Markets, Philosophy, and Myth*, 112–13 (1994).
47. *For a New Liberty*, 256.
48. Id., 255.
49. Id., 259.
50. Id.
51. Matt Zwolinski, "Libertarianism and Pollution," 32 *Phil. & Pub. Pol'y* Q. 9, 9 (Fall/Winter 2014).
52. David Friedman, *The Machinery of Freedom: Guide to Radical Capitalism* 168 (2nd ed. 1989).
53. Rothbard, "Law, Property Rights, and Air Pollution," 83.
54. Id., 87–88.
55. Id., 70.
56. Id., 88.
57. Herbert L. Needleman, "The Removal of Lead from Gasoline: Historical and Personal Reflections," *Env. Res. Sec.* A84 20 (2000).
58. Jennifer Doleac, "New Evidence that Lead Exposure Increases Crime," Brookings, June 1, 2017.
59. Nozick so argues in *Anarchy, State, and Utopia*, 28–29. Rothbard is committed to the same view.
60. Zwolinski, *Libertarianism and Pollution.*
61. On the question of pollution, the 2020 Libertarian Party platform is Rothbardian: Governments are unaccountable for damage done to our environment and have a terrible track record when it comes to environmental protection. Protecting the environment requires a clear definition and enforcement of individual rights and responsibilities regarding resources like land, water, air, and wildlife. Where damages can be proven and quantified in a court of law, restitution to the injured parties must be required.
62. Richard A. Epstein, *Principles for a Free Society*, 194 (1998).
63. The excitement and adventure of a stateless world are admiringly elaborated in Barnett, *The Structure of Liberty*, 284–97.
64. Robert A. Heinlein, *Farnham's Freehold*, 314–15 (1964).
65. E.J. Dionne, Jr., *Why Americans Hate Politics*, 272 (1991).

66. Ralph Raico, "How Nozick Became a Libertarian," Feb. 5, 2002, https://www.lewrockwell.com/2002/02/ralph-raico/how-nozick-became-a-libertarian/.
67. Friedrich Nietzsche, *The Gay Science*, 193, 205 (1887; Walter Kaufmann trans. 1974).
68. *Anarchy, State, and Utopia*, 33.
69. Id., 52.
70. Id., 5.
71. Id., ix.
72. Id., 231.
73. Id., 344 n.2, citing Boris Bittker, *The Case for Black Reparations* (1973).
74. Id., 79.
75. Zwolinski, "Libertarianism and Pollution."
76. Rothbard was right, from the standpoint of his anarchism, to regret the ratification of the Constitution. See Andrew Koppelman, *The Tough Luck Constitution and the Assault on Health Care Reform*, 38–67 (2013).
77. Rothbard, *Ethics of Liberty*, 231–53.
78. For catalogs, which include many flaws I haven't discussed, see Jonathan Wolff, Robert Nozick: *Property, Justice, and the Minimal State* (1991); Haworth, *Anti-Libertarianism*.
79. Jonathan Wolff does observe that Nozick's proposal, to allow rights violations so long as compensation is paid, entails that "Nozick does not . . . believe that we should punish all rights violations." Wolff, Robert Nozick, 60. He "does not give any arguments for the principle of compensation, nor is he able to derive it from other libertarian assumptions." Id., 68.
80. Christine M. Korsgaard, "Taking the Law into Our Own Hands: Kant on the Right to Revolution," in *Reclaiming the History of Ethics: Essays for John Rawls* 301–2 (Andrews Reath et al. eds., 1997).
81. Id., 303. Kant's view is elaborated in Arthur Ripstein, *Force and Freedom: Kant's Legal and Political Philosophy*, 267–86 (2009).
82. Korsgaard, "Taking the Law," 303. In fairness to Nozick, I acknowledge that when he wrote, Kant's political philosophy was generally dismissed. Korsgaard and Ripstein had not yet published their work, which overturned that evaluation. But this excuse is not available to those today who embrace Nozick's neo-Kantian argument. Thanks to Sam Fleischacker for clarification on this point.
83. This commitment to the rule of law stands in a complex relation to lawbreaking and disruption, which evidently play a crucial role in bringing about democratic change and respect for the rights of the poorest citizens. There is that to be said for anarchistic thinking. See James C. Scott, *Two Cheers for Anarchism* (2012).
84. Onora O'Neill explains the Kantian view: "One type of principle that can be adopted by one agent yet cannot be adopted by all is a principle whose enactment destroys or disables or undercuts agency in at least some others

on at least some occasions and so renders those others at least temporarily unable to adopt that same principle." "The Great Maxims of Justice and Charity," in *Constructions of Reason*, 228 (1989).

85. Immanuel Kant, "The Metaphysics of Morals," in *Practical Philosophy*, 468 (Mary J. Gregor ed. 1996).
86. *Anarchy, State, and Utopia*, 34.
87. We saw in chapter 2 the inadequacy of Nozick's conception of property. I here will ignore the further difficulty that Nozick undermines his libertarianism in the last part of his book. There he envisions a plurality of autonomous communities, which can have very coercive institutions so long as there are exit rights. He does not pause to consider that post-New Deal America may be one such community.
88. Ayn Rand, *The Fountainhead*, 504–5 (1943; Signet 1952).
89. This is emphasized in Will Wilkinson, "Jonathan Chait on Ayn Rand," Sept. 16, 2009, https://willwilkinson.net/2009/09/16/jonathan-chait-on-ayn-rand/.
90. Rand, *Atlas Shrugged*, 381.
91. Roy A. Childs, "Ayn Rand and the Libertarian Movement," in *Liberty Against Power: Essays*, 265 (Joan Kennedy Taylor ed. 1994).
92. Elspeth Reeve, "How to Tell Paul Ryan Wants to Be Veep: He's Rejected His Former Idol Ayn Rand," *Atlantic Wire*, Apr. 26, 2012.
93. Anne C. Heller, *Ayn Rand and the World She Made* xii, 287 (2009).
94. S. Douglas Beets, "BB&T, Atlas Shrugged, and the Ethics of Corporation Influence on College Curricula," 13 *J. Acad. Ethics*, 311 (2015).
95. Gary Johnson, *Seven Principles of Good Government* 31 (2012). For voluminous other examples of her influence on the contemporary right, see Jonathan Chait, "Wealthcare," *New Republic*, Sept. 13, 2009.
96. Gregory Salmieri, "An Introduction to the Study of Ayn Rand," in *A Companion to Ayn Rand* 3 (Allan Gotthelf and Gregory Salmieri eds. 2016).
97. Kirsten Powers, "Donald Trump's 'kinder, gentler' version," *USA Today*, Apr. 11, 2016.
98. Ayn Rand, *Atlas Shrugged*, 975 (1957; Signet 1996).
99. Id., 381.
100. Id., 973.
101. Id., 380.
102. Doherty, *Radicals for Capitalism*, 543.
103. *Man's Rights*, in *Capitalism: The Unknown Ideal*, 322 (1967).
104. Paul Ryan, *A Roadmap for America's Future* (2010).
105. Lucy Madison, "Fact-checking Romney's '47 percent' comment," CBS News, Sept. 25, 2012.
106. Chait, "Wealthcare."
107. "The Objectivist Ethics," in *The Virtue of Selfishness*, 33 (1964).
108. See *Atlas Shrugged*, 973; Ayn Rand, "The Nature of Government," in *Capitalism: The Unknown Ideal*, 329.

109. "Government Financing in a Free Society," in *The Virtue of Selfishness*, 116.
110. *Atlas Shrugged*, 356.
111. Jennifer Burns, *Goddess of the Market: Ayn Rand and the American Right* 273 (2009).
112. Id., 104–6.
113. Ayn Rand's *Marginalia: Her Critical Comments on the Writings of Over 20 Authors*, 151, 153 (Robert Mayhew ed. 1995). John Tomasi argues that Rand is concerned about those on the bottom, because she argues that unregulated capitalism will make them better off. Free Market Fairness 135–36 (2012). This may be true of low income workers if one makes some mighty bold assumptions about the dysfunctionality of the welfare state. It is no help to those who don't earn enough to keep themselves alive, which is true of many who need expensive medical treatment.
114. *Atlas Shrugged*, 13. Jennifer Burns observes that Rand's "invocation of the self made man is muted by other messages in Rand's novel, particularly her fondness for inherited wealth, family businesses, and aristocracy." "'The Root of All Good': Ayn Rand's Meaning of Money," 4 *J. Cultural Economy*, 329, 340 (2011).
115. Though it is irrelevant to the evaluation of her published work, it is unsurprising that Rand could not comprehend a disciple's distress when Rand carried on an affair with the woman's husband. Gail Wynand's devastation, in *The Fountainhead*, at losing his wife to Howard Roark is more convincing.
116. *Atlas Shrugged*, 972.
117. Randians are divided about how to interpret her. Some think that she really believes that self-preservation is always at stake. See Chris Matthew Sciabarra, *Ayn Rand: The Russian Radical* 243 (2d ed. 2013). It is mysterious how she could think that.
118. *The Objectivist Ethics*, 23.
119. "What is Capitalism?," in *Capitalism: The Unknown Ideal*, 18.
120. George Kateb, "The Night Watchman State," 45 *American Scholar* 816, 824–25 (Winter 1975–76).
121. Sciabarra, *Ayn Rand*, 240–45.
122. John Gray, *Liberalism* 45–50 (2d ed. 1995).
123. Andrew Koppelman, "Is Marriage Inherently Heterosexual?," 42 *Am. J. of Jurisprudence* 51 (1997).
124. E.g., Martha Nussbaum, *Creating Capabilities: The Human Development Approach* (2013). How much redistribution that requires will depend on how much prosperity is likely to be delivered by a free market. Nussbaum relies on contestable ideas of human flourishing, but that is consistent with Rawls. See Andrew Koppelman, "Why Rawls Can't Support Liberal Neutrality: The Case of Special Treatment for Religion," 79 *Rev. of Politics* 287 (2017).
125. She is aware of Hume's argument, but is under the impression that she has defeated it. *The Objectivist Ethics*, 17.

Sarah Conly, *Against Autonomy: Justifying Coercive Paternalism*, 72 (2013). The points made below are elaborated, with a more careful philosophical apparatus, in Andrew Koppelman, "Drug Policy and the Liberal Self," 100 *Northwestern U. L. Rev.* 279 (2006).

Mark Kleiman reports one survey:

> Respondents were asked both whether they had ever tried a given drug and whether they had ever "felt 'hooked' on" that drug. Nicotine was the outlier: 59 percent of those who had ever smoked a cigarette reported that they had been dependent at one time or another. The only other form of drug taking with a capture ratio greater than 1 in 5 was smoking cocaine (22 percent). The ratios for the other three powerful mass-market drugs were remarkably close together: 17.1 percent for alcohol, 16.6 percent for powder cocaine, and 13.7 percent for marijuana.

Mark A.R. Kleiman, *Against Excess: Drug Policy for Results* 41–42 (1992); see also Erich Goode, *Drugs in American Society* 129–30 (5th ed. 1999)(of people who have taken an alcoholic drink at least once in their lives, 62 percent have also done so in the past month; the figures for other drugs are cigarettes, 40 percent; marijuana, 15 percent; heroin, 9 percent; cocaine, 8 percent; stimulants, 9 percent; and hallucinogens, 7 percent); Douglas N. Husak, *Drugs and Rights*, 124 (1992)("Daily users of cocaine constitute less than 5 percent of all persons who use it annually and less than 2 percent of persons who have ever tried it" and "the figures do not differ radically when cocaine is smoked in the form of crack").

These figures are misleading to the extent that they do not account for the importance of culture and environment in determining the severity of the consequences of capture. Becoming an addict is likely to be more destructive and more difficult to reverse if addicts are an isolated and liminal population rather than being integrated into normal society.

11. The most striking illustration I know of is Walter Pahnke's "Good Friday experiment." On that holiday in 1962, Pahnke administered capsules to twenty Protestant divinity students, who then attended a religious service. Half the capsules contained psilocybin, an extract of hallucinogenic mushrooms; the other half contained a placebo. Six months after the experiment, the subjects who had taken the hallucinogen, to a far greater extent than the control subjects, reported having had a mystical experience that produced persisting positive changes in attitude and behavior. Moreover, a follow-up set of interviews, conducted twenty-four to twenty-seven years after the original experiment, found that these effects persisted. "The experimental subjects [most of whom had been members of the clergy all of their lives, and so should be as qualified as anyone to know a religious experience when they have one] unanimously described their Good Friday psilocybin experience as having had elements of a genuinely mystical nature and characterized it as one of the highpoints of their spiritual life." Most of the control subjects,

126. *Atlas Shrugged*, 972. Here, too, she is not writing of mere biological survival but of man's "proper" survival.
127. Matt Zwolinski, "Ayn Rand's Ethical Egoism," in "Debate, Is Ayn Rand right about rights?," Apr. 16, 2017, http://www.learnliberty.org/blog/debate-is-ayn-rand-right-about-rights/. This fallacy is not peculiar to Rand. There is a tendency in many libertarian thinkers to begin with the first-person interest in property, and to silently convert it into a third-person obligation of others to respect what I have claimed. Jan Narveson, for instance, argues that labor gives one title to the whole product of one's labor, because "the various things one can do with that whole thing are what the agent saw herself to be in the way of enabling herself to do; that's what her action was *all about*." *The Libertarian Idea*, 83. This does not mean that the first Asian who came to Alaska got title to all of North America, because "it cannot be plausibly argued that her activity, what she saw herself to be doing, was using a whole continent or anything like it." Id., 85. Does this mean that, if she *had* understood her activity in that way, she would have had that title?
128. Eric Mack, "The Fundamental Moral Elements of Rand's Theory of Rights," in *The Philosophic Thought of Ayn Rand* 122, 152 (Douglas J. Den Uyl and Douglas B. Rasmussen eds. 1984).
129. Quoted in James Tully, A Discourse on Property: John Locke and his Adversaries 47 (1980).
130. Mack, "The Fundamental Moral Elements;" Jan Narveson, "Ayn Rand as Moral & Political Philosopher," 23 *Reason Papers* 96 (Fall 1998).
131. *The Objectivist Ethics*, 31.
132. Id., 32.
133. Id., 31.
134. *The Fountainhead*, 681.
135. David Schmidtz, *Elements of Justice* (2006), carefully distinguishes them.
136. Leslie Green, "Pornographies," 8 J. *Pol. Phil.* 27, 43–46 (2000). "Part of what is at stake when people age, when they are severely disabled, when they are chronically unemployed, is the fear that they are not, or are no longer, useful." Id., 46.
137. Thanks to Samuel Freeman for pointing this out.
138. *The Objectivist Ethics*, 26–27.
139. Heather Long, "56% of Americans think their kids will be worse off," *CNN Money*, Jan. 28, 2016.
140. *The Fountainhead*, 681.
141. "Patents and Copyrights," in *Capitalism: The Unknown Ideal*, 133. Quotations that follow are from this five-page essay.
142. Rand's defense of intellectual property doesn't work even given her premises. See Timothy Sandefur, "A Critique of Ayn Rand's Theory of Intellectual Property Rights," 9 *J. Ayn Rand Stud.* 139 (2007).
143. John Locke, *Two Treatises of Government*, 2.34, 291 (Peter Laslett ed. 1988).

144. John Locke, *A Letter Concerning Toleration*, 47 (James H. Tully, ed. 1983) (1689).
145. U.S. Const., Article I, Sec. 8.
146. Schmidtz, *Elements of Justice*, 40–49.
147. *The Constitution of Liberty*, 95.
148. Id., 118–30.
149. Friedrich Hayek, Law, Legislation, and *Liberty, v. 2:* The Mirage of Social Justice 63 (1976).
150. *Atlas Shrugged*, 961.
151. Letter to the Editor, *N.Y. Times*, Nov. 3, 1957, quoted in Harriet Rubin, *Ayn Rand's Literature of Capitalism*, *N.Y. Times*, Sept. 15, 2007.
152. An alternate reading might be that these people are innocently but inevitably experiencing the consequences of bad political principles, but elsewhere she explains who among them are the "guiltiest men." "Patents and Copyrights," 134.
153. *Atlas Shrugged*, 559.
154. Burns, *Goddess of the Market*, 34–36; Heller, *Ayn Rand and the World She Made*, 84.
155. Heller, *Ayn Rand and the World She Made*, 193.
156. Burns, *Goddess of the Market*, 59.
157. Heller, *Ayn Rand and the World She Made*, 131.
158. Id., 335.
159. David Brooks, *Bobos in Paradise: The New Upper Class and How They Got There* (2000).
160. The head of a steel company wrote to Rand in 1957: "For twenty-five years I have been yelling my head off about the little-realized fact that eggheads, socialists, communists, professors, and so-called liberals do not understand how goods are produced. Even the men who work at the machines do not understand it." Burns, *Goddess of the Market*, 168. He was right.
161. "America's Persecuted Minority: Big Business," in *Capitalism: The Unknown Ideal*, 48.
162. Friedrich Hayek, *The Road to Serfdom*, 39 (1944; rev. ed. 1976).
163. *Ayn Rand's Marginalia*, 149.
164. "The Anti-industrial Revolution," in *The New Left: The Anti-Industrial Revolution* 142 (2d rev. ed. 1975).
165. Introduction, in *The Virtue of Selfishness*, viii.
166. *Atlas Shrugged*, 941.
167. "The Ethics of Emergencies," in *The Virtue of Selfishness*, 44.
168. "What is Capitalism?," 26.
169. "The Ethics of Emergencies," 43.
170. Id., 48.
171. *The Road to Serfdom*, 120.
172. Id., 120–21.

173. *A Theory of Justice*, 9.
174. Iris Marion Young, *Justice and the Politics of Diff* masi similarly argues that Rawls tends "to empha *status* of citizens over that of their *agency*." Tom 265.
175. John Rawls, *Justice as Fairness: A Restatement*, 140
176. *Afterword*, in *Atlas Shrugged*, 1070.
177. Burns, *Goddess of the Market*, 19–20; Heller, *Ayn R Made*, 60–1, 68, 159.
178. Friedrich Nietzsche, *Beyond Good and Evil*, §68, trans. 1966).
179. Conor Lynch, "Libertarianism Is for White Men: T the Right's Favorite Movement," Salon, June 10, 2015; derstanding Libertarian Morality: The Psychological Identified Libertarians," 7 *PLoS ONE* (Aug. 21, 2012) .org/10.1371/journal.pone.0042366.
180. *The Journals of Ayn Rand*, 70 (David Harriman ed. 19 controversial because it has been alleged that the editor the material, but the Ayn Rand Institute kindly allowed n nal entry in Rand's handwriting. This passage is accurate.
181. This attractive aspect of Rand's vision is missed by many c critics. See Andrew Koppelman, "Involving Orcs," revie *Ayn Rand and the Culture of Greed*, by Lisa Duggan, *New R* 2019.
182. Doherty, *Radicals for Capitalism*, 14.
183. Richard Epstein's book *Principles for a Free Society* is more c and would be a better introduction to libertarianism for und
184. Nietzsche, *Beyond Good and Evil*, §5, 12.
185. Doherty's delightful history of the libertarian movement, *Radi talism*, is filled with more entertaining eccentrics than a Dicke

CHAPTER 4: NANNY

1. Friedrich Hayek, "The Use of Knowledge in Society," in *The Essen* 223 (Chiaki Nishiyama and Kurt R. Leube eds., 1984).
2. John Stuart Mill, *On Liberty*, 68 (Gertrude Himmelfarb ed., Peng 1974) (1859).
3. Friedrich Hayek, *The Road to Serfdom*, 59 (1944; rev. ed. 1976).
4. Friedrich Hayek, *The Constitution of Liberty*, 145 (1960).
5. Murray Rothbard, *For a New Liberty: The Libertarian Manifesto*, 1 ed. 1978).
6. David Boaz, *The Libertarian Mind: A Manifesto for Freedom*, 132 (20
7. Libertarian Party 2020 Platform, https://www.lp.org/platform/.

8.
9.
10.

on the other hand, "could barely remember even a few details of the service." Rick Doblin, Pahnke's " 'Good Friday Experiment': A Long-Term Follow-up and Methodological Critique," 23 J. of *Transpersonal Psych.* 1, 13 (1991). The experiment has not been repeated, because changing drug laws soon made it illegal to do so.

12. W. Travis Hanes and Frank Sanello, *Opium Wars: The Addiction of One Empire and the Corruption of Another*, 34 (2002).
13. For a review of the inconclusive evidence, see Robert J. MacCoun and Peter Reuter, *Drug War Heresies: Learning from Other Vices, Times, and Places*, 331–37 (2001).
14. Steven B. Duke and Albert C. Gross, *America's Longest War: Rethinking Our Tragic Crusade Against Drugs* (1993).
15. Deirdre McCloskey, *Crossing: A Memoir*, xiii–xiv (1999).
16. For survey and critique, see Andrew Koppelman, "Neutrality and the Religion Analogy," in *Religious Exemptions* (Kevin Vallier and Michael Weber, eds., 2018); Andrew Koppelman, "The Fluidity of Neutrality," 66 *Rev. of Politics* 633 (2004).
17. Murray Rothbard, *Toward a Reconstruction of Utility and Welfare Economics*, 28 (1956).
18. Gary Becker and Kevin Murphy, "A Theory of Rational Addiction," 96 *J. Pol. Econ.* 675, 691 (1988).
19. Homer, *Odyssey*, book IX, 139 (Richmond Lattimore, tr. 1967).
20. *Against Autonomy*, 9.
21. Mark A.R. Kleiman, "Neither Prohibition nor Legalization: Grudging Tolerance in Drug Control Policy," 121 *Daedalus* 53, 55 (1992).
22. Id., 59.
23. All these defects of rationality are elaborated in Kleiman, *Against Excess*, 30–45.
24. For one sophisticated economist's analysis of the problems presented by the plurality of the self, see Thomas Schelling, "The Intimate Contest for Self-Command," 60 *Pub. Interest*, 94–118 (1980).
25. As this is written in 2021, some states are in fact moving to grudging toleration or complete legalization of marijuana, which however remains technically illegal under federal law.
26. Frederick Schauer, "Slippery Slopes," 99 *Harv. L. Rev.* 361 (1985).
27. Norman H. Clark, *Deliver Us from Evil: An Interpretation of American Prohibition* 146–48 (1976); Mark Edward Lender and James Kirby Martin, *Drinking in America: A History*, 136–47 (rev. ed. 1987).
28. In 1922, Congress spent $6.75 million for a force of 3,060 Prohibition Bureau employees, including agents, clerks, and stenographers. Some districts had no automobiles or boats. Clark, *Deliver Us From Evil*, 161. "By 1926, state legislatures in the United States were appropriating annually a total of only $698,855 for Prohibition enforcement, an amount estimated as

approximately one-eighth of that which the same governments were spending to police their laws for the control of fish and game. Some states were spending nothing at all." Id., 163.

29. Mill, *On Liberty*, 151.
30. See Tamar Schapiro, "What is a Child?," 109 *Ethics* 715 (1999).
31. See Michael Massing, *The Fix*, 143–65 (1998).
32. Mark Edward Lender and James Kirby Martin, *Drinking in America: A History* (rev. ed. 1987). It became so because social norms had changed. Alcohol use leads to aggression and sexual arousal in some cultures but not others. Craig McAndrew and Robert Edgerton, *Drunken Comportment* (1969). Ethan Nadelmann observes that

    > while certain types of drugs are more difficult to use in moderation than others, the principal determinants of destructive drug use patterns involve not the pharmacology of the drug but the set and setting in which the drug is consumed. That is why alcohol consumption among conquered aboriginal groups and cocaine consumption among some inner-city populations have more in common with one another than either does with patterns of alcohol or cocaine consumption among less vulnerable sectors of the population.

    Ethan A. Nadelmann, "Thinking Seriously About Alternatives to Drug Prohibition," 121 *Daedalus* 85, 102 (1992).
33. Daniel Kahneman, *Thinking Fast and Slow* (2011).
34. Cass R. Sunstein and Richard H. Thaler, *Nudge: Improving Decisions About Health, Wealth, and Happiness* 5 (rev. ed. 2009).
35. Id., 105–13.
36. There is also a powerful case for moving beyond default rules to a more inflexible paternalism, which is what Social Security does. Ryan Bubb and Richard H. Pildes, "How Behavioral Economics Trims Its Sails and Why," 127 Harv. L. Rev. 1593 (2014).
37. Gregory Mitchell, "Libertarian Paternalism is an Oxymoron," 99 *Nw. U. L. Rev.* 1255–56 (2005).
38. Conly, *Against Autonomy*, 11, 90.
39. Mario J. Rizzo and Glen Whitman, *Escaping Paternalism: Rationality, Behavioral Economics, and Public Policy* 17 (2020).
40. This is emphasized in id.
41. Conly, *Against Autonomy*, 115.
42. Jacob S. Hacker and Paul Pierson, *American Amnesia: How the War on Government Led Us to Forget What Made America Prosper* 137 (2016).
43. There were no available national statistics on poverty among the elderly in the mid-1930s, but the Social Security Administration summarized a number of state-level statistics, the modes of which clustered around the 50 percent level. Social Security Administration, Social Security in

America: The factual background of the Social Security Act as summarized from staff reports to the Committee on Economic Security 149–54 (1937).

44. George A. Akerlof and Robert J. Shiller, *Phishing for Phools: The Economics of Manipulation and Deception*, 154 (2015).
45. Kathleen Romig, "Social Security Lifts More Americans Above Poverty Than Any Other Program," Center on Budget and Pol'y Priorities, Feb. 20, 2020.
46. Akerlof and Shiller, *Phishing for Phools*, 155.
47. Quoted in Sunstein, *Simpler*, 167.
48. See generally Akerlof and Shiller.
49. A notable example is the proliferation of risky financial products that led to the crash of 2008: "A major part of the reason Wall Street developed ever more complex products was precisely because it was so hard for clients—and regulators—to figure them out." Hacker and Pierson, *American Amnesia*, 285.
50. Epic Systems v. Lewis, 138 S.Ct. 1612 (2018).
51. See Judith Resnik, "Diffusing Disputes: The Public in the Private of Arbitration, the Private in Courts, and the Erasure of Rights," 124 *Yale L. J.* 2804 (2015).
52. Katherine V. W. Stone and Alexander J. S. Colvin, "The Arbitration Epidemic: Mandatory arbitration deprives workers and consumers of their rights," Economic Policy Institute, Dec. 7, 2015, 21.
53. Id., 21–22.
54. Id., 23.
55. Id., 19.
56. Doctor's Associates, Inc. v. Casarotto, 517 U.S. 681 (1996).
57. Jessica Silver-Greenberg and Robert Gebeloff, "Arbitration Everywhere, Stacking the Deck of Justice," *N.Y. Times*, Oct. 31, 2015.
58. American Express v. Italian Colors Restaurant, 570 U.S. 228, 236 (2013).
59. Elizabeth G. Thornburg, "Contracting with Tortfeasors: Mandatory Arbitration Clauses and Personal Injury Claims," 67 *L. & Contemp. Probs.* 253, 255 (2004).
60. Jessica Silver-Greenberg and Michael Corkery, "In Arbitration, a 'Privatization of the Justice System,'" *N.Y. Times*, Nov. 1, 2015.
61. This became notorious when Fox News argued that an arbitration clause barred suit by an employee who claimed sexual harassment by the broadcaster's chair. See Emily Martin, "Keeping Sexual Assault Under Wraps," *U.S. News*, Sept. 28, 2016.
62. Thomas L. Knapp, "Arbitration Isn't the Problem," Nov. 5, 2015, William Lloyd Garrison Center for Libertarian Advocacy Journalism.
63. Two classic catalogs of Hayekian complaints are Henry Hazlitt, *Economics in One Lesson* (1946), and Murray Rothbard, "Power and Market," in Man, Economy, and State, 1089–1144 (2d ed. 2009).

64. See Deepak Gupta and Lina Khan, *Arbitration as Wealth Transfer*, American Constitution Society Issue Brief, Feb. 2016.
65. Silver-Greenberg and Gebeloff, "Arbitration Everywhere."
66. James W. Child, "Can Libertarianism Sustain a Fraud Standard?," 104 *Ethics* 722 (1994). Nozick's difficulties in thinking about fraud are noted in Jonathan Wolff, *Robert Nozick: Property, Justice, and the Minimal State* 85–86 (1991).
67. *The Constitution of Liberty*, 144. For similar analyses, more closely tied to the actual legal doctrine of fraud, see Randy E. Barnett, *The Structure of Liberty: Justice and the Rule of Law*, 102–6 (1998); Richard A. Epstein, *Simple Rules for a Complex World*, 81–82 (1995).
68. *The Road to Serfdom*, 39. Bruce Caldwell explains why Hayek cannot simply assume that people act in their own best interests in market transactions:

    > Hayek's central question is as follows: What set of institutional arrangements might best assist fallible individuals to make better decisions and better use of their knowledge? This is a very Austrian question, and it is one that some new institutionalist economists also ask. It is emphatically not the sort of question that springs naturally to the mind of those working with models populated by *homo economicus*.

    Bruce Caldwell, *Hayek's Challenge: An Intellectual Biography of F. A. Hayek* 286–87 (2004).
69. *Black's Law Dictionary*, 10th ed., ed. Bryan A. Garner (2014), s.v. "fraud."
70. Id., quoting John Willard, *A Treatise on Equity Jurisprudence* 147 (Platt Potter ed., 1879).
71. Id.
72. Rebecca Tushnet, "It Depends on What the Meaning of 'False' Is: Falsity and Misleadingness in Commercial Speech Doctrine," 41 *Loyola L.A. L. Rev.* 227 (2007).
73. Luigi Zingales, *A Capitalism for the People*, 167 (2012). Zingales shows how, in countries with low levels of trust, economic cooperation is confined within families, and economic growth is stunted.
74. E.J. Dionne, Jr., *Why Americans Hate Politics*, 282 (1991).
75. Id., 281.
76. Conly, *Against Autonomy*, 42.

CHAPTER 5: LIBERTY

1. Friedrich Hayek, *The Constitution of Liberty*, 29 (1960).
2. Glenn Kessler, "Rand Paul's rewriting of his own remarks on the Civil Rights Act," *Wash. Post*, Apr. 11, 2013. In fact, as early as college, he wrote that "every piece of anti-discrimination legislation passed over the past few decades, ignores one of the basic, inalienable rights of man—the right to discriminate." Conor Lynch, "Libertarianism is for white men," *Salon*, Jun 10, 2015.

3. John Locke, *A Letter Concerning Toleration*, 46 (James H. Tully, ed. 1983) (1689).
4. Id., 29.
5. See also Samuel R. Bagenstos, "The Unrelenting Libertarian Challenge to Public Accommodations Law," 66 *Stan. L. Rev.* 1205 (2014).
6. Ayn Rand, *The Virtue of Selfishness: A New Concept of Egoism* 134 (1964).
7. Murray Rothbard, For a New Liberty: The Libertarian Manifesto 206 (rev. ed. 1978). For a similar view, see Charles Murray, *What it Means to Be a Libertarian: A Personal Interpretation*, 79–89 (1997).
8. Robert Bork, "Civil Rights—A Challenge," 149 *New Republic*, Aug. 31, 1963, 22. Other contemporaneous examples of the same reasoning are collected in Linda C. McClain, *Who's the Bigot? Learning from Conflicts over Marriage and Civil Rights Law*, 121 (2020).
9. See Deirdre McCloskey, *The Bourgeois Virtues: Ethics for an Age of Commerce* (2006).
10. Nathan B. Oman, "Doux Commerce, Religion, and the Limits of Antidiscrimination Law," 92 *Ind. L. J.* 693, 712 (2017).
11. Richard Epstein, *Forbidden Grounds: The Case Against Employment Discrimination Laws* (1992).
12. Id., 28–58.
13. *Capitalism and Freedom* 108–15 (1962).
14. Alan Ebenstein, *Friedrich Hayek: A Biography* 294–95 (2003).
15. Friedrich Hayek, Law, Legislation, and Liberty, *v. 2: The Mirage of Social Justice*, 100 (1976).
16. The only source his biographer cites for his views on antidiscrimination laws is a few remarks in a 1961 interview in South Africa. Ebenstein, *Friedrich Hayek*, 294–95.
17. Samuel Issacharoff, "Contractual Liberties in Discriminatory Markets," 70 *Tex. L. Rev.* 1219, 1242–43 (1992); "Symposium, Forbidden Grounds: The Case Against Employment Discrimination Laws," 31 *San Diego L. Rev.* 1 (1994 John J. Donohue III, "Is Title VII Efficient?," 134 *U. Pa. L. Rev.* 1411, 1415–19 (1986).
18. James J. Heckman and J. Hoult Verkerke, "Racial Disparity and Employment Discrimination Law: An Economic Perspective," 8 *Yale L. & Pol'y Rev.* 276, 281 (1990).
19. Elizabeth Anderson, *The Imperative of Integration* (2010) is a thorough survey of the persisting effects of racism in America.
20. John D'Emilio, "Capitalism and Gay Identity," in Ann Snitow et al. eds., *Powers of Desire: The Politics of Sexuality* (1983).
21. It also matters whether the blockage comes from isolated actors in the market or a single dominant entity. In a case involving the Boy Scouts, the Supreme Court, reasoning in a libertarian spirit, treated the largest youth organization in the world as though it were a small private club. See Andrew

Koppelman with Tobias Barrington Wolff, *A Right to Discriminate? How the Case of* Boy Scouts of America v. James Dale *Warped the Law of Free Association* (2009).

22. See Tarunaibh Khaitan, *A Theory of Discrimination Law* (2015).
23. Joseph Fishkin, "The Anti-Bottleneck Principle in Employment Discrimination Law," 91 *Wash. U. L. Rev.* 1429, 1444–52 (2014).
24. See Joseph Fishkin, *Bottlenecks: A New Theory of Equal Opportunity* (2014).
25. Andrew Koppelman, *Antidiscrimination Law and Social Equality*, 181–90 (1996).
26. See Jonathan Haidt, *The Righteous Mind: Why Good People are Divided by Politics and Religion*, 170–177 (2012).
27. See Koppelman, *Antidiscrimination Law*, 220–64; Andrew Koppelman, "A Free Speech Response to the Gay Rights/Religious Liberty Conflict," 110 *Northwestern U. L. Rev.* 1125 (2016).
28. Andrew Koppelman, *Gay Rights vs. Religious Liberty? The Unnecessary Conflict* (2020).
29. David Boaz, *The Libertarian Mind: A Manifesto for Freedom*, 119 (2015).
30. There is a deeper problem with Boaz's assertion, going beyond the scope of this book. Humans are always born into the world with duties to those who raised them. Any social contract presumes that the parties have mutual obligations that precede contract: "If they are in a position to decide their common future, it is because they already have one: because they recognize their mutual togetherness and reciprocal dependence, which makes it incumbent upon them to settle how they might be governed under a common jurisdiction in a common territory." Roger Scruton, *How to Be a Conservative*, 23 (2014).
31. Libertarian Party 2020 Platform, https://www.lp.org/platform/.
32. On pornography, see Andrew Koppelman, "Does Obscenity Cause Moral Harm?," 105 *Columbia L. Rev.* 1635 (2005).
33. See Diaz v. Pan American World Airways, Inc., 442 F.2d 385 (5th Cir. 1971).
34. Kimberly Yuracko, "Private Nurses and Playboy Bunnies: Explaining Permissible Sex Discrimination," 92 *Calif. L. Rev.* 147, 196 (2004).
35. Id., 205.
36. Id., 205–9.
37. Regina v. Brown, [1993] 2 All E.R. 75 (U.K. House of Lords).
38. Laskey, Jaggard and Brown v. the United Kingdom Judgment of 19 February 1997, Reports of Judgments and Decisions, Eur. Court HR, 1997-I at 119.
39. William N. Eskridge, Jr., *Gaylaw: Challenging the Apartheid of the Closet* 261 (1999).
40. Id., 260–61.
41. Id., 84.

42. The most recent reported American prosecution for consensual sadomasochistic assault is People v. Samuels, 250 Cal. App. 2d 501, 58 Cal. Rptr. 439 (1st Dist. 1967). Consent was declared to be no defense to sadomasochistic assault in State v. Collier, 372 N.W. 2d 303 (Iowa 1985), and Commonwealth v. Appleby, 380 Mass. 296, 402 N.E. 2d 1051 (1980), but in both those cases defendants' claims of consent were contrary to the testimony of their victims.
43. Cheryl Hanna, "No Right to Choose: Mandated Victim Participation in Domestic Violence Prosecutions," 109 *Harv. L. Rev* 1849 (1996).
44. See generally Debra Satz, *Why Some Things Should Not Be For Sale: The Moral Limits of Markets* (2010).
45. Koch was quoting libertarian activist Baldy Harper. Daniel Schulman, *Sons of Wichita: How the Koch Brothers Became America's Most Powerful and Private Dynasty*, 100 (2014).
46. Martha C. Nussbaum, *Hiding from Humanity: Disgust, Shame, and the Law*, 107–15 (2004).
47. Karl Marx, "On the Jewish Question," in *The Marx-Engels Reader*, 42 (Robert C. Tucker ed., 2d ed. 1978).
48. Edmund Burke, *Reflections on the Revolution in France* 194 (Conor Cruise O'Brien ed. 1968).
49. Id.
50. Friedrich A. Hayek, *Individualism and Economic Order* 5 (1948).
51. Charles Taylor, Sources of the Self (1989).
52. Garry Wills, *A Necessary Evil: A History of American Distrust of Government* (1999).
53. Richard Weiss, *The American Myth of Success: From Horatio Alger to Norman Vincent Peale* 5 (1969).
54. Gwen Ifill, "Clinton's Standard Campaign Speech: A Call for Responsibility," *N.Y. Times*, Apr. 26, 1992.
55. John Ermisch et al., eds., *From Parents to Children: The Intergenerational Transmission of Advantage* (2012); Pew Charitable Trusts Economic Mobility Project, *Economic Mobility: Is the American Dream Alive and Well?* 9–10 (May 2007).

CHAPTER 6: MOOCHERS

1. Friedrich Hayek, *Law, Legislation, and Liberty, v. 3: The Political Order of a Free People*, 6 (1979).
2. See Geoffrey Kabaservice, *Rule and Ruin: The Downfall of Moderation and the Destruction of the Republican Party, from Eisenhower to the Tea Party* 1–16 (2012).
3. Id. at 72–122.

4. Rick Perlstein, *Before the Storm: Barry Goldwater and the Unmaking of the American Consensus*, 462 (2001)(quoting Goldwater speech, coauthored by William Rehnquist and political theorist Harry Jaffa).
5. Kim Phillips-Fein, *Invisible Hands: The Businessmen's Crusade Against the New Deal*, 140–41 (2009).
6. Eric Foner, *The Story of American Freedom*, 320–21 (1998).
7. Phillips-Fein, *Invisible Hands*, 264.
8. Michael Lewis, *The Fifth Risk* (2018).
9. Daniel A. Farber, "Regulatory Review in Anti-Regulatory Times," 94 *Chi.-Kent L. Rev.* 383 (2019); Brad Plumer and Coral Davenport, "Science Under Attack: How Trump Is Sidelining Researchers and Their Work," *N.Y. Times*, Dec. 28, 2019.
10. Coral Davenport, "Counseled by Industry, Not Staff, EPA Chief is Off to a Blazing Start," *N.Y. Times*, July 1, 2017.
11. Theda Skocpol and Vanessa Williamson, *The Tea Party and the Remaking of Republican Conservatism* (2012).
12. David Frum, "Crashing the Party," 93 *Foreign Aff.* 37 (2014).
13. David Frum, "When Did the GOP Lose Touch With Reality?," *New York*, Nov. 20, 2011.
14. Matthew Continetti, "The Paranoid Style in Liberal Politics," *Wash. Examiner*, Apr. 4, 2011.
15. Jane Mayer, Dark Money: *The Hidden History of the Billionaires Behind the Rise of the Radical Right*, 9 (rev. ed. 2017).
16. Quoted in James K. Glassman, "Market-Based Man," *Philanthropy*, Fall 2011.
17. "Transcript: Obama's Interview Aboard Air Force One," *N.Y. Times*, Mar. 7 2009.
18. Rebekah Metzler, "Obama: I Am Not a Socialist," *U.S. News*, Nov. 19, 2013.
19. Sheri Berman, *The Primacy of Politics: Social Democracy and the Making of Europe's Twentieth Century* (2006); Sheri Berman, "Unheralded Battle: Capitalism, the Left, Social Democracy and Democratic Socialism," *Dissent* (Winter, 2009).
20. A prominent exception is Elizabeth Anderson. See "So You Want to Live in a Free Society (1): What Hayek Saw," *Left2Right*, May 27, 2005; "How Not to Complain About Taxes (III): 'I deserve my pretax income,'" *Left2Right*, Jan. 26, 2005.
21. This conflation goes back to Goldwater. See E. J. Dionne Jr., *How the Right Went Wrong*, 53 (2016).
22. Michael Grunwald, *The New New Deal: The Hidden Story of Change in the Obama Era*, 56 (2012).
23. John Locke, *Two Treatises of Government*, 1.42, 170 (Peter Laslett ed. 1988).
24. Id.
25. Friedrich Hayek, *The Road to Serfdom*, 120–21 (1944; rev. ed. 1976).
26. Friedrich Hayek, *The Constitution of Liberty*, 298 (1960).

27. Jonathan Cohn, *The Ten Year War: Obamacare and the Unfinished Crusade for Universal Coverage*, 139–51 (2021).
28. Andrew Koppelman, *The Tough Luck Constitution and the Assault on Health Care Reform*, 5 (2013).
29. Lawrence R. Jacobs and Theda Skocpol, *Health Care Reform and American Politics: What Everyone Needs to Know*, 135 (2010).
30. Stuart M. Butler, "Assuring Affordable Health Care for All Americans," Heritage Foundation, 1989.
31. *The Road to Serfdom*, viii.
32. Michael Lind, "Here's how GOP Obamacare hypocrisy backfires," *Salon*, Oct. 28, 2013.
33. Seven-Sky v. Holder, 661 F.3d 1, 53 (D.C. Cir. 2011)(Kavanaugh, J., dissenting as to jurisdiction).
34. Donald Cohen, "The History of Privatization," Talking Points Memo, 2016.
35. Michael Cohen, *How for-profit prisons have become the biggest lobby no one is talking about*, Wash. Post, Apr. 28, 2015.
36. Justice Policy Institute, *Gaming the System: How the Political Strategies of Private Prison Companies Promote Ineffective Incarceration Policies* (Oct. 2011).
37. David Dayen, "The True Cost," Talking Points Memo, 2016.
38. Sharon Dolovich, *State Punishment and Private Prisons*, 55 *Duke L. J.* 437 (2005).
39. Timothy S. Jost, "Health Care Reform and A Failed Vision of Bipartisanship," 35 *Health Aff.* 1748 (Oct. 2016).
40. Tim Phillips, "President Obama's health care law is unraveling," *Daily Caller*, Feb. 29, 2012.
41. Quoted in Paul Starr, *Remedy and Reaction: The Peculiar American Struggle over Health Care Reform* 213 (2011).
42. Tom Daschle with David Nather, *Getting It Done: How Obama and Congress Finally Broke the Stalemate to Make Way for Health Care Reform* 152, 187 (2010); Letter of Douglas Elmendorf, Director, Congressional Budget Office, to Rep. Bruce Braley, Dec. 29, 2009, available at http://www.cbo.gov/sites/default/files/cbofiles/ftpdocs/108xx/doc10872/12-29-tort_reform-braley.pdf.
43. A few outlier Republicans, such as Senator Olympia Snowe, might have supported the law, but after many discussions Majority Leader Harry Reid could not pin her down on what it would take to get her vote. Daschle, *Getting It Done*, 220.
44. In fact, it is an ordinary exercise of Congress's long-established choice of means for carrying out its enumerated powers. See Andrew Koppelman, "'Necessary,' 'Proper,' and Health Care Reform," in *The Health Care Case: The Supreme Court's Decision and Its Implications*, 105 (Nathaniel Persily et al., eds., 2013).

45. It might however have the unanticipated consequence of hamstringing the federal government's capacity to respond to pandemics, since compulsory testing and vaccination might be resisted by some who are not engaged in any self-initiated action. Andrew Koppelman and Steven Lubet, "Is the Roberts Court going to let coronavirus kill us?," *Just Security*, Apr. 17, 2020.
46. See Randy Barnett, *The Structure of Liberty* (1998). This book, Barnett's principal work of political philosophy, begins with a Hayekian exploration of the benefits of property and contract for facilitating social cooperation and managing information. Halfway through, it becomes a Rothbardian fantasy of how these benefits could be delivered without a state, via a pattern of private contracts. When I described Barnett's philosophy in *The Tough Luck Constitution* (76–90), I did not understand the Rothbard connection. He is a better philosopher than Rothbard, but duplicates many of Rothbard's errors, notably his uncritical optimism about what anarchy would look like.
47. Koppelman, *The Tough Luck Constitution*, 16.
48. Cohn, *The Ten Year War*, 292–93.
49. Philip Klein, *Overcoming Obamacare: Three Approaches to Reversing the Government Takeover of Health Care*, 87 (2015).
50. See, e.g., id., passim. I say this dubitante, because the consumer-driven model on which they are based rests on an implausibly idealized psychology and underestimates the opacity of insurance markets to consumers. See Timothy Stoltzfus Jost, *Health Care at Risk: A Critique of the Consumer-Driven Movement* (2007).
51. Sarah Kliff, "Why Obamacare enrollees voted for Trump," *Vox*, Dec. 13, 2016.
52. There were a number of different estimates of the law's effects. Here is one: the Congressional Budget Office estimated that in the following decade, 23 million Americans would lose their insurance, and taxes would be cut by $661 billion. Congressional Budget Office, Cost Estimate: H.R. 1628, American Health Care Act of 2017, May 24, 2017.
53. Christopher Leonard, Kochland: *The Secret History of Koch Industries and Corporate Power in America*, 537–41 (2019).
54. Rand Paul and Mark Meadows, "Let's fully repeal ObamaCare, then have an open debate on how to replace it," Fox News, Mar. 6, 2017.
55. Koppelman, *The Tough Luck Constitution*, 122–29.
56. Id., 139–42.
57. Rachel Garfield, Kendal Orgera, and Anthony Damico, "The Coverage Gap: Uninsured Poor Adults in States that Do Not Expand Medicaid," Kaiser Family Foundation, Jan. 2021.
58. Alexander Hertel-Fernandez, Theda Skocpol, and Daniel Lynch, "Business Associations, Conservative Networks, and the Ongoing Republican War over Medicaid Expansion," 41 J. *Health Politics, Policy & Law*, 239 (2016).
59. Sarah Miller et. al, "Medicaid and Mortality: New Evidence from Linked Survey and Administrative Data," *NBER Working Paper* No. 26081 (rev. Aug. 2019).

60. Bruce Caldwell, *Hayek's Challenge: An Intellectual Biography of F. A. Hayek* 226–29 (2004).
61. Grunwald, *The New New Deal*, 10.
62. Id., 14.
63. Id., 218.
64. *The Road to Serfdom*, 38–39.
65. See, for example, Henry Hazlitt, *Economics in One Lesson* 31–36 (rev. ed. 1979).
66. Hacker and Pierson, *American Amnesia*, 102–3.
67. Id., 39; Matt Hourihan, "A Snapshot of U.S. R&D Competitiveness: 2020 Update," *Am. Assn. for the Advancement of Science*, Oct. 22, 2020, https://www.aaas.org/news/snapshot-us-rd-competitiveness-2020-update; James Pethokoukis, "US federal research spending is at a 60-year low. Should we be concerned?," *American Enterprise Institute* blog, May 11, 2020, https://www.aei.org/economics/us-federal-research-spending-is-at-a-60-year-low-should-we-be-concerned/.
68. Hacker and Pierson, *American Amnesia*, 41.
69. James McBride and Anshu Siripurapu, "The State of U.S. Infrastructure, Council on Foreign Relations," Nov. 8, 2021, https://www.cfr.org/backgrounder/state-us-infrastructure.
70. Hacker and Pierson, *American Amnesia*, 41.
71. Theda Skocpol and Alexander Hertel-Fernandez, "The Koch Network and Republican Party Extremism," *14 Perspectives on Politics* 681, 694 (2016); Hiroko Tabuchi, "How the Koch Brothers Are Killing Public Transit Projects Around the Country," *N.Y. Times*, June 19, 2018.
72. Maureen Groppe, "'Stop the Spending Spree': Fiscal conservatives mobilize to block Biden's jobs and families plans," *USA Today*, May 13, 2021.
73. Federation of American Societies for Experimental Biology, NIH Research Funding Trends (Sept. 2019).
74. Id.
75. Quoted in Dionne, *Why the Right Went Wrong*, 335.
76. Hacker and Pierson, American Amnesia, 63–69.
77. Julian Davis Mortenson and Nicholas Bagley, "Delegation at the Founding," 121 *Colum. L. Rev.*, 277 (2021).
78. Gundy v. United States, 139 S. Ct. 2116, 2130 (2019)(plurality opinion).
79. Murray Rothbard, "Law, Property Rights, and Air Pollution," 3 *Cato J.* 55, 70, 87–88 (Spring 1982).
80. Daniel Schulman, *Sons of Wichita: How the Koch Brothers Became America's Most Powerful and Private Dynasty*, 106 (2014).
81. Daniel Fisher, "Inside the Koch Empire: How The Brothers Plan To Reshape America," *Forbes*, Dec. 24, 2012.
82. In 1978 he declared:

> Our greatest strength is that our philosophy is a consistent world view and will appeal to the brightest, most enthusiastic, most capable

> people, particularly young people. But to realize that strength, we have to state it in a radical, pure form. Now, if we don't, if we temporize, if we state it in a conservative form, then we're going to lose the appeal of that. And the temptation is particularly great because the other side of that is our greatest weakness; that is, because we have a radical philosophy, we don't appeal to people who are in positions of influence, people with status or wealth. We don't have business people, for example. So the temptation is, let's compromise, let's temporize, let's be much more gradual than we should be. As a result, we could destroy the appeal to the comers of this world, and therefore we destroy the movement.

"Reflections and Prognostications," *Reason*, May 1978.

83. Yasha Levine and Mark Ames, "Charles Koch to Friedrich Hayek: Use Social Security!," *The Nation*, Oct. 17, 2011.
84. Stephen Moore, "Private Enterprise," *Wall St. Journal*, May 6, 2006. In his most recent book, however, Koch says that the authors "who have had the most influence on me are probably Abraham Maslow and Friedrich Hayek," Maslow for teaching self-actualization and Hayek for showing that "human well-being and progress come through a spontaneous order of cooperation and competition." Charles Koch with Brian Hooks, *Believe in People: Bottom-Up Solutions for a Top-Down World*, 257 (2020). The gesture toward Hayek is less revealing than his earlier, repeated references to Mises and Harper.
85. Charles Koch, *Good Profit: How Creating Value for Others Built One of the World's Most Successful Companies* 13–14 (2015).
86. Moore, *Private Enterprise*.
87. Timothy Noah, "Charles Koch, Listen to Your Guru!," *Politico*, Nov. 30, 2015. In advanced capitalist countries, there is considerable variability in the relation between economic growth and wages. Lane Kenworthy, *Social Democratic Capitalism*, 88–89, 146–51 (2020).
88. F. A. Harper, *Why Wages Rise*, 73 (1957).
89. Id., 72.
90. Koch, *Good Profit*, 14.
91. Ludwig von Mises, *Human Action: A Treatise on Economics*, 851 (Mises Institute 1998).
92. Id., 237.
93. Ludwig von Mises, *The Ultimate Foundation of Economic Science* 44 (1962).
94. Mises, *Human Action*, 715.
95. Id.
96. Henry Hazlitt, *Economics in One Lesson*, 32 (1979; 1st ed. 1946).
97. Id.
98. "Review of Hayek, The Constitution of Liberty," *Christian Economics*, Aug. 1, 1960.
99. Id.
100. Ludwig von Mises, *Socialism*, 431 (rev. ed. 1951; Liberty Fund 1981).

101. Quoted in Jennifer Burns, *Goddess of the Market: Ayn Rand and the American Right*, 177 (2009).
102. Mises, reviewing Rothbard's work, expressed no reservations about the economics. Ludwig von Mises, "A New Treatise on Economics," *New Individualist Review*, Autumn, 1962.
103. *Human Action*, 651.
104. Id., 653.
105. Id.
106. It is hard to be certain, because the only source of data is Koch's self-reporting to *Forbes* magazine.
107. Leonard, *Kochland*, 1–2.
108. Sons of Wichita, 245.
109. Fisher, *Inside The Koch Empire*.
110. *Believe in People* 9; Charles Koch, *The Science of Success* 27 (2007); *Good Profit*, 5.
111. Leonard, *Kochland*, 5–6, 50, 148–49.
112. Wallace S. Moyle, "The Derivations of Charles Koch," *American Affairs*, Feb. 20, 2020.
113. Leonard, *Kochland*, 371–88, 517–26.
114. *Sons of Wichita*, 249.
115. Id., 211–21.
116. Id., 184.
117. Perhaps Koch, following Mises, thinks that liability, not regulation, should forestall such reckless risk taking, but that instrument is ineffective in a world of limited liability corporations. Koch has carefully proliferated such corporations within the structure of his business, so that the ruinous liability of one branch cannot damage the entire structure.
118. *Good Profit*, 82. He attributes the pipe's weakness to "corrosion . . . caused by bacteria in the soil that acted more quickly than leading U.S. experts had ever found." Id., 83. Had the jury agreed, it could not have awarded a penny.
119. See, for example, his *Freakonomics* interview, June 21 and 22, 2017.
120. "Reflections and Prognostications," *Reason*, May 1978.
121. Charles Koch, "The Business Community: Resisting Regulation," 7 *Libertarian Rev.* 30, 32 (Aug. 1978). This argument could rationalize the Kochs' acceptance of targeted tax abatements, which otherwise look like the crony capitalism they denounce.
122. Brian Doherty, *Radicals for Capitalism: A Freewheeling History of the Modern American Libertarian Movement*, 316 (2007). Koch's radical inclinations are sometimes tempered by a streak of cautious incrementalism. Asked by an interviewer what he would do if he could push a button that would instantly end all illegitimate state actions, he declined. "We'd have

mass chaos. I want to go just as fast and as far as we continue to get better results but we must do it in a way that the change demonstrates that people will be better off. I don't see how we'll get far down the road if we take steps that make people worse off." Id., 606. His recent support for legislation that would deprive millions of health insurance suggests that he has revisited this question.

123. Mayer, *Dark Money*, xiv.
124. Jane Mayer, "New Koch," *New Yorker*, Jan. 25, 2016; Ian Austen, "A Black Mound of Canadian Oil Waste Is Rising over Detroit," *N.Y. Times*, May 17, 2013.
125. Koch, "The Business Community."
126. The pattern of lying is detailed in Mayer, Dark Money, 150-56.
127. Koch, *Science of Success*, 44.
128. Mayer, *Dark Money*, 169.
129. *Science of Success*, 44.
130. Barack Obama, *A Promised Land*, 261 (2020).
131. Leonard, *Kochland*, 225.
132. Id., 526.
133. Mayer, "New Koch."
134. Skocpol and Hertel-Fernandez, *The Koch Network and Republican Party Extremism*, passim; Alexander Hertel-Fernandez, *State Capture: How Conservative Activists, Big Businesses, and Wealthy Donors Reshaped the American States—and the Nation* (2019).
135. Skocpol and Hertel-Fernandez, "The Koch Network and Republican Party Extremism," 690.
136. *Sons of Wichita*, 266–68.
137. Daniel Carpenter and David A. Moss, *Introduction*, in *Preventing Regulatory Capture: Special Interest Influence and How to Limit It* (Carpenter and Moss eds. 2013).
138. Hacker and Pierson, *American Amnesia*, 288.
139. Mayer, *Dark Money*, 244.
140. Hacker and Pierson, *American Amnesia*, 94.
141. Jonathan H. Adler, "Taking Property Rights Seriously: The Case of Climate Change," 26 *Soc. Phil. & Pol'y*, 296 (2009).
142. *Science of Success*, 124.
143. Leonard, *Kochland*, 400.
144. Jane Mayer, "'Kochland' Examines the Koch Brothers' Early, Crucial Role in Climate-Change Denial," *New Yorker* Daily Comment, Aug. 13, 2019.
145. Mayer, Dark Money, 198.
146. Theda Skocpol, "Naming the Problem: What It Will Take to Counter Extremism and Engage Americans in the Fight Against Global Warming" (Jan. 2013).
147. Leonard, *Kochland*, 416–18, 451–54.

148. Skocpol and Hertel-Fernandez, "The Koch Network and Republican Party Extremism," 693.
149. Coral Davenport and Eric Lipton, "How G.O.P. Leaders Came to View Climate Change as Fake Science," *N.Y. Times*, June 3, 2017.
150. Hacker and Pierson, *American Amnesia*, 288–96.
151. Leonard, *Kochland*, 433.
152. Id., 439–40.
153. Mayer, *Dark Money*, 243–77.
154. For comprehensive reviews of the misinformation, see Constantine Boussalis and Travis G. Coan, "Text-mining the signals of climate change doubt," 36 *Global Environmental Change* 89 (2016); Peter Jacques et al., "The organisation of denial: Conservative think tanks and environmental skepticism," 17 *Env. Politics*, 349 (2008).
155. Jim Tankersley and Chris Mooney, "What Charles Koch really thinks about climate change," *Wash. Post.* June 6, 2016.
156. Stephen J. Dubner, "Why Hate the Koch Brothers? (Part 2)," *Freakonomics*, June 22, 2017.
157. George F. Will, "Global Warming Advocates Ignore the Boulders," *Wash. Post*, Feb. 21, 2010.
158. Charles Krauthammer, "Carbon Chastity," *Wash. Post*, May 30, 2008.
159. Mayer, *Dark Money*, 257.
160. Brian Doherty, "Trump's Dangerous Anti-Libertarian Nationalism," *Reason*, Feb. 17, 2017; Will Wilkinson, "Revitalizing Liberalism in the Age of Brexit and Trump," Niskanen Center, Nov. 30, 2016.
161. Leonard, *Kochland*, 556–57.
162. Koch, *Science of Success*, x.
163. Kate Tuttle, "Jane Mayer discusses her book 'Dark Money' and its ongoing relevance," *Los Angeles Times*, Apr. 12, 2017.
164. John Rawls, *Justice as Fairness: A Restatement* 138 (2001).
165. Lane Kenworthy, "Economic Inequality and Plutocracy," 51 *Contemp. Sociology* 6 (2022); Task Force on Inequality and American Democracy, American Political Science Association, "American Democracy in an Age of Rising Inequality," 2 *Perspectives on Politics* 651, 661–62 (2004).
166. Martin Gilens and Benjamin I. Page, "Testing Theories of American Politics: Elites, Interest Groups, and Average Citizens," 12 *Persp. on Politics* 564 (2014).
167. Jeffrey Winters, *Oligarchy* (2011).
168. David Bernstein, *Only One Place of Redress: African Americans, Labor Regulations, and the Courts from Reconstruction to the New Deal* (2001).
169. Jake Rosenfeld, *What Unions No Longer Do* (2014). The dysfunctions of the American labor movement are to some extent the consequence of earlier proto-libertarian judicial interventions, which made the fate of labor legislation uncertain and channeled the labor movement into a few bottleneck industries such as coal and steel. See William E. Forbath, "Courts,

Constitutions, and Labor Politics in England and America: A Study of the Constitutive Power of Law," 16 *L. & Soc. Inquiry* 1 (1991).

170. See Brink Lindsey, "The End of the Working Class," Niskanen Center, Aug. 30 2017.
171. "Households and nonprofit organizations; net worth, Level," Federal Reserve Bank of St. Louis, https://fred.stlouisfed.org/series/HNONWRQ027S.
172. Nicholas Eberstadt, "Our Miserable 21st Century," *Commentary*, Feb. 15, 2017.
173. Nicholas Eberstadt, *Men Without Work: America's Invisible Crisis* (2016).
174. He offered a better statement of the situation before he was elected: "What ails working-and middle-class blacks is not fundamentally different from what ails their white counterparts: downsizing, outsourcing automation, wage stagnation, the dismantling of employer-based health care and pension plans, and schools that fail to teach young people the skills they need to compete in a global economy." *The Audacity of Hope*, 245 (2006).
175. Even in an extended interview on his legacy, he did not dwell much on this issue, even though he otherwise was frank about the limitations of the recovery. Andrew Ross Sorkin, "President Obama Weighs His Economic Legacy," *N.Y. Times Magazine*, Apr. 28, 2016.
176. Benjamin I. Page, Larry M. Bartels, and Jason Seawright, "Democracy and the Policy Preferences of Wealthy Americans," 11 *Persp. on Pol.* 51 (2013).
177. Hacker and Pierson, *American Amnesia*, 255.
178. Id.
179. Skocpol and Hertel-Fernandez, *The Koch Network and Republican Party Extremism*, 685–86.
180. Mayer, *Dark Money*, 293.
181. Id., 350.
182. One also thinks of the corrupt politician Kip Chalmers, in *Atlas Shrugged*, too stubborn to see that he is directing his train to its, and his, doom.
183. Edmund Burke, *Reflections on the Revolution in France*, 342 (Conor Cruise O'Brien ed. 1968).
184. Thus, for example, Benjamin Disraeli, explaining in 1874 why the massive expansion of the franchise in England need not doom conservatism:

> We have been told that a Conservative working man cannot be Conservative, because he has nothing to conserve—he has neither land nor capital; as if there were not other things in the world as precious as land and capital! . . . there are things in my opinion even more precious than land and capital, and without which land and capital themselves would be of little worth. What, for instance is land without liberty? And what is capital without justice? The working classes of this country have inherited personal rights which the nobility of other nations do not yet possess. Their persons and their homes are sacred. They have no fear of arbitrary arrests or domiciliary visits. They know

> that the administration of law in this country is pure, and that it is no respecter of individuals or classes. They know very well that their industry is unfettered, and that by the law of this country they may combine to protect the interests of labour; and they know that though it is open to all of them to serve their sovereign by land or sea, no one can be dragged from his craft or his hearth to enter a military service which is repugnant to him. Surely these are privileges worthy of being preserved! Can we therefore be surprised that a nation which possesses such rights should wish to preserve them? And if that be the case, is it wonderful that the working classes are Conservative?

Alexander Charles Ewald, *The Right Hon. Benjamin Disraeli, Earl of Beaconsfield, K.G., and His Times*, v. 4, 313 (1881–82).

185. Both versions are on display in Russell Kirk, *The Conservative Mind* (7th ed. 2001). Kirk, whose work is a foundational text of American conservatism, never notices the fundamental difference between the two. His hero Burke regarded the well-being of the worst off as the standard for political legitimacy, not just a strategy for preserving hierarchy and tradition. See chapter 2, note TK (quoting Burke). On the continuing attractions of Burkean conservatism, see Andrew Koppelman, "Liberal Conservatism," review of *How to Be a Conservative*, by Roger Scruton, *New Rambler*, Aug. 26, 2020.

186. *Anarchy, State, and Utopia*, 43 (1974).

CONCLUSION

1. Llewellyn H. Rockwell Jr., "What Would Murray Say about the Coronavirus?," LewRockwell.com, Mar. 4, 2020, quoting Murray Rothbard, *The Ethics of Liberty*, 78, 238-39 (NYU Press 1998).
2. Id.
3. Walter E. Block, "A Libertarian Analysis of the COVID19 Pandemic," 24 J. *Libertarian Stud.* 206, 212 (2020). Block engages a number of libertarian writers, but Rockwell is, in my view, the most uncompromising Rothbardian of the lot.
4. Id., 214.
5. Id., 217.
6. Murray Rothbard, "Law, Property Rights, and Air Pollution," 3 *Cato J.* 55, 87 (Spring 1982).
7. This describes not only Rothbard, but also Nozick and Rand.
8. The narrative that follows is drawn from James Fallows, "The 3 Weeks that Changed Everything," *Atlantic*, June 29, 2020, and Oliver Milman, "Trump administration cut pandemic early warning program in September," *Guardian*, Apr. 30, 2020.
9. Jonathan Chait, "Richard Epstein Can't Stop Being Wrong About the Coronavirus," *New York* Intelligencer, Apr. 21, 2020.

10. David Willman, "The CDC's failed race against covid19: A threat underestimated and a test overcomplicated," *Wash. Post*, Dec. 26, 2020; Shawn Boburg et al., "Inside the coronavirus testing failure: Alarm and dismay among the scientists who sought to help," *Wash. Post*, Apr. 3, 2020.
11. Florida v. U.S. Dep't of Health and Human Servs., 716 F.Supp.2d 1120, 1162 (N.D. Fla. 2010) (quoting Plaintiff's argument).
12. Virginia ex rel. Cuccinelli v. Sebelius, 728 F.Supp.2d 768, 788 (E.D. Va. 2010).
13. Florida ex rel. Bondi v. U.S. Dept. of Health and Hum. Svcs., 780 F.Supp.2d 1256, 1289 (N.D. Fla. 2011).
14. Jared Goldstein, "Broccoli and the Conservative Imagination," *Balkinization* blog, May 1, 2012, http://balkin.blogspot.com/2012/05/broccoli-and-conservative-imagination.html.
15. That could be seen in the plaintiffs who challenged the law, many of whom insisted that they could reasonably manage without insurance because they were healthy. Kaj Ahlburg, a retired investment banker, declared that he could afford to be uninsured. He did not say what he thought would or should happen to those who did not have his resources. Mary Brown owned a small auto repair shop in Florida, and told reporters she did not want to put her resources into health insurance. Her attorney said, "I wouldn't care to speculate about what she'd do if she became ill. That's how she chooses to lead her life." While the litigation was pending, she filed for bankruptcy with $4,500 in unpaid medical bills. Keith Seinfeld, "Port Angeles mystery man becomes lead plaintiff against Obama's health law," KNKX, Mar. 12, 2012; David G. Savage, "Plaintiff challenging healthcare law went bankrupt—with unpaid medical bills," *Los Angeles Times*, Mar. 8, 2012; "Plaintiffs Sue for Right to Remain Uninsured," NPR *All Things Considered*, Jan. 19, 2011; Harris Meyer, "Why do the uninsured want to stay uninsured? They won't say," *The Health Care Blog*, Jun 1, 2010.
16. Tom Hals and Jan Wolfe, "U.S. judge says Florida can't ban cruise ship's 'vaccine passport' program," *Reuters*, Aug. 9, 2021.
17. Kristi Noem, "Update on South Dakota's COVID19 response," *Rapid City J.*, Oct. 21, 2020.
18. Nathaniel Weixel, "More GOP governors embrace mask mandates, but holdouts remain," *The Hill*, Nov. 21, 2020.
19. Chris Cillizza, "Another tragic statistic to come out of the pandemic," CNN, Sept. 1, 2021.
20. Walker Bragman and Alex Kotch, "How The Koch Network Hijacked The War On COVID," *Daily Poster*, Dec. 22, 2021; Isaac Stanley-Becker, "Koch-backed group fuels opposition to school mask mandates, leaked letter shows," *Wash. Post*, Oct. 1, 2021; Jonathan Easley, "Koch-backed group launches ads urging lawmakers to reject COVID-19 relief bill," *The Hill*, Feb. 23, 2021. While it resisted shutdowns, Americans for Prosperity told its own staff to work from home. Lee Fang, "Charles Koch Network Pushed

$1 Billion Cut to CDC, Now Attacks Shelter-in-Place Policies for Harming Businesses," *The Intercept*, Mar. 26, 2020.

21. Charles Koch, "How individual actions can make a difference during the coronavirus pandemic," *Fortune*, May 18, 2020; Charles Koch and Brian Hooks, "An American approach to the coronavirus crisis: Find innovative ways to contribute," *USA Today*, Mar. 28, 2020.
22. Emily Singer, "Hawley wants to block federal funding for schools that require vaccines for students," *Am. Independent*, Aug. 10, 2021.
23. Charles Davis, "Ted Cruz says a vaccine mandate is 'authoritarianism,' but he supports them in Texas," *Business Insider*, July 30, 2021.
24. "Sununu signs 'medical freedom' immunization bill," *AP News*, July 25, 2021. The statute is more sober in the fine print. "It does not, however, supersede the state law regarding vaccinations as a prerequisite for admission to school. . . . The new law also does not apply to county nursing homes, the state psychiatric hospital or other medical facilities operated by the state or other governmental bodies. And it allows mandatory immunizations in prisons and jails when there is a significant health threat." Id.
25. https://twitter.com/tatereeves/status/1436081918982897667 (Sept. 9, 2021).
26. Don Albrecht, "Vaccination, politics and COVID-19 impacts," 22 *BMC Public Health* (2022), https://doi.org/10.1186/s12889-021-12432-x; David Leonhardt, "Red Covid," *N.Y. Times*, Sept. 27, 2021.
27. National Federation of Independent Business v. Department of Labor, Occupational Safety and Health Administration, 142 S.Ct. 661 (2022). On the decision's reasoning, see Andrew Koppelman, "The Supreme Court's Embarrassing OSHA Decision," Smerconish.com, Jan. 25, 2022; Andrew Koppelman, "The Supreme Court, vaccination and government by Fox News," *The Hill*, Jan. 14, 2022.
28. See, e.g., Paul Krugman, "When Libertarianism Goes Bad," *New York Times*, Oct. 22, 2020.
29. That conclusion has led some prominent libertarian authors, notably Jason Brennan, Jessica Flanigan, and Ilya Somin, to support vaccine mandates. Jonathan Cohn, "Opponents Of COVID19 Vaccine Mandates Have a Curious Definition of 'Freedom,'" *HuffPost*, Aug. 7, 2021. The U.S. Supreme Court, at a time when it was zealous to protect economic liberties, see Lochner v. New York, 198 U.S. 45 (1905), nonetheless unanimously upheld compulsory vaccination for smallpox. "Real liberty for all could not exist under the operation of a principle which recognizes the right of each individual person to use his own, whether in respect of his person or his property, regardless of the injury that may be done to others." Jacobson v. Massachusetts, 197 U.S. 11, 26 (1905).
30. Masks are a lot cheaper than the cab fare home from the tavern, and then there's the hassle of going back for your car next morning. And DWI laws affect you much more intimately, dictating what you can put into your body.

See Andrew Koppelman, *COVID19, masks and the freedom to drive drunk*, *The Hill*, Nov. 29, 2020.

31. See Andrew Koppelman, "Theorists, Get Over Yourselves: A Response to Steven D. Smith," 41 *Pepperdine L. Rev.* 937 (2014).
32. The fantasy of autarky can also involve the capacity to separate from people one doesn't like. That has been the attraction of racist variants of libertarianism, in both the United States and Europe. Because these are fringe elements of libertarian thought, unmoored from any of the philosophical frameworks we have examined (Rothbard sometimes appealed to it, but only as a weapon for resisting the state), I have given them no attention in this book. They do however reveal something about the attractions of libertarianism for at least some of its adherents.
33. Edward O. Wilson, "Karl Marx was right, socialism works," interview with Human Ethology Bulletin, Mar. 27, 1997, http://www.froes.dds.nl/WILSON.htm.
34. Martha C. Nussbaum, *Hiding from Humanity: Disgust, Shame, and the Law*, 14 (2004).
35. The same fantasy is evident in the growing vogue for rights to carry guns. The attraction of that right is its promise of personal safety. Second Amendment enthusiasts thus express their frustration with the police while obscuring the fact that many regimes with more stringent gun regulation do a better job of delivering that safety.
36. Douglass C. North, John Joseph Wallis, and Barry R. Weingast, *Violence and Social Orders: A Conceptual Framework for Interpreting Recorded Human History* (rev. ed. 2013).

INDEX

abolitionists, 113
addiction, 154–57
Affordable Care Act. *See* Obamacare
Ahlburg, Kaj, 298*n*15
alcohol, 282*n*32, 299*n*30
altruism, 146–47
Americans for Prosperity, 197, 201–3, 209, 217, 219–20, 226, 298*n*20
Americans for Tax Reform, 3
anarcho-capitalism, 107–8, 119–24
anarchy, 11, 111, 113–19
Anarchy, State, and Utopia (Nozick), 124–25
Anderson, Elizabeth, 45–46
anticapitalism, 8
antidiscrimination. *See* discrimination
Anti-New Deal business movement, 109
antitrust laws, 53–54, 119
arbitration, 164–68
aristocracy, 117
Aristotle, 137–38
Atlas Shrugged (Rand), 6, 17, 131–33, 136–37, 142, 144–46
Austrian School, 208–9

Barnett, Randy, 17, 30, 199, 272*n*23, 290*n*46
Beck, Glenn, 2–8, 132
Becker, Gary, 155
Bezos, Jeff, 42–43
Biden, Joseph, 16, 23, 66, 191–92, 235
Bismarck, Otto von, 21
Blair, Tony, 34
Block, Walter, 231
Boaz, David, 46, 152, 180, 286*n*30
Bonaparte, Napoleon, 227
Bork, Robert, 174–75
Brexit, 59
British Labour Party, 34
Brown, Mary, 298*n*15
Buchanan, James, 255*n*109, 270*n*138
Buchanan, Pat, 111
Burgin, Angus, 26, 65–66
Burke, Edmund, 184–85, 227, 266*n*92, 297*n*185
Burns, Jennifer, 276*n*114
Bush, George H. W., 219
Bush, George W., 162, 192, 232

Caldwell, Bruce, 284*n*68
capitalism
  anarcho-capitalism, 107–8, 119–24
  anticapitalism, 8
  in Chile, 61
  to Democrats, 13, 171
  discrimination in, 178
  Hayek on, 228
  laissez-faire, 12
  markets in, 14–16, 63–64
  Marxism and, 13
  morality in, 103–4
  philosophy of, 30–31, 89–90

capitalism (*cont'd*)
politics of, 6–7, 23–24
in popular culture, 130–33
regulation of, 70
slavery and, 63
socialism compared to, 25–26
society with, 14–15, 265*n*73
technology from, 105–6
in United States, 37
virtues of, 23
wealth from, 19–20
Cato Institute, 17, 110, 113, 152, 216, 220
Centers for Disease Control, 232–33
Chait, Jonathan, 134–35
charity, 148
Chile, 61
China, 53, 64, 154, 203, 232
Christie, Chris, 226
Citizens for a Sound Economy, 217–18
Civil Rights Act, 65, 173–78, 188
Civil War, 88, 135
Clark, John Bates, 89–93, 264*n*72
classic liberalism, 109–10, 247*n*21
Clean Air Act, 48, 121, 212
climate change, 110, 218–23
Clinton, Bill, 23, 186, 189, 195, 205, 219
Clinton, Hillary, 225
coal, 218
communism, 41, 60–61, 112, 135
community, 43–44, 147–49
compensation, 128
competent regulation, 53
Conard, Edward, 260*n*210
"Confessions of a Right-Wing Liberal" (Rothbard), 112
Conly, Sarah, 153–54, 156
conservatives. *See* Republicans
contracts, 164–69
corruption, 7, 57–58, 255*n*113
courts, 10–12, 123, 167–68, 171, 181–82, 256*n*122
COVID, 110, 230–36, 290n45, 299*n*24
Crane, Ed, 221
Cranick, Gene, 1–4, 8, 232, 237
Cranick, Paulette, 3
credit scores, 178–79
criminal laws, 82
Cruz, Ted, 235

deception. *See* fraud
Declaration of Independence, 76, 78
Deepwater Horizon oil spill, 55
DeMint, Jim, 197
democracy, 49–51, 60, 188, 274*n*83
Democrats, 4–8, 13–14, 23, 27, 34–35, 171, 187
Denmark, 41, 64
Department of Transportation, 164
DeSantis, Ron, 234
Dewey, Thomas, 188, 192
Dionne, E. J., 125, 171–72
discrimination, 13, 23–24, 168, 173–81
Disraeli, Benjamin, 296*n*184
distributive justice, 92–93
Dole, Robert, 194
drugs, 23, 108, 152–58, 280*n*10, 280*n*11, 282*n*32

Earned Income Tax Credit (EITC), 92, 141, 265*n*81
economics. *See also* capitalism
Americans for Tax Reform, 3
Austrian School, 208–9
of communism, 60–61
to Democrats, 4–5, 27
discrimination from, 178–79
externalities in, 47–48
freedom in, 14–15
in globalization, 58–64
of government, 6–7, 13–14, 203–4, 215
during Great Depression, 25
growth in, 249*n*52
of Hayek, 35–38, 74, 222–23
of healthcare, 20
in libertarianism, 14–16, 50
of markets, 18–19, 70–71
Nobel Prize in, 14, 30
planning, 25–26
in politics, 25–27, 188
of pollution, 218–23
of poverty, 7
of privatization, 53–54
of property, 9–10
psychology of, 133
with regulation, 10, 67–68
in religion, 87
of Social Security, 162–63
in United States, 25–26, 53–54
of welfare, 76
Economics in One Lesson (Hazlitt), 209
education, 48–49, 151
Eisenhower, Dwight, 188, 192
EITC. *See* Earned Income Tax Credit
elitism, 117

employment, 58–59
England, 25–27, 34, 59, 62, 296*n*184. *See also* Locke
entitlement, 36–37, 92, 95, 99–100, 267*n*102
Environmental Protection Agency, 48, 50, 121–22, 190, 216
Epstein, Richard, 66–70, 109–10, 123, 176, 178, 259*n*193
Eskridge, William, 182
Europe, 191–92, 203, 220, 300*n*32
externalities, 47–49, 210–11, 219

Farnham's Freehold (Heinlein), 123–24
Filmer, Robert, 85–86
Fink, Richard, 219
Finland, 64
fire departments, 1–4, 246*n*4
For a New Liberty (Rothbard), 112
foreign policy, 118
The Fountainhead (Rand), 17, 130–33, 142, 149
France, 61
fraud, 168–71
free markets. *See* markets
free speech, 180
Free to Choose (Friedman, M.), 65–66
freedom
  addiction related to, 155–56
  in courts, 256*n*122
  discrimination as, 174–80
  with drugs, 154–58
  in economics, 14–15
  from government, 9–10, 21–22
  Hayek on, 108, 152, 173
  ideology of, 29–30
  labor and, 79–82
  in libertarianism, 151–54, 173–74, 183–86, 299*n*29
  morality of, 114
  with paternalism, 161–68
  philosophy of, 125–26, 138–39, 237
  poverty and, 9, 186
  property and, 129–30
  regulation and, 22–23, 66–70, 164–65, 272*n*41
  to Rothbard, 152, 183–84
  for self-harm, 157–58
  in society, 38–39, 97, 158–61
  to Supreme Court, 172
Freeman, Samuel, 86
Friedman, David, 121
Friedman, Milton, 32, 64–66, 92, 258*n*178
Frum, David, 190

Gates, Bill, 19
gay rights, 13
George Mason University, 110
Germany, 21, 25–28, 42
Ginsburg, Ruth Bader, 194, 234
Goldberg, Jonah, 2, 4
Goldwater, Barry, 107, 188–89
Gorsuch, Anne, 122
Gorsuch, Neil, 165, 167
government
  in anarchy, 115–19
  authority of, 126–27, 129–30
  corruption of, 57–58
  in democracy, 50–51
  by Democrats, 23
  duty of, 76–78
  economics of, 6–7, 13–14, 203–4, 215
  in England, 25–27
  exploitation by, 151–52
  freedom from, 9–10, 21–22
  to Hayek, 194–95
  healthcare from, 192–93, 194–95
  ideology of, 70–71
  inequality for, 38–43
  justice from, 129
  to Koch, Charles, 206–8
  in liberalism, 28–29
  in libertarianism, 52–57, 205, 208–17
  lobbying of, 219–20
  morality of, 71–72
  Obamacare for, 11–12
  paternalism by, 24, 168–72
  politics of, 9, 20–21, 58–64
  pollution for, 127–28
  poverty for, 15
  to Rand, A., 143–49
  redistribution by, 52–53
  regulation by, 32–33, 48–49, 67–68
  reliance on, 143–44
  society and, 2–3, 43–46, 185–86
  taxation by, 207–8
  of United States, 143, 185, 290*n*45
  welfare from, 4–5
Gowdy, Trey, 220
Gray, John, 58
Great Depression, 14, 25
Great Enrichment, 33, 47, 49, 105, 117–18, 227

gross domestic product, 51
grudging toleration, 157
guns, 300*n*35

Harper, F. A., 207–8, 211
Hawley, Josh, 235
Hayek, Friedrich
  Barnett on, 290*n*46
  Beck and, 5–6, 8
  Burke and, 184–85
  on capitalism, 228
  communism to, 135
  criticism of, 284*n*68
  economics of, 35–38, 74, 222–23
  on education, 151
  on freedom, 108, 152, 173
  government to, 194–95
  Great Enrichment to, 47, 49
  healthcare to, 193
  ideology of, 14–16, 64–65, 111
  on inequality, 36–37, 253*n*68
  on inheritance, 41
  justice to, 272*n*23
  to Koch, Charles, 207
  on labor, 141–42, 175
  libertarianism and, 8–9, 12, 24, 30–35, 109, 150
  Locke and, 76–77, 82, 210
  on markets, 29–35, 57–58, 70–71, 188, 219
  Marx and, 252*n*64
  Mises and, 207–10
  morality of, 59–60, 110, 264*n*71
  Nozick and, 149
  Obama and, 192, 225
  paternalism to, 170
  philosophy of, 1, 8–9, 18, 70, 71–73, 201–3, 252*n*22, 252*n*44, 255*n*106
  politics of, 72–73
  on poverty, 136
  on property, 45–46, 66–67, 119–20
  Rand, A., and, 7, 144, 147
  Rawls, J., and, 104–5, 142, 223–24
  on redistribution, 44–45
  on regulation, 26–27, 46–47, 60–64, 167–68, 256*n*117
  reputation of, 138
  Rothbard and, 174, 271*n*15
  social justice to, 253*n*76
  Social Security for, 248*n*32
  on society, 37–38, 104, 155
  on survival, 119
  on technology, 187
  on wealth, 25
  welfare to, 43–44, 51–52
Hazlitt, Henry, 209
healthcare, 20, 167, 192–201, 236–37, 263*n*55, 290*n*52, 298*n*15. *See also* Obamacare
Heinlein, Robert, 123–24
Hess, Karl, 107–8
Hitler, Adolf, 25
Hobbes, Thomas, 139, 268*n*117
Homer, 156
homosexuality, 182–83
Human Action (Mises), 207
human rights, 181–82
Hume, David, 100–101, 138–39
Humphrey, Hubert, 189

ideology. *See specific topics*
immigration, 148
incrementalism, 293*n*122
India, 203
Industrial Revolution, 33
inequality
  for government, 38–43
  Hayek on, 36–37, 253*n*68
  Locke on, 83–84, 88–89, 105
  in markets, 87–94
  politics of, 41–42
  in privatization, 62–63
  Rawls, J., on, 102–3
  redistribution of, 22, 76–77
  in society, 40–41, 136–37
  in United States, 19–20, 223–24
Inglis, Bob, 219–20
inheritance, 41, 104, 269*n*132
intellectual property, 20, 142–43, 278*n*152
International Monetary Fund, 63–64
Interstate Commerce Commission, 50
isolationism, 25–26

Javits, Jacob, 189
Jefferson, Thomas, 76, 78, 86
Jobs, Steve, 19
Johnson, Gary, 17, 132
Johnson, Lyndon, 189
judges. *See* courts
justice, 82, 92–93, 129, 143–48, 228–29, 272*n*23

Kant, Immanuel, 125–30, 140, 268*n*117, 274*n*82, 275*n*84

Kavanaugh, Brett, 195
Kennedy, John F., 145
Keynes, John Maynard, 202
Kleiman, Mark, 156–57, 160, 280*n*10
kludgeocracy, 55–56
Koch, Charles
  for Cato Institute, 17, 220
  climate change to, 123
  COVID for, 235
  democracy to, 188
  freedom to, 183
  fundraising by, 20–21, 197
  government to, 206–8
  for incrementalism, 293*n*122
  libertarianism and, 206–7
  Obama to, 190–91
  philosophy of, 291*n*82, 292*n*84, 293*n*117
  in politics, 208–17
  reputation of, 10, 187
  Rothbard and, 113
Koch, Chase, 214
Koch, David, 191, 197, 206
Koppelman, Andrew, 11
Korsgaard, Christine, 128–29
Kymlicka, Will, 267*n*102

labor
  in Civil Rights Act, 177–78
  EITC with, 141
  entitlement from, 95
  freedom and, 79–82
  Hayek on, 141–42, 175
  laws, 176–77
  Locke on, 115, 118–19, 141, 143, 261*n*7
  National Labor Relations Act, 62
  philosophy of, 277*n*127
  as property, 80, 82–83
  psychology of, 87–94
  Rand, A., on, 139–40
  by servants, 88–89
  taxation of, 91, 265*n*82
  unions, 91–92
  in United States, 224–25, 281*n*28, 295*n*169
laissez-faire capitalism, 12
LeFevre, Robert, 215–16
Lenin, Vladimir, 31, 62, 145
liberalism, 5, 28–29, 75, 109–10, 153, 184–86, 247*n*21
liberals. *See* Democrats
libertarianism. *See specific topics*
liberty. *See* freedom
Limbaugh, Rush, 132
Lindsey, Brink, 56
literature, 130–33. *See also specific topics*
lobbying, 217–20, 225–26
Locke, John
  Filmer to, 85–86
  Hayek and, 76–77, 82, 210
  on inequality, 83–84, 88–89, 105
  influence of, 185
  interpretation of, 268*n*117
  Kant and, 128
  on labor, 115, 118–19, 141, 143, 261*n*7
  to Nozick, 97–98, 265*n*84
  philosophy of, 75–77, 79–82
  on property, 22–23, 93, 137, 139
  Rawls, J., and, 24, 94–96, 135, 150, 266*n*85, 266*n*90
  reputation of, 261*nn*4–5
  Rothbard and, 78–79, 85, 100, 110
  on society, 136, 174
  on wealth, 86–87, 102, 263*n*48
Lugar, Richard, 219

Mack, Eric, 81–82, 269*n*132
MacLean, Nancy, 255*n*109
Madison, James, 63
Mafia Commission, 116–17
manufacturing, 58–59
markets
  in capitalism, 14–16, 63–64
  contracts in, 167
  economics of, 18–19, 70–71
  failure of, 177–78
  Friedman, M., on, 65–66
  Hayek on, 29–35, 57–58, 70–71, 146, 188, 219
  ideology of, 24
  inequality in, 87–94
  property in, 97
  regulation of, 46–52
  risk of, 283*n*49
  Rothbard on, 155
  with Social Security, 61
  society and, 35–38, 57–58, 171–72
  trade in, 140
  wealth from, 46–47
Marx, Karl, 26, 62, 96–97, 184, 236, 252*n*64, 261*n*5, 267*n*98
Marxism, 13, 21, 27–28, 134–35, 187
Mayer, Jane, 216, 222
McCarthy, Joseph, 107, 111
McCloskey, Deirdre, 33, 155, 259*n*182

McConnell, Mitch, 226
Meadows, Mark, 75, 200
Medicaid, 3, 18, 201
Medicare, 3, 5, 51–52, 99, 217
Mexico, 203
Microsoft, 217–18
Mill, John Stuart, 152–53, 158
Mises, Ludwig von, 31–32, 111, 197–98, 207–11
Monsanto, 54
Mont Pelerin Society, 32
morality
  Aristotle on, 137–38
  authority for, 236–37
  in capitalism, 103–4
  from culture, 50–51, 104–5
  of freedom, 114
  of government, 71–72
  of Hayek, 59–60, 110, 264*n*71
  in libertarianism, 113–19, 198–99
  of social contract theory, 94–97, 128
  of Social Security, 68
  in society, 175–76
  survival in, 80–81
Moyle, Wallace S., 212

Narveson, Jan, 272*n*41, 277*n*127
National Industrial Recovery Act, 31
National Labor Relations Act, 62
nationalism, 24, 60–61
neoliberalism, 247*n*21
New Deal, 27, 30–31, 65, 109, 145, 161–62
Niebuhr, Reinhold, 63
Nietzsche, Friedrich, 125–26, 148
Nixon, Richard, 188–89, 194
Noem, Kristi, 234–35
nonaggression, 113–22, 128, 180
Norquist, Grover, 3
North Korea, 60–61
Norway, 41–42, 64
Nozick, Robert
  for anarchy, 124–25
  on authority, 91
  Clark and, 264*n*72
  on entitlement, 99–100
  Hayek and, 149
  Kant and, 129–30
  Locke to, 97–98, 265*n*84
  philosophy of, 14, 24, 274*n*79, 274*n*82
  on property, 102, 275*n*87
  Rand, A., and, 110, 157
  Rawls, J., and, 124–25, 268*n*107
  Rothbard and, 17–18, 125–29
  on society, 98–99
  taxation to, 115
Nussbaum, Martha, 236–37, 276*n*124

Obama, Barack
  Biden and, 16, 191–92
  government of, 23
  Hayek and, 192, 225
  legacy of, 196*n*175
  politics of, 35–36, 193, 196*n*174
  privatization to, 197
  for regulation, 163–64, 216
  to Republicans, 190–91, 197–99, 201–4
  Trump and, 48, 224
Obamacare
  in courts, 10–11
  for government, 11–12
  for libertarianism, 187
  philosophy of, 16, 35–36
  politics of, 3, 110, 234, 236–37
  Republicans and, 21, 192–201
  in Supreme Court, 194, 200–201
  taxation in, 209–10
Obion County, 1–4
O'Connor, Sandra Day, 177
Odyssey (Homer), 156
Olsen, Mancur, 118
Oman, Nathan, 176
O'Neill, Onora, 275*n*84

Pahnke, Walter, 280*n*11
paternalism. *See specific topics*
Paul, Rand, 17, 75, 173–75, 200
Paul, Ron, 17, 111, 189
Perot, Ross, 111
philosophy. *See specific topics*
Pinochet, Augusto, 61
Polanyi, Karl, 60
policymakers, 56, 160
politics
  of anarcho-capitalism, 119–24
  authenticity in, 108–9
  authority in, 100
  of capitalism, 6–7, 23–24
  of Civil Rights Act, 174–76, 188
  of climate change, 218–23
  of democracy, 60
  of Democrats, 34
  of discrimination, 23
  economics in, 25–27, 188
  in England, 296*n*184

of globalization, 15
of government, 9, 20–21, 58–64
of Hayek, 72–73
of healthcare, 192–201
ideology in, 4–5, 10
of inequality, 41–42
kludgeocracy in, 55–56
Koch, Charles, in, 208–17
of libertarianism, 4–8, 21–24, 100–106, 108, 111–13, 171–72, 206–17
lobbying in, 217–18
of Obama, 35–36, 193, 196*n*174
of Obamacare, 3, 110, 234, 236–37
opportunism in, 221–22
philosophy in, 28–29, 101, 236–37
of property, 79–82
of regulation, 47–48, 213–14
of Republicans, 2–4, 188–92, 289*n*43
of Rothbard, 111–13, 119–23
strategy in, 297*n*185
of Trump, 59, 189–90, 196
in United States, 1–4, 12–13, 24, 88, 134, 185–86, 187–88
of Upper Big Branch Mine disaster, 54–55
of violence, 128–30
of wealth, 38–43
wealth in, 223–29
of welfare, 64–66
pollution, 120–22, 127–28, 206, 212, 214–15, 218–23, 273*n*61
popular culture, 130–33
possessions. *See* property
poverty
economics of, 7
freedom and, 9, 186
for government, 15
Hayek on, 136
for libertarianism, 250*n*10
in Marxism, 21
philosophy of, 71
programs, 55–56
Social Security and, 282*n*43
in United States, 162
prisons, 195–96
privatization
corruption in, 255*n*113
economics of, 53–54
inequality in, 62–63
to Obama, 197
philosophy of, 211–12
of prisons, 195–96
of property, 93–94
of Social Security, 10
socialism and, 39–40
society with, 64–66, 116
progressive taxation, 39, 43
property
in communism, 41
economics of, 9–10
externalities related to, 219
freedom and, 129–30
Hayek on, 45–46, 66–67, 119–20
intellectual, 20, 142–43, 278*n*152
labor as, 80, 82–83
laws, 47, 67–68, 128–29
in libertarianism, 74–79, 97–100
Locke on, 93, 137, 139
in markets, 97
Nozick on, 102, 275*n*87
philosophy of, 28, 83–84, 114–15
politics of, 79–82
privatization of, 93–94
Rand, A., on, 134–43
Rawls, J., on, 97–98, 130
redistribution of, 89–90, 118–19
rights, 95–96, 99–102, 105–6, 115–19, 123–24, 135–36, 203, 272*n*23
Rothbard on, 210–11
Supreme Court on, 85

racism, 175–77, 179–80, 188–89, 300*n*32. *See also* discrimination
Rand, Ayn
Burns on, 276*n*114
government to, 143–49
Hayek and, 7, 144, 147
on libertarianism, 130–34
Nozick and, 110, 157
philosophy of, 17, 107
on property, 134–43
on racism, 174
reputation of, 6
Rothbard and, 14, 16, 24, 149–50
to Ryan, P., 199–200
Tomasi on, 276*n*113
rationality, 159–61, 163–64
Rawls, Bobby, 94
Rawls, John
Burke and, 266*n*92
Hayek and, 104–5, 142, 223–24
ideology of, 228
on inequality, 102–3
justice to, 147–48
for libertarianism, 96–97, 106

Rawls, John (*cont'd*)
  Locke and, 24, 94–96, 135, 150, 266*n*85, 266*n*90
  Marx and, 267*n*98
  Nozick and, 124–25, 268*n*107
  on property, 97–98, 130
  on redistribution, 103–4
  reputation of, 138
  on social contract theory, 22, 76–77, 98–99
  on social justice, 270*n*138
  on survival, 136, 266*n*87
Rawls, Tommy, 94
Reagan, Ronald, 30, 112, 122, 189, 195, 205, 224
reciprocity, 140–41
redistribution
  in globalization, 68–69
  by government, 52–53
  Hayek on, 44–45
  of inequality, 22, 76–77
  of property, 89–90, 118–19
  Rawls, J., on, 103–4
  reciprocity and, 140–41
  from taxation, 101–2
  of wealth, 89–90, 133
Reeves, Tate, 235
reform, 200, 211
regulation
  of capitalism, 70
  competent, 53
  in democracy, 49–50
  of drugs, 282*n*32
  economics with, 10, 67–68
  English Corn Laws, 62
  freedom and, 22–23, 66–70, 164–65, 272*n*41
  by government, 32–33, 48–49, 67–68
  Hayek on, 26–27, 46–47, 60–64, 167–68, 256*n*117
  ideology of, 51, 71–72
  laws, 52
  in libertarianism, 54–55, 119–24
  of markets, 46–52
  Obama for, 163–64, 216
  politics of, 47–48, 213–14
  of sex, 180–83
  in society, 22
  taxation as, 219
  of technology, 49
  of tobacco, 218
  welfare, 65–66
Reid, Harry, 289*n*43
religion, 87, 137–38, 174–75, 184, 280*n*11
Republicans
  Barnett on, 30
  Democrats and, 7–8, 9, 13–14
  ideology of, 10–11
  libertarianism to, 17, 201–4
  lobbying with, 225–26
  Obama to, 190–91, 197–99, 201–4
  Obamacare and, 21, 192–201
  philosophy of, 107–8
  politics of, 2–4, 188–92, 289*n*43
  taxation to, 16–17
respect, 158–59
retirement, 160
rights. *See* freedom
The Road to Serfdom (Hayek), 6, 27, 31, 34–35, 146
"Roadmap for America's Future" (Ryan, P.), 134
Roberts, John G., 168
Rockwell, Lew, 230–31
Rodgers, Daniel, 70–71
Romney, Mitt, 134, 204
Roosevelt, Franklin, 27, 30–31, 161–62, 184
Rosenbaum, Alisa. *See* Rand, Ayn
Rothbard, Murray
  at Cato Institute, 216
  on discrimination, 174
  freedom to, 152, 183–84
  Freeman on, 86
  Hayek and, 174, 271*n*15
  influence of, 199, 230–31
  Locke and, 78–79, 85, 100, 110
  on markets, 155
  Mises and, 197–98
  for nonaggression, 115–19
  Nozick and, 17–18, 125–29
  Paul, Ron, and, 189
  philosophy of, 14, 16–17, 72, 196, 206, 227
  politics of, 111–13, 119–23
  on property, 210–11
  Rand, A., and, 14, 16, 24, 149–50
  reputation of, 124–25
  Zwolinski on, 114
Rousseau, Jean-Jacques, 268*n*117
Ryan, Alan, 89
Ryan, Paul, 10, 17, 131, 199–200, 226

Sade, Marquis de, 145
sadomasochistic sex, 181–83
Sanders, Bernie, 5, 35, 192, 247*n*13
Scalia, Antonin, 11, 85
Scanlon, T. M., 95, 103
Schumpeter, Joseph, 58
self-preservation, 79–80
servants, 88–89, 91
sex, 180–83, 248*n*31
Sher, George, 82
Simmons, A. John, 81
slavery, 63, 113, 135, 261*n*4
Smalley, Danielle, 213–14
Smith, Adam, 266*n*91
Snowe, Olympia, 289*n*43
social contract theory
  Boaz on, 286*n*30
  history of, 75–76
  in libertarianism, 94–97
  morality of, 94–97, 128
  philosophy of, 100–106
  Rawls, J., on, 22, 76–77, 98–99
  self-preservation in, 79–80
social justice, 253*n*76, 270*n*138
Social Security
  economics of, 162–63
  for Hayek, 248*n*32
  justice and, 143–44
  laws, 188
  markets with, 61
  Medicaid and, 18
  Medicare and, 51–52, 99, 217
  morality of, 68
  from New Deal, 161–62
  philosophy of, 3, 5, 8, 44–45
  poverty and, 282*n*43
  privatization of, 10
  for society, 161
  in United States, 51–52
socialism, 5–8, 25–28, 35, 39–40, 45, 235
socialization, 57–58
society
  with capitalism, 14–15, 265*n*73
  community in, 43–44, 147–49
  drugs in, 23, 152–53
  entitlement in, 36–37
  freedom in, 38–39, 97, 158–61
  in Germany, 42
  government and, 2–3, 43–46, 185–86
  Hayek on, 37–38, 104, 155
  history of, 83–84
  inequality in, 40–41, 136–37
  laws in, 154–58
  Locke on, 136, 174
  markets and, 35–38, 57–58, 171–72
  Marx on, 96–97
  morality in, 175–76
  Nozick on, 98–99
  philosophy of, 33–34, 97–100
  with privatization, 64–66, 116
  progress in, 72–73
  rationality in, 163–64
  regulation in, 22
  respect in, 158–59
  Social Security for, 161
  surplus in, 102
  survival in, 104–5, 137–38
  violence in, 122
  wealth in, 36–37
South Korea, 53, 60–61
Soviet Union, 28, 112, 135
Spencer, Herbert, 28
Spooner, Lysander, 113
Stalin, Joseph, 21, 25, 91
Stevenson, Adlai, 111
Stone, Jason, 213–14
Strauss, Leo, 87
Sumner, William Graham, 28
Sunstein, Cass, 51, 160
Supreme Court, 11–13, 165–67, 205, 248*n*31, 285*n*21
  freedom to, 172
  Obamacare in, 194, 200–201
  on property, 85
Sweden, 41, 64

Taft, Robert, 188
taxation
  EITC, 92, 141, 265*n*81
  externalities and, 210–11
  by government, 207–8
  for healthcare, 290*n*52
  inheritance and, 104, 269*n*132
  of labor, 91, 265*n*82
  laws for, 116
  loopholes in, 212–13
  to Nozick, 115
  in Obamacare, 209–10
  philosophy of, 133–34
  progressive, 39, 43
  redistribution from, 101–2
  as regulation, 219

taxation (*cont'd*)
to Republicans, 16–17
of wealth, 38–39
Tea Party, 190
technology, 49, 105–6, 187
Teles, Steven, 55–56
Tennessee, 1–4
Thaler, Richard, 160
Thatcher, Margaret, 30
Theory of Justice (Rawls, J.), 124
Thomas, Clarence, 66
tobacco, 218
Tomasi, John, 83, 256*n*122, 276*n*113
totalitarianism, 12, 145
The Tough Luck Constitution (Koppelman), 11
trade, 117–18, 140
Trump, Donald
on climate change, 221–22
Clinton, H., and, 225
COVID for, 232–33
influences of, 17
leadership of, 200
nationalism by, 24
Obama and, 48, 224
politics of, 59, 189–90, 196
reputation of, 10, 111, 132, 187

unions, 91–92, 167–69, 224
United States. *See specific topics*
Upper Big Branch Mine disaster, 54–55

vaccinations. *See* COVID
Verrilli, Donald, 11–12
violence, 122, 128–30, 139, 169, 183
virtue, 141

Waldron, Jeremy, 80, 100
Walker, Scott, 226
Wallace, George, 188
welfare, 4–5, 43–44, 51–52, 64–66, 76
"What Would Murray Say About the Coronavirus?" (Rockwell), 230–31
Why Wages Rise (Harper), 207–8
Will, George, 221
Williamson, Kevin, 4
Wilson, E. O., 236
Wolff, Jonathan, 274*n*79

Young, Iris Marion, 148

Zingales, Luigi, 171
Zwolinski, Matt, 114, 120–21, 127, 139, 277*n*127